D0206170

STREET ADDICTS
in the Political Economy

STREET ADDICTS

in the Political Economy

Alisse Waterston

Temple University Press
Philadelphia

Temple University Press, Philadelphia 19122
Copyright © 1993 by Temple University. All rights reserved
Published 1993
Printed in the United States of America

The paper used in this publication meets the minimum
requirements of American National Standard for Information
Sciences—Permanence of Paper for Printed Library Materials,
ANSI Z39.48-1984 ⊗

Library of Congress Cataloging-in-Publication Data
Waterston, Alisse, 1951–
    Street addicts in the political economy / Alisse Waterston.
        p.   cm.
    Includes bibliographical references (p.   ) and index.
    ISBN 0-87722-992-9 (cloth)
    1. Narcotic addicts—United States—Social conditions.
  2. Narcotic addicts—United States—Economic conditions.
  3. Homeless persons—United States—Drug use.   I. Title.
HV5825.W3814   1993
305.9'0824—dc20   92-5259

Contents

Preface

New York City is home to at least two hundred thousand opiate addicts (Gillman 1989:28; New York Academy of Sciences 1989:7). While opiate use is certainly not a new phenomenon, the experiences of addicts change with developments in the political economy surrounding them. In New York City, such major changes as economic restructuring, the flight of industry, cutbacks in government assistance programs, the politicization of ethnicity, and the gentrification of neighborhoods have set the stage for mass "individual" failure in the form of unemployment (or marginal employment), homelessness, criminal involvement, and drug addiction (Hopper 1988; Block et al. 1987; Hopper, Susser, and Conover 1986; Smith 1984; Susser 1982; Tabb 1982; Alcaly and Mermelstein 1977; Schiller 1977; Herbstein 1983).

No matter how poor we may judge their personal choices to be, the addicts portrayed in this book think and act within social settings circumscribed by contemporary political and economic trends. Whether the setting is a city shelter, a street corner, a drug clinic, or a jail, addicts are structurally vulnerable to the larger sociocultural system within which they live.

It may be difficult to imagine this kind of vulnerability, since drug addicts are cast as the city's most deviant population and blamed for the poor quality of urban life. As shelter residents, criminals, patients, and low-level, informal-sector workers, street addicts are subject not only to the constraints of their personal drug habits but also to the handicaps of positions of relative powerlessness within a wider social arena.

I suggest that the most widely accepted conceptualization of street addicts by social scientists, policymakers, and, perhaps, the general American public does not reflect the true nature of addict life. In the traditional conceptualization, street addicts and their "subcultures" are peripheral, marginal, and deviant. To dispel the "myth of marginality," I present a portrait of addicts as people whose lives are constantly shaped by relations within a range of so-called private and public arenas, and who, despite limitations, devise strategies in response. Certain institutional and private forces should therefore be seen as both constraints and tools to be used within any given situation. These forces include various drug-abuse programs and clinics, city shelters, the criminal-justice system, the employment picture, prospects and conditions, race, gender, and sexuality. Addicts' lives are then better understood as a constant interaction between the addicts and extrinsic forces, their "tools." This understanding moves us away from the traditional construction of addicts as deviant, a "scareword . . . a stereotype that serves to embrace and isolate a group" (Haskell 1988:18–20).

In this effort to uncover the cultural construction of street drug addicts, I have found it useful to consider several theoretical issues: the role of deviance ideology and social differentiation in the reproduction of class conflict and inequality; the part played by social institutions in the reproduction of class relations; the influence of ideology, institutions, and social categories in the formation of cultural and personal meaning; the imperceptibility of social-control mechanisms and techniques of class domination; and the place of individual and collective consciousness in effecting social change. In all, I attempt to capture some thoughts, feelings, and experiences of street addicts and interpret them within the framework of reproduction theory (Willis 1977; MacLeod 1987; Giroux 1983; Bourdieu and Passeron 1977; Harris and Young 1981). This study may therefore be characterized as an "articulation of richly described experiences of everyday life with larger systems and the subtle expressions of ideology" (Marcus and Fischer 1986:78), with particular reference to street drug addicts in New York City.

METHODOLOGY

Unlike traditional social scientists, I do not presume an independent existence of this "group" (i.e., members of a drug subculture). Instead, my treatment of the "unit" selected for study includes descriptions of addicts' involvement in various aspects of city life: from work-force participation to the criminal-justice system, from health and welfare institutions to personal networks. This is consistent with a major theme of this work: While drug use is a significant hindrance for these individuals, addicts are more than drug abusers. They are members of the class of working poor that has emerged in the city (particularly in the past fifteen years), they are city residents who have been displaced by gentrification, and they are a diverse group of people whose common bond (drug use) does not account for all their experiences as workers, men/women, homosexuals/heterosexuals, blacks/whites/Latinos, homeless/housed, and members of various personal networks.

This book is based on ethnographic data collected from 1984 to 1987 by a multidisciplinary team of social-science researchers. My work is built on two studies designed and directed by the sociologist Paul Goldstein of Narcotic and Drug Research, Inc. (NDRI), in New York City. Dr. Goldstein was interested in examining the relationship between drugs and violence among a male and female sample of 285 polydrug street addicts (152 men and 133 women). Two of the significant demographic characteristics of the total sample are that a majority (70 percent) are members of racial or ethnic minorities and that more than half the sample were homeless at the time of the research.[1]

Given the unusual circumstance of this study, in which an anthropologist constructed an ethnographic work using data collected by others, I suggest that the study be considered an "experiment in writing and understanding," following George Marcus and Michael Fischer in *Anthropology as Cultural Critique* (1986). While I made several trips to the Lower East Side to observe the final stages of the interview process, to visit the neighborhood, and to speak informally with residents, I immersed myself in street-addict life primarily by reading and rereading written dialogue between interviewers and addicts. In the relative isolation of my home-office, I pored over more than five thousand pages of transcript and slowly developed a sense of individual personalities, as well as of shared concerns, among the group. I also began to see connections between addicts' experiences and understandings and larger, external systems.

For this study, 98 interviews (5,373 pages) with 55 individuals (41 men and 14 women) were used. They constitute most of the interviews in the study that were tape-recorded and transcribed. The demographic composition of this subsample closely resembles that of the larger sample of 285 individuals. In terms of race/ethnicity, for example, figures for the subsample closely parallel the total sample (total sample: 48 percent black, 30 percent white, 20 percent Hispanic, and 2.5 percent other; subsample: 42 percent black, 31 percent white, 25 percent Hispanic, 3 percent other). There is a similar parallel for the variable "education" (total sample: 43 percent less than high school graduation, 27 percent high school graduation, 29 percent some college or college graduation, 1 percent unknown; subsample: 42 percent less than high school graduation, 24 percent high school graduation, 33 percent some college or college graduation). The gender ratio in the subsample does not parallel that of the larger sample. This is primarily due to funding limitations and time constraints, which restricted the number of tape-recorded and transcribed interviews of women during the second phase of the study.

I was not present for the primary data-gathering process.[2] As a result of this circumstance, the study lacks information that comes from an array of communication modes: how people act, feel, and look and what they say and do in actual situations. Some descriptions of systems and structures may therefore seem unduly static (e.g., the organization of drug work, patterns of shelter life), although I would argue that this is to some degree inevitable in any attempt to capture and describe the "ethnographic moment."

In using this approach, I was also constrained by the research agenda and strategies of the two projects. The major limitation seemed a possible overemphasis on negative aspects of street-addict life (e.g., problems, hardships, and violence as related to drugs). A look at other accounts of addicts' experiences, however, suggests that this emphasis may reflect actual conditions rather than research bias (Bourgois 1989; Williams 1989; Sullivan 1989; Johnson et al. 1985).

Taken together, these issues raise questions about the reliability of social-science research in general. The very methodology used here makes explicit the inherent subjectivity of any such research strategy. Based as it is on secondary sources, this book does not claim to present an unbiased picture. Instead, the analysis should be seen as an interpretation of a particular slice of life from which new and more refined theoretical hypotheses may be generated. Despite the limitations of this uncommon approach to ethnographic research and writing, I believe that this study advances our knowledge of the street addicts whose voices are heard on these pages.

PLAN OF THE BOOK

The thesis I present counters the prevailing perspective on street addicts in academic, political, and media circles in the United States. In Chapter I, I introduce my theoretical position and set out the basic argument. The chapter contains a critical review of the social-science literature on drugs and a critical evaluation of United States drug policy of the past 100 years. The chapter ends with a statement on the importance of exploring the role of economic, political, and ideological forces in shaping the nature and context of the street-addict experience.

Chapters II to VI are organized around the major aspects of street-addict life: housing, work, the criminal-justice system, medical and drug treatment, and interpersonal relations. Chapter II, on homelessness and city shelters, introduces the Lower East Side of Manhattan, where many addicts live and where the research was conducted. Experiences related to homelessness and city shelters are analyzed in terms of broad processes of housing restructuring and displacement and the role of public facilities in social control and dispossession. Chapter III describes various aspects of the work lives of street addicts, from past disappointments to more current opportunities in informal legal and illegal industries. The discussion includes analysis of street addicts as a laboring segment within a differentiated market; it also considers issues of culture and ideology, the manipulation of products and people, and the organization of work. Chapter IV details processes of social differentiation and social reproduction as played out within the criminal-justice system. Interactions between street addicts and police, lawyers, judges, and fellow inmates are presented and shown as characterized by varying degrees of conflict. Chapter V looks at drug treatment and medical care. It shows that although addicts are generally treated more humanely by drug-treatment and medical personnel than by the police and the judiciary, in many ways the health-care system represents another bureaucratic effort to set limits on behavioral alternatives. In Chapter VI, the most intimate aspects of street addicts' experiences are presented. Early childhood, the nature of family relations, adult intimate affiliations, and street friendships are recalled by addicts who have come of age during a period of significant social change. These experiences are analyzed in terms of dominant ideology and the social reproduction of class and gender structures.

Chapter VII "Drugs, Culture, and Society," briefly describes the cultural contexts of drug initiation, use, and addiction. It also presents social criticism from the perspective of some street addicts, which in some ways corresponds with the arguments of this book. The chapter concludes with a summary discussion of the economic, ideological, and political roles of street addicts and how these connect to broad processes of social reproduction. This study suggests the need for a change in our perception of the drug situation and offers specific political and policy recommendations.

Acknowledgments

This book is a culmination of a decade of support and inspiration from my family, friends, colleagues, and teachers, who have helped me better understand the world we live in. From my first day as a graduate student in a small class on Forty-second Street, I have felt a deep appreciation for the chance to study and learn. Over the years, it had often been difficult to sustain this opportunity. I am very grateful to all those who have helped me along the way.

First, I want to extend my sincere appreciation to the men and women whose stories are heard on these pages. I am deeply grateful that they so generously shared their lives with us and hope that my depiction does them some justice.

The Graduate School and University Center, City University of New York, deserves special acknowledgment for offering me a quality education as well as a three-year University Fellowship. I am also grateful to Narcotic and Drug Research, Inc. (NDRI), for naming me a postdoctoral research fellow and for granting me a five-year predoctoral fellowship, providing both financial and collegial support.

There are many colleagues to thank at NDRI. First, a special thank-you goes to Paul Goldstein for so graciously making the data from the DRIVE and FEMDRIVE studies available to me. As principal investigator, Paul organized his team of researchers to produce data of exceptional quality. I also thank my friend Barry Spunt for patiently introducing me to the ins and outs of the DRIVE/FEMDRIVE research project. I am very grateful to Patricia Bellucci for helping me access data and showing me the way with computers. I also thank Tom Miller and Paul Simons for providing helpful information.

I owe a special debt to two people at NDRI who have been unfailing in their support of my efforts. As director of the program of Behavioral Sciences Training in Drug Abuse Research, Bruce Johnson invited me to join NDRI and has given advice and assistance of immeasurable value. I extend as well my deep appreciation to my good friend Gregory Falkin. A true mentor, Greg always showed great confidence in my endeavors.

Ida Susser has been a great source of support as well as an important intellectual guide. I thank her for being a special friend and an inspiring role model. I am also very grateful to Jane Schneider, whose intellectual rigor and steadfast encouragement have been most helpful. I extend special thanks to Eric R. Wolf, whose work is always inspiring and whose comments are always insightful.

I wish to express many thanks to William Kornblum for being a good friend over the years. Bill was always available, whether I needed a sounding board for ideas or a sympathetic ear. I also appreciate the help of Carol Stack, Leith Mullings, Roger Sanjek, Charles Winick, and Saskia Sassen.

I extend heartfelt thanks to Michael Ames, editor-in-chief at Temple University Press, whose enthusiasm for this book has been very encouraging. Many thanks also go to Eleanor M. Miller for her useful comments on the manuscript and to Frank Austin for his valuable assistance.

My friends and colleagues at City University and at NDRI have been an important source of camaraderie over the years. I especially want to acknowledge my good friends Aisha Khan, Wendy Hoeffler, Allyson Purpura, and Elite Ben Yosef and to express my appreciation to Ronnie Catan, Cherni Gillman, Joan Wertheim, John Baumann, Deborah Hillman, and Regina Arnold. I extend many thanks to my special friend Terry Williams for his unwavering encouragement.

None of my efforts would have been possible without the love and support of my family and close friends. My son, Matthew, has been my mainstay over the past decade. As my child, my companion, and my helper, Matthew gave me a special kind of sustenance. I am grateful to Tina Fox for always being there to help with domestic emergencies, and I extend special thanks to Sheila Hanna and the staff of Eastchester Child Development Center for being my extended family. I am also grateful to Linda Justiniano and to Jessica, David, and Adrienne Waterston for their moral support over the years. I owe more than I can ever say to my best friend, Claudia Brandt Arioli. I thank her dearly for helping me in all things.

I express my love and gratitude to my husband, Howie, who has been my true friend. I thank him for believing in me, for helping me, and for his enduring patience. He has been my best critic, editor, and computer expert and has stood by me no matter how frustrating my efforts became or impractical they seemed.

Finally, I thank my mother, Louise, and my father, Michael, for giving me so much love and support. Without their help I would have been unable to pursue my studies. I thank my father for teaching me about being a mensch, and I am grateful to my mother for so much. I learned from her about "only connect" and about how to follow my heart. To my parents, in love and gratitude, I dedicate this work.

STREET ADDICTS
in the Political Economy

CHAPTER I

Toward a Political Economy of Drugs

> What is always needed in the appreciation of art, or life, is the larger perspective. Connections made, or at least attempted, where none existed before, the straining to encompass in one's glance at the varied world the common thread, the unifying theme through immense diversity, a fearlessness of growth, of search, of looking, that enlarges the private and the public world. And yet, in our particular society, it is the narrowed and narrowing view of life that often wins.
>
> ALICE WALKER
> *In Search of Our Mother's Gardens*

The prevailing social-science perspective on street drug abuse derives from an empiricist paradigm that has shaped the nature of research findings and analysis. As noted by its critics, this distinctly Western approach to social research has serious flaws. In declaring the poverty of empiricism, Robin Blackburn says, "The assumption that there exists a realm of facts independent of theories which establish their meaning is fundamentally unscientific" (1973:10). In fact, the purpose and procedure of science is to question the readily apparent and disclose what was before unknown: "Science proceeds by challenging the deceptive obviousness of everyday observation and common sense . . . [the obvious] is misleading and treacherous" (Blackburn 1973:10). What we choose to study, how we label and delineate our subject, and the implicit concepts used to shape our significant questions, all reflect a prior set of ideas that influence the outcome of our investigation. To assume that this does not occur reflects what Blackburn calls "ideology in the social sciences," which consequently "arrests social thought at inadequate and superficial concepts" (1973:9–10). Leith Mullings (1987:3–4) provides an example of shortcomings that occur when social scientists adopt unawares a social category for a unit of analysis. Urban anthropologists in the sixties

> were, to a great extent, influenced by the indigenous categories of their own society which held that [ethnicity] was primordial, and a priori bounded the unit of analysis. The problem was not that these studies were based on what were alleged to be ethnic groups, but rather that they failed to sort out what should be separate variables: the way in which ethnicity is conditioned by economic and political relationships, and the role of the larger social, political, and economic structure in defining the unit they selected for analysis.

In this example, social scientists falsely assumed the independent existence of ethnic groups, without considering the forces (including their own pronouncements) that shaped the emergence and character of the group at the "moment" of observation. This form of ethnocentrism, reinforced by training in Western science, is perhaps more difficult to overcome among social scientists on their home turf, where social groups and cultural meanings appear to be almost natural.

Marx, a major critic of the positivist approach, pointed out that "scientific truth is always a paradox if judged by the everyday appearance of things" (1951:384; Ollman 1971:228).

Social scientists who believe that "the facts speak for themselves" ultimately obscure underlying social determinants while providing ideological rationales for the existing social order (Diamond, Scholte, and Wolf 1975:872). As Bertell Ollman explains, "Misinterpretation results from focusing too narrowly on facts which are directly observable and from abstracting these appearances from the surrounding conditions and results which alone give them their correct meaning, a meaning that often runs counter to the obvious one" (1971: 228). These critics argue for a broader conceptual framework within which to comprehend social relations, one that must replace a social science intent on naming, classifying, defining. Referring again to our example of ethnic groups, a social-relations approach would consider political power, economic inequality, and cultural forms as significant factors in understanding ethnicity. On the other hand, a positivist approach, relying on appearances, would present a particular ethnic group as a "discrete and reified entity," which would therefore be "a distortion . . . of the dynamic factors in the situation" (Diamond, Scholte, and Wolf 1975:872; Ollman 1971: 228–29).

These are not the only difficulties associated with formal empiricism. Charges that the various academic disciplines have become "timid . . . technical exercises" and "empty abstractions" concerned primarily with trivia stem from an overreliance on detailed fact-finding, rationalized as objective science (Blackburn 1973:10; Shaw 1973). Eric Wolf, in fact, argues that the historical separation of the social sciences into several academic disciplines had more to do with political, economic, and ideological concerns than with any inherent march toward the truth (1982:7–8). It is no wonder, then, that critics consider the organization of academia a "symptom of alienation" and find the social-science "yield . . . increasingly commonplace" (Diamond, Scholte, and Wolf 1975:872; Wolf 1982:ix; see also Ollman 1971).

A major aspect of the critique of empiricism, then, is that all understanding contains "interested beliefs." This is not to suggest that critics consider on-the-ground observations of human behavior and thought irrelevant. Rather, the dialectical method suggested by Marx recommends that such categories as "objective" and "subjective" be eliminated from social-science discourse, since this kind of naming stalls us at fruitless either/or arguments and seeks to separate the inseparable. As we conduct our social-science work, we must study not only the thoughts and behaviors of a social group but also the processes involved in the social construction of the group. Scientists in the empiricist tradition tend to be concerned only with the first aspect; dialecticians are also concerned with the latter. Since it has often been the case that social scientists perform their work from the vantage point of the dominant social class, and that the dominant class has been a major force in constructing social groups, an ironic and ethically problematic situation arises as social scientists ignore their own contributions to that social construction (Valentine 1968; Wolf 1969; Leacock 1971; Shaw 1973; Nicolaus 1973; Ollman and Vernoff 1982; Castells 1977). Our challenge is to discard the false dichotomies and dualistic practices of our culturally constructed scientific tradition, while evaluating the possible relevance of such practices to the structuring and shaping of the social phenomena under study. Sandra Harding makes this point for feminist theory, explaining that as long as such false dichotomies as culture/nature, reason/passions, public/private, and so on "structure social relations, our lives and our consciousnesses . . . we cannot afford to dismiss them as irrelevant" (1986:657–63).

The epistemological issues raised in this discussion serve not only as a guide to my critical review of the literature on drug use in urban America but also as the basis for the theoretical-conceptual and methodological approach of this study. In the literature review below, I demonstrate how various studies follow in the positivist tradition and therefore suffer the flaws and weaknesses highlighted above. I am particularly concerned with assumptions about the unit of study and with the tendency to focus on disassembled facts. I also explore some consequences of the approach for interpretations and explanations of findings and for, literally, the "group" under study.

MAINSTREAM SOCIAL SCIENCE IN PERSPECTIVE

Social-science interest in drug users emerged from the topical concerns and methodological specialties of the Chicago school of urban studies. Social scientists at the University of Chicago during the period between World War I and the end of the 1930s set a particular direction for urban studies in the United States that continues to be felt. The focus at that time was on urbanism, or characteristic life in the city, which directed the urban scientist to describe the city environment. In addition, impetus from the social-survey movement ("systematic empirical investigation") and a concern with social progress shaped the major features of urban studies that began in Chicago (Hannerz 1980:21; Castells 1977).

Behind this interest in the urban environment was a belief that "the city was a force in world history, capable of shaping and releasing human nature in new ways" (Hannerz 1980:24). The city was held to be accountable, therefore, for the ill will, immorality, and vice characteristic of many urban dwellers described in sociological accounts. From this perspective, it was but a minor leap to studies of social problems and, eventually, to the development of "social deviance" as a subspecialty of the social sciences.

A tendency in the early Chicago studies was to highlight the seamy side of urban life. Urging students to report on decay and disorganization in cities, Robert E. Park nurtured sociological studies of minorities, gangs, opium addicts, hoboes, and juvenile delinquents. Each study seemed to contain a world unto its own, while also representing inevitable, undesirable features of city life. The false reasoning that dictated the sociological course of action was: since social problems are endemic to urbanism, urban social scientists must document, in ethnographic or statistical detail, these social problems. While this approach seems an "objective" endeavor to document the social phenomena "out there," several "interested beliefs" may be identified. For one, it is difficult to assess how particular behaviors and attitudes had come to be determined problematic; perhaps the determination reflects the scientist's personal standards or those embraced by the dominant class. In addition, the tendency was for the scientist to study "social problems" as exhibited by the lower classes, new immigrants, and American blacks. In this way, modern urban studies reinforced the idea of a connection between social problems and the lower classes. The assumption of this link, coupled with such explanatory models as urbanism, a "natural" competition for space in cities, culture conflict, and social deviance, constitutes a sociological paradigm of the positivist tradition. As critics have pointed out, this paradigm ignores the economic, political, and ideological context within which the social worlds of the urban lower classes was embedded. For example, Manuel Castells explains that the spatial order of the city is not the "physical given," suggested by the paradigm, but "a certain historically-constituted social relation" (1977:vii). Moreover, Mullings argues that features of urban culture are better understood as the social effects of industrial capitalism (1987:2). But despite such criticisms, I believe that many urban social scientists continue to rely on the traditional paradigm as a foundation for their research.

The influence of the Chicago school on anthropology and sociology centers on the notion of urban culture as "a specific system of social relations [produced] by the ecological context of the city" (Castells 1975:75). The anthropology of Robert Redfield borrows from this tradition. In his rural/urban dichotomy, folk society (the traditional domain of anthropology) is characterized by a set of traits opposite to those of urban society. The folk-urban continuum, although projecting an inevitable evolutionary progression of society, suggests that there is little to be desired in the urban way of life. Sociologists examined the urban end of things, describing such features as anomie, superficial social relations, individualization, secularization, anonymity, social heterogeneity, isolation, lack of participation, and immorality—in short, social disorganization. Armed with a distorted version of cultural relativism, urban anthropologists and sociologists observed these traits primarily among the poorer and darker-skinned members of the urban population who clung to a self-limiting class culture.

In some ways, the "culture of poverty" notion contradicts the folk-urban dichotomy. If the city produces the flip side of the romantic rural ideal, then how is it that only some groups exhibit the negative traits? I believe this contradiction was "resolved" in several ways. First, as S. L. Schlossman has pointed out, the idea of a poverty culture among recent immigrants in American cities was not new to the twentieth century. Instead, the concept developed after the Irish immigration of the 1840s and 1850s, as government and private charity officials believed that "[immigrant] youth faced temptations of deviancy because of pernicious home and community surroundings" (Schlossman 1974:153). Schlossman cites statements and reports issued by various organizations during the period that suggest an "inextricable relation" between delinquency, immigration, and urbanism (1974:155–58). That "inextricable relation" appears firmly embedded in the minds of early twentieth-century social scientists, who, as previously noted, studied minorities, gangs, opium addicts, hoboes, and juvenile delinquents.

The ecological orientation of early urban sociology took a similiar direction. Interest in the "natural" competition for physical space in the urban environment reflected a definition of the city as an area densely populated *with* immigrants/blacks/poor people. The following quotation from two Chicago sociologists illustrates the typical argument. Here, belief in the inextricable relation between certain groups, social disorganization, deviancy, and poverty culture is revealed, as is the understanding that "social relations are causal in their own right, apart from their economic, political, or ideological context" (Wolf 1982:9):

> We assumed that the city had a characteristic organization and way of life that differentiated it from rural communities. Like rural communities, however, it was composed of natural areas, each having a particular function in the whole economy and life of the city, each area having its distinctive institutions, groups, and personalities. Often there were wide differences between communities which

were very sharply demarcated. . . . The natural areas could be significantly studied in two aspects: their spatial pattern [and] their cultural life. . . . For example, [one map] showed that juvenile delinquents were concentrated in certain areas of the city and that they tended to thin out in other areas. . . . Delinquents were concentrated in what we call the areas of deterioration and transition; they thinned out and almost disappeared in the better residential neighborhoods. Statistical data and map-plotting tell us much, but they don't tell us all. . . . Studies of all the different social and health conditions related to the distribution of juvenile delinquency found the highest correlate with juvenile delinquency was tuberculosis. Now, of course, we know that tuberculosis doesn't cause juvenile delinquency; nor does juvenile delinquency cause tuberculosis. *But it meant that the same community conditions that give rise to tuberculosis, give rise to juvenile delinquency—nonwhite population, immigrant population, bad housing.* (emphasis mine; Burgess and Bogue 1964:7–9)

In the same article, the authors note that some groups go through an adjustment process that then leads to personal and community reorganization (1964:10). It is therefore possible to have "urbanization without breakdown," particularly if outsider groups assimilate and conform to certain norms. Social problems occur as groups have trouble letting go of values and life-styles inimical to successful adaptation, upward mobility, and moral strength.

As we have seen, there is a parallel interest in social problems by nineteenth-century city planners upset with juvenile delinquency, broken homes, debauchery, criminality, and intemperance and by twentieth-century urban anthropologists and sociologists upset with "educational failure," "matriarchy," "delinquency," "crime," and "drug addiction" (Valentine 1968:30; Schlossman 1974). This suggests the firmly established place of social problems as a topic of study in urban social science. As the disciplines became more highly specialized and technically sophisticated, so did the study of social problems. From this tradition, and with these new developments, emerged a subfield in sociology, the study of deviance. This specialty adopted many of the assumptions and biases of its parent field, and it also suffers similiar problems in establishing causality and explanation. The social-deviance field is particularly relevant to this study since "drug use" has been a substantive area of the deviance literature for several decades.

SOCIAL DEVIANCE AS A DOMINANT PARADIGM

In the general literature on social deviance, individuals and groups who blatantly disregard the stated norms of conduct and attitude are viewed as socially pathological and qualitatively distinct from other members of society or other social groups (Becker 1964 and 1963; Bell 1971; Clinard 1964; Erikson 1966; Matza 1969 and 1964). Beginning in the 1950s, students of social deviance attempted to bring a new "objectivity" to their studies by *not* expressing personal judgment on the behaviors under question. According to David Matza, "neutrality, buttressed as it is by the philosophy of science, is the sentiment toward deviant phenomena commended by most contemporary sociologists. We are to empathize with neither the correctional enterprise nor its deviant subjects" (1969:37). By this time, however, the subjective values of social scientists were no longer necessary for constituting deviant behavior, since the concept was now firmly established.

From this new perspective on social deviance, "society" defines what behaviors violate accepted norms. However, acceptable and unacceptable norms and behaviors are assumed social facts and are therefore not subject to analysis or historical reconstruction. Instead, sociologists of deviance from the "labeling" school are most concerned with what happens to those groups of persons "channeled into a deviant role" (Gove 1975:11). While these new studies did shift attention from individual character disorders or psychopathology, the emphasis on deviance and deviant groups remained.

A significant consequence of this emphasis was to effectively eliminate "society" (or significant "rule makers" and "rule-implementing" institutions) from the unit of study, focusing instead on the more narrow "microgroup" of deviants. Proponents of labeling theory seemed to move in an important direction by suggesting that "whether or not an act is deviant depends on how others who are socially significant in power and influence define the act" (Bell 1971:11). Instead of exploring this notion more fully, however, most studies were content to describe deviant groups—prostitutes, addicts and alcoholics, homosexuals, delinquents, minorities. Persons who find themselves locked into one or more deviant "subcultures" are "those on the margins of society . . . those least able to resist a deviant label and therefore most likely to be channeled into a deviant role [where they] develop a deviant world view and the knowledge and skills that go with it" (Gove 1975:11–13). In addition, certain sociological traits found to correlate with persons labeled deviant ("biological anomaly, disrupted home, bad companions, too little legitimate opportunity, too much pressure") smack of causality

(Bell 1971:13; Dai 1937; Erikson 1966). As a result, our understanding of the labeling process ("how deviants come to be differentiated by imputations about them by others") has not advanced, and sociological traits have merely replaced certain refuted psychological attributes (Kitsuse 1980:390).

In his review of David Matza's "The Disreputable Poor," Charles Valentine illustrates that, notwithstanding claims to scientific objectivity, studies that focus on "deviants" tend to perpetuate pejorative images of certain social groups (1968: 45–47). Valentine describes Matza's piece as an "exercise in learned and sophisticated stereotyping . . . outstanding chiefly for the large number of derogatory conceptions it brings together" (1968:45). Matza argues that the "dregs" culture of the urban poor reflects consequences of labeling and stigmatizing by "other members of society" (Matza 1966:311). While these "other members of society" are not identified, the disreputable poor are described as "persons spawned in poverty . . . people who remain unemployed, or casually or irregularly employed . . . who differ in a variety of ways . . . who cannot be easily reformed or rehabilitated . . . are resistant and recalcitrant" (Valentine 1968:45–46; Matza 1966: 312–17). In effect, Matza's attention to poverty culture (assumed to be empirically "true") prevails at the expense of understanding historical processes related to poverty, employment, and "marginality" and perpetuates what Valentine considers a "blame the victim" ideology. Matza's work illustrates some of the limitations associated with the study of social deviance.

Most social-science studies of drug users have tended to incorporate many of the assumptions and approaches of studies in social deviance. In fact, empirical examples of drug users and drug subcultures are frequently cited to illustrate social deviance (Simmons 1969; Rubington 1967; Schur 1965; Becker 1964 and 1963; Finestone 1957; Treadway 1930). Bingham Dai's early "Chicago school" study on opium addiction helped usher in this tradition. The author is most curious about "them [addicts] as a group and the world they live in . . . the underworld environment [which is] a breeding ground of new drug users" (1937:645). Dai's study contains the major conceptual and methodological tools associated with Chicago social science as well as a basic suggestion of social deviance. Later works, such as Howard Becker's *Outsiders* (1963) and Edwin Schur's *Crimes without Victims* (1965) contain extensive discussions of drug users as examples of rule- and law-breakers who consequently suffer social ostracism. Robert Bell's textbook (1971) includes "drugs" as a chapter under group and subcultural deviance. A common theme throughout these works is that an all-consuming life-style associated with illicit behavior comes with the deviance label; for users of drugs, "addiction [becomes] a total way of life," and new "cures" should be devised to "help them become more productive members of society" (Bell 1971:216; Schur 1965:160). Once again, attention to the subculture prevails, and remedies are directed at deviant actors.

Studies that have specifically focused on drug users and their subcultures in American society have explicitly or implicitly adopted this perspective. The major conceptual models found in the earlier, core drug literature fall into two main categories: (1) the criminal model, presenting the criminal addict, who "represents a destructive force confronting the people of America"; and (2) the medical model, presenting addiction-prone-personality profiles (Anslinger 1951; Chein et al. 1964; Cloward and Ohlin 1960; Inciardi 1986; Kavaler et al. 1968; Laurie 1967; Morgan 1966). These models are steeped in the history of medicalization and criminalization of drug use and users in the United States during this century, processes coinciding with the segregation of and attempts to marginalize new immigrants and American blacks (Inciardi 1986; Klein 1983; Kramer 1976; Musto 1973). In a certain way, social scientists and policymakers have together constructed images of social problems and problem populations.

Perhaps, then, the most fundamental flaw in the deviant literature in general, and in the drug literature in the deviant tradition, is an overemphasis on the microgroup. In the case of drug users, some scholars of deviance argue that the criminalization of drugs is an important factor in the emergence of the deviant subculture (Becker 1963; Schur 1965). While I have no dispute with the assertion that the criminalization of drugs contributes to the nature of drug use, I differ with an approach that accentuates the supposed *end-product* of labeling while ignoring *ongoing* relations between users and the social institutions with which they must deal. From the deviance perspective, criminalization results in the emergence of an all-encompassing drug subculture that has an enormous impact on the user's life, self-concept, and identity—as if the subculture provides the only identity and reason for being and seems to be the major factor in a drug user's life. While we do not get a sense of the user's actual experiences in the criminal-justice system, we do learn about the rules, values, ways of doing things, and language of his subculture. In my view, this approach leads to an exaggerated picture of users' lives, as well as an overstatement of differences between users and nonusers. As a result, it contributes to the ghettoization of the group and to the construction of a false separation between "them and us." In these portraits, the deviant subculture seems to insert itself in the middle of the metropolis, and we have no sense of it being part of anything larger than its own demiworld. It is ironic that deviance theorists, interested in examining the consequences of labeling, have been party to the social construction of the tag "deviant other." By focusing too narrowly on the "facts" about their unit of study, deviance theorists are guilty of distortion and, ultimately, of obscuring underlying determinants of those "facts."

U.S. DRUG POLICY IN REVIEW

Social scientists are not solely responsible for constructing the "addict as deviant" view; rather, the perspective has been shaped by scientists' historically formed interactions with users themselves, the media, and policymakers. A major theme that emerges from the history of drug policies in the United States during the twentieth century is that many important decisions, laws, and government mandates have had less to do with possible hazards of particular drugs (to users and the general public) than with foreign relations and international markets, battles for federal control and states' rights, power struggles between national interest groups and "big" government, and the social control of labor. While some groups acted with sincere concern for the affected populations (however paternalistic such concern may have been), their efforts often resulted in strange and contradictory alliances with other, more mercenary factions. In all cases, however, hidden interests were articulated through what was best for addicts, society at large, or national security. Meanwhile, the evils, benefits, or benign attributes of particular drugs were hidden or highlighted as appropriate for the political point being made at the time.

A significant overall pattern in the history of drug policy is that at times of social discontent—particularly during periods of economic depression—certain drugs became associated with particular ethnic, racial, and (lower) class groups. After a period of intense propaganda in which the awful drug was firmly linked with the problematic social group, new drug initiatives followed (Klein 1983; Kramer 1976). According to the historian David Musto (1987 [1973]:65):

> Prominent newspapers, physicians, pharmacists, and congressmen believed opiates and cocaine predisposed habitués toward insanity and crime. They were widely seen as substances associated with foreigners or alien groups. Cocaine raised the specter of the wild Negro, opium the devious Chinese, morphine the tramps in the slums; it was feared that use of all these drugs was spreading into the "higher classes."

Moreover, as specific drugs became associated with the leisure and social activities of the (white) middle class, they were no longer perceived as "so bad."

The first context for drug policy in the United States was the period from after the Civil War to the turn of the century. At this time, the industrial revolution was in full play, as urban areas expanded with manufacturing industries and new immigrant groups and as frontier settlement was facilitated by the laying of the railroads. At the same time, new chemical substances were being "discovered." Laudanum (tincture of opium) was an old favorite, followed by morphine (1803). After 1850, cocaine attracted notice, and chloral hydrate and heroin were discovered (H. W. Morgan 1974; Musto 1973). These chemicals were freely distributed, primarily in over-the-counter pain remedies, allergy tonics, and beverages like wine of coca and the original "classic" Coca-Cola (Musto 1981:5; Musto 1973:3; Inciardi 1986). Unregulated patent medicines, such as Dover's Powder and Scotch Oats Essence, were commonly given to restless babies and nervous women (Ehrenreich and English 1978; Musto 1981; Stephens 1987; Inciardi 1986). While such remedies were readily available, self-medication slowly gave way as physicians recommended or prescribed medicines in both urban and rural areas (H. W. Morgan 1974:11). By the late nineteenth century, opiate use was such an ordinary, common occurrence that *Good Housekeeping* magazine dubbed it an activity "peculiarly American" (Musto 1973:279).

This period in U.S. history is also marked by growing tensions between the classes—particularly between immigrant and American black labor on the one hand and the growing industrial giants on the other. Drug use became an arena within which these tensions were played out and defused, giving rise to "the drug problem." With the railroads completed, and with the depression of the 1890s, Chinese workers became, as Musto points out, "a labor surplus and a threat to American citizens" (1973:6). Suddenly, attention was directed at the drug habits of lower-class Chinese. Although opiate use was commonplace among Americans in general, the evils of (Chinese) opium smoking became front-page news and cause for great concern (Klein 1983:34; Musto 1973:3; Reinarman 1983:17). Just as alarming were reports of black men driven mad by the cocaine found in such Parke Davis Company products as Coca Cordial and cocaine cigarettes (Musto 1973:7). As several authors suggest, propaganda campaigns against blacks coincided with efforts after Reconstruction to inhibit black economic and political gains. Craig Reinarman quotes a popular media refrain of the period: "Most of the attacks on white women of the South are the direct result of a cocaine-crazed Negro brain" (1983:17).

Along with the propaganda campaigns that indicted both threatening minorities and the drugs associated with them came new efforts to control psychoactive substances. While the social control of labor was one hidden agenda behind these efforts, other important interests rallied around the nation's commitment to find solutions to the "drug problem." The drug issue brought into alliance groups far apart on other issues and principles. Among the significant players were progressive reformers, physicians, and pharmacists, as well as representatives of American interests abroad.

Progressive reformers, advocates of federal intervention in an array of social and economic spheres, were concerned with protecting consumers from the unlabeled contents of widely used consumer goods. Musto (1973:11) explains that while some reformers focused on the manufacturers of potentially harmful products (e.g., patent medicines), xenophobic factions within the progressive movement directed efforts at regulating users. Progressive reformers found allies in physicians and pharmacists around the drug issue, an association Musto attributes to the growing professionalization of the medical and pharmaceutical fields (1973:13–23). As health care fell from female hands, giving way to the elite masculine profession of medicine in the nineteenth century, doctors and pharmacists became more concerned about setting exclusionary standards and practices for their profession (Ehrenreich and English 1978). The narcotics problem provided an opportunity for health professionals to establish control over the practice of medicine. With the help of federal intervention, over-the-counter medicines would be strictly controlled, and self-medication with narcotics would no longer be permitted. Legislation would secure the appropriation of medical knowledge and function by physicians and pharmacists, therefore advancing the social, economic, and political status of the medical field. An interesting contradiction in the collaboration between reformers and physicians/pharmacists is that while both advocated federal intervention over states' rights, they each anticipated very different outcomes of that intervention. Reformers pushed for improvements in consumers' access to information, while doctors and pharmacists hoped to limit consumer knowledge and reinforce patients' dependency on them. The Pure Food and Drug Act of 1906 was not only government's response to lobbying efforts but also a first step in federal control of narcotics.

International politics and economic considerations were also significant factors in the drive for federal narcotics control. As Musto argues, a major force in the push for domestic narcotic legislation was "American imperialism, [particularly] the drive at the China market" (1973:24). The connection between domestic legislation and imperialist interest was primarily centered on public-relations efforts to win favor over antiforeign and anti-imperialist sentiments. As a United States representative in this effort, Hamilton Wright hoped to convince China of U.S. sincerity by offering to help the Chinese overcome their devastating opium problem. To show good faith, he helped set up an international forum (the Shanghai Opium Commission of 1906) to address the issue and pushed for the Smoking Opium Exclusion Act, which forbade the importation of prepared opium into the United States (Musto 1981:7; 1973:30–53).

Eager to demonstrate U.S. consistency and benevolent concern, and thereby win China's favor, Wright and his supporters engaged in a major crusade over the next six years to enact more stringent and comprehensive antinarcotic legislation in the United States. During this period, propaganda campaigns against drugs reached new heights in which "Statistics were usually interpreted to maximize the danger of addiction, dramatize a supposed crisis in opiate consumption, mobilize fear of minorities, and never waver from exuberant patriotism" (Musto 1973:33). In general, State Department representatives pushed for the criminalization of narcotics and federal police powers in the states.

Other interests joined the developing fray. Advocates of states' rights, for example, objected to federal police powers in the states, and physicians and pharmacists once again took a stand on national legislation. Contrary to their earlier position supporting federal intervention, medical interests came to oppose government legislation. Physicians recognized that criminalizing narcotics would redefine drug use, moving it away from the "disease model" and out of their hands. The more important motive behind the medical lobbying against intervention in narcotics, however, was the growing threat of a federally imposed form of socialist medicine and national health insurance being proposed at the time (Burrow 1963: 141–45; Musto 1973).

The conflict between those attempting to clear the path for capitalist expansion into new markets and domestic groups eager to protect their own interests found expression in "the drug problem." The major sides in the struggle took different policy positions, each supported by "scientific" data. Advocates of criminalization (e.g., State Department representatives) produced facts and figures demonstrating drug use to be the cause of urban blight, crime, and moral decay. Advocates of medical interests, on the other hand, borrowed from advances in medicine and psychology to show that drug use was a health and mental-health issue. Both positions were imbued with a sense of moral righteousness, which helped to advance policy objectives. After several years of complex political maneuverings, pledges, and compromises, the Harrison Act was passed in 1914. While the legislation specifically required narcotics merchants to register with and pay tax to the Bureau of Internal Revenue, it was still somewhat vague on "legitimate medical uses" of narcotics and the extent of federal police powers in regulating narcotics traffic. Since much was left up to interpretation, federal agents began to arrest "dope doctors," while other doctors continued to prescribe narcotics to their "patients."

Although differences between the medical and criminal approaches suggest widely different perspectives on the "drug problem," it is important to keep in mind that both share an assumption about the social control of narcotics users. Dorie Klein argues that, as two sides of the same coin, both positions are "part of a larger state project of social control . . . an attempt to effect a real and symbolic order" (1983:31–33). Historically, discussion has been limited to the "criminal" versus "medical" models; attention is therefore directed away from deeper conflicts, such as those involving class and race. From the time of the Harrison Act (1914) to the present, the "medical" and "criminal" sides have seesawed in gains and losses, as evidenced by the legislation, Supreme Court decisions, general policies, and specific programs of the past sixty years.

Soon after the Harrison Act became law, champions of "criminalization" made a gain over their rivals as physicians were stripped of their right to prescribe maintenance dosages of narcotics. Such "progress" cleared the way for the criminalization of marijuana in the 1930s, when "locoweed" became associated with Mexican "outlaws," who were "an unwelcome surplus in regions devastated by unemployment during the Great Depression" (Musto 1973:218; Reinarman 1983:15). Later, when marijuana became associated with middle-class white youth in the 1960s, images of "reefer madness" appeared absurd and soon disappeared. To this day, drug users are forbidden to "self-medicate" or to have physicians prescribe narcotics for them. One exception to this prohibition is the synthetic narcotic analgesic methadone. Starting in the early 1960s, a medical approach again began to win favor as punitive methods failed to curb urban decay, crime, and addiction among minorities. Although legal maintenance of users' drug of first choice (e.g., heroin) was considered too radical a proposition, methadone maintenance was presented as an acceptable alternative. While the drug produces its own high, it also blocks the euphoric sensations of heroin. To gain acceptability, the latter characteristic of methadone was touted, and medical maintenance became legitimate once again.

This brief historical review reveals that drug policies "do not necessarily follow from drug-related problems" (Reinarman 1983:9). While individual physicians, law-enforcement officials, government representatives, and citizen-activists may have been sincere in their efforts to address a perceived "drug problem," broader political and economic considerations weighed heavily in the social construction of the "problem" and how it should best be addressed. Given these factors, it is difficult to assess the benefits or harmfulness of particular drugs, especially when they are used in moderation. As Reinarman points out, "Distinctions between 'good' and 'bad' drugs were rooted in ideology as much as in evidence of inherent risk" (1983:10). Moreover, since policies and practices have been justified on moralistic grounds, the "truth" of the matter is further confused.

For example, advocates of the medical approach encouraged a stereotype of the addict as weak—psychologically and physiologically enslaved by his drug craving (characteristics later refuted by anthropologist Ed Preble [1969]). As H. W. Morgan explains, "The word 'slave' illustrated the popular belief that [the addict] was not a free agent. . . . The user was passive, devoid of free will . . . often compared to the helpless child" who, without his drug, "was given to fits of uncontrollable passion or violence" (1974:21). Since users are at the "mercy of uncontrollable needs" from which they can never *really* be freed, it would be unethical to outlaw professional treatment (e.g., physician maintenance) of such patients. On the other hand, advocates of criminalization argued that, although addicts may be at the mercy of uncontrollable cravings, they commit horrendous crimes against society in their selfish quest for relief and should be duly punished for them. In addition, they argued, users (dope-crazed fiends) commit crimes as a result of ingesting drugs. Because of the harmful effects to users and society, it would be immoral to permit drug use. To criminalize drugs (by outlawing possession, sale, distribution, paraphernalia, etc.) would therefore be the ethical response to the situation. It is difficult to assess the veracity of the statements and "facts" presented to support policy positions since, as we have seen, the drug issue has been manipulated by advocates with hidden agendas.

DEVELOPMENT AND STASIS IN DRUG RESEARCH

The past twenty years have seen a blossoming in the drug-use field, with a significant increase in data and publications. These newer studies have used more sophisticated qualitative and quantitative research techniques, and they have tended to adopt a view that sees the addict as "victim" as well as "victimized" (Akins and Beschner 1979). Nevertheless, the "addict as deviant" assumption remains, as does a tendency to associate the most troublesome users with ethnic and racial minorities. Moreover, the "addict as victim" view often locates causality within the family, community, or culture of the addict without connecting these to any larger context (P. Morgan 1983; Quinney 1977; Reinarman 1983; Timmer 1982).

As already noted, there is a tendency in the deviance literature to lapse into negative, stereotypical portrayals of subjects. This is confounded by an enduring practice of attributing observed behaviors and attitudes to the "subculture." For example, in "The 'Street Addict Role,' " Richard Stephens and Stephen Levine define three patterns of behavior typical of street addicts: the "cool cat," conning, and an antisocial attitude. The patterns are further defined by these features: "lack of social concern or social conscience; need to always look out for number one; importance of outward appearances; importance of image; a street code such that sources are not revealed and addicts do not inform on other addicts, etc." Besides the contradiction of the last characteristic by the first (since protecting sources and friends is an expression of social concern and conscience), traits are fully attributed to the subculture, made up of "heroin-using, slum-dwelling, minority group members" (Stephens and Levine 1971:351–57). But it is also possible to see these traits as a reflection of alienated social relations, a feature of capitalist production (Ollman 1971). Given that the traits may also be "found" on Wall Street, in city hall, and in Trump Tower, the alternative explanation may be even more plausible. However, such alternatives are difficult to pursue by social scientists of a mind captivated by the concept of deviance.

Another example of recent research that illustrates these tendencies is a 1981 study by Richard Clayton and Harwin Voss, *Young Men and Drugs in Manhattan*. The goal of the project behind this highly technical work was to "examine the etiology and natural history of drug use" (1981:v). The authors began with an assumption that heroin use in urban areas was "epidemic," requiring "data to answer epidemiological questions" (1981:157). In addition, they make explicit their assumptions that "growing up in areas of Manhattan known to have high rates of drug use would facilitate the use of illicit drugs . . . that a drug subculture existed in these areas . . . [and] that involvement in the sale of illicit drugs is an indicator of involvement in a drug subculture" (1981:161). While these are all problematic assumptions, Clayton and Voss nevertheless continue to "test" their "causal model" that explains illicit drug use. Employing the sophisticated statistical technique of path analysis, the authors demonstrate the significance for illicit drug use of such variables as family and peer influence, early deviance and school adjustment, involvement in drug sales and drug availability, and labeling (1981:131 and 161–71). Among their criteria of causality, Clayton and Voss include the following statement: "The relationships between the independent (X) and dependent (Y) variables must not be spurious; that is, the relationship must not be the result of both X and Y being caused by a factor or factors antecedent to them" (1981:132). The authors explain that to test for spuriousness is rather difficult, but they proceed to eliminate the problem statistically (1981:133). However, since the researchers do not consider factors beyond the causal model, their own criteria of causality are not yet satisfied. Relations of causality seem to be substituted with variables that correlate statistically; consequently, scientific explanation remains inadequate and superficial.

Many of the more recent works have successfully refuted some of the distorted portrayals and incorrect conclusions that mark the earlier studies. Based on more accurate descriptions of addict life as experienced on the street, they include analyses of the drug economy, socialization processes, patterns of stratification, folklore, and street slang (Agar 1973; Cleckner 1977; Coombs, Fry, and Lewis, eds. 1976; Feldman 1968; Fiddle 1967; Finestone 1957; Hughes and Jaffe 1971; Johnson et al. 1985; Johnson 1980; Preble and Casey 1969). Perhaps the best example is the anthropologist Ed Preble's study "Taking Care of Business" (Preble and Casey 1969).

Preble's work was original and pioneering on several fronts. For one, he was a veteran field-worker who spent almost twenty-five years "hanging out" with street addicts in Manhattan. These efforts gave a new legitimacy to participant-observation as a significant research technique among drug researchers, who have since adopted some of Preble's methods as standard procedure. In addition, his extensive knowledge of street activities and individual users provided a sound basis for refuting the psychological and sociological profiles found in the drug literature. Discarding the notion of "the heroin addict" or "the addict personality," Preble instead provides detailed accounts of heroin marketing and distribution and of occupational specialization in the industry.

Although Preble's study and others like it are invaluable for providing quality information and important insights, unfortunately "Taking Care of Business" never leaves the ghetto community. In fact, Preble explains that his study "follows the activities of lower class heroin users in their adaptation to the social and economic institutions and practices connected with the use of heroin" (1969:2). Lacking is a theoretical statement tying the social and economic institutions of heroin to the larger capitalist-based political economy of which the illegal-drug industry is a part. Because drug users and the street subculture are still presented as distinct and autonomous social phenomena, the deviance perspective is essentially maintained and perpetuated. The unacknowledged "fit" between studies in social deviance and community- or subculture-bound field studies rests on a common outcome of their approaches: distancing and exoticizing the subject. This is reminiscent of Simone de Beauvoir's "other"—"one part in a totality of which two components are necessary to one another" (1952:xxiii). Addicts are depicted as the scary, strange, exotic, powerless "other," while the second component, and the dialectical relationship between them, is neither drawn nor examined.

In this brief review of the intellectual roots of drug research, it is clear that, in general, the topical interests and explanatory models are consistent with positivist principles. Although the deviance perspective hints at the notion of the social and cultural construction of groups, such a relativist stance appears as a contextual given and is not subject to analysis. Instead, virtually all attention is paid to deviants and their subcultures, the end products of labeling. Essentially, most drug researchers assume the existence of an external, objective reality known variously as "drug addicts," "substance abusers," "street addict subculture," and the like, which, because it exists "out there," is the appropriate unit of study. As scientists, their objective is to capture the "essential" nature of the subject, which requires the accumulation of empirical, so-called value-free facts about "them." As drug research becomes more sophisticated, we have more and more information on users' unusual life-styles and evidence of activities and conditions that correlate with addiction: crime, violence, family breakdown, psychological despair and low self-esteem, and the persistent rigidity of their drug-cultural beliefs and rituals.

In a discussion of "the fad of cultures," Charles Valentine notes the social-science tendency to assign the term "culture" to what are really social categories. As he explains, "Any number of specific units have been loosely characterized as distinctive by virtue of various 'culture patterns' " (1968:105). Valentine lists a dozen categories that have come under the subculture rubric, a fact he notes with astonishment. One consequence of this practice is to delimit an illusory boundary around the group, leaving a false impression that an autonomous system operates within. Accordingly, the tendency to ignore connections between the group and any larger system is great, and explanation is limited to the dictates of culture or its carriers. Valentine suggests that drug users be understood as a behavioral class, and therefore a "stratum, segment or constituent unit within the larger system—the society as a whole" (1968:106). Although most drug researchers assume the empirical truth of drug subculture(s), the subculture is, in fact, defined primarily through substance using/abusing behaviors. The political and policy implications of these studies are similiar to those of the "culture of poverty" projects: mystification of underlying causes and conditions of drug phenomena and a "blame the victim" ideology (which includes blaming drug users for an array of social problems). As Valentine argued more than twenty years ago, discussions that emphasize difference and distinctness obscure "structural articulations to the rest of the system, attributes shared with other subunits, and elements common to the society as a whole" (1968:106; see also Leeds 1973; Lomnitz 1977; Perlman 1976; Portes 1983; Sassen Koob 1981 and 1984).

There is a hand-in-hand relationship between "the drug problem" (particularly as flaunted by politicians and the media) and increased interest in drug research. Many drug researchers are highly dependent on government funding to carry out their projects, although they do maintain relative autonomy from their funding sources. Nevertheless, there is a certain congruence between the interests of state policymakers and the scientific findings and interpretations of drug researchers. There is general agreement among most researchers and the state about a drug problem in need of solution. As part of the equation, users constitute a problem population and drug researchers are problem solvers. One consequence of this assumption is to discourage examination of basic social forces, such as economic activities, class conflict, and labor-market composition, as these factors relate to the population being studied. Since these important forces are ignored and obscured, we are left with what Eleanor Leacock calls "sociocentric interpretations of data" and a fragmented picture of drug users (1971:24).

In some sense, for researchers to examine these social forces is to bite the hand that feeds them. This is not to say a conscious conspiracy is operating; instead, it reflects the ideological role of social research, made a little easier by scientists who believe in their own objectivity (Blumberg 1973:105–12). In a discussion of the ideological role of the social sciences, Martin Shaw (1973:33–34) explains the collaborative relationship between professional researchers and "the powers that be" as follows:

[Social scientists] . . . think that to be called bourgeois
ideologists means that they are charged with being capitalism's yes-men. Ideology, however, is not apology, although
it may and often does entail it. Ideologies are world-views
which, despite their partial and possibly critical insights,
prevent us from understanding the society in which we
live and the possibility of changing it. They are world-
views which correspond to the standpoint of classes and
social groups whose interests in the existing social system
and incapacity to change it makes it impossible for them
to see it as a whole.

My reading of the drug literature suggests that most studies
are caught in this predicament. Little research considers "underlying social determinants"; most studies instead focus
"too narrowly on facts which are directly observable" (Diamond, Scholte, and Wolf 1975:872; Ollman 1971:228). Like
"culture of poverty" theorists of the past, researchers still
view drugs "as a disabling way of life. . . . [Therefore] the
current emphasis is on people and the development of their
social competence rather than on structural change" (Gladwin 1967:34–35). I believe the agenda for drug research is to
fill the conceptual gap presented in this review, thereby coun-
tering the problematic implications for theory and practice.
This book explores an alternative perspective on drug users
and is guided by Mullings's statement that "what one does
with the unit selected for study has significant consequences
. . . [and the phenomena] cannot be understood without examination of how they are embedded in the political economy of
the wider society" (1987:6).

Given the regularity with which recent political platforms
and media reports have been concerned with the "drug crisis

facing the nation," it is imperative that an alternative approach be fully explored. The history of U.S. drug policies suggests it best to maintain a cynical eye toward media reports and political statements on the latest "drug epidemic" or "drug craze." Over the past several years, we have seen almost daily news items on rising drug abuse, particularly among low-income minorities. These abuses are now associated with groups who are the most recent immigrants to the United States—arrivals from the Caribbean and South America (e.g., Jamaicans, Dominicans, Colombians). Once again, new vicious and violent gangs are hitting our cities, dope-crazed (minority) teens are a frightening menace, and rampant drug use threatens the strength of our country.

This is not to say that it is necessarily empirically false that such groups are involved in "illicit" drug use or trade. Rather, it is to say that limiting the discussion to those associations perpetuates old myths, propagates new ones, functions as the same mechanism of social control as it did during earlier "crises," and obscures the systemic workings of international political economy. Moreover, there is little difference between earlier "official" responses to the drug problem and more recent proposals. The dialogue on "what to do" about rampant domestic drug abuse is contained within the two traditional alternatives (criminal-justice and medical responses) and a more recently developed third response—educational intervention. While education has the potential to provide a sound basis for enlightened decision making, it is often the case that educational materials contain more propaganda than accurate information. On the international level, U.S. response alternates between offering paternalistic guidance and assistance to those (Third World) nations plagued by drug syndicates and threatening to effect coercive measures in the "war against drugs."

ALTERNATIVE APPROACHES: THE LARGER PERSPECTIVE

Recently, a few researchers have begun to conceptualize drug phenomena from a political-economic perspective. For example, a prominent drug journal devoted an entire issue to "The Political Economy of Drugs and Alcohol" (*Journal of Drug Issues* [Winter] 1983). A multidisciplinary team of contributors discuss a range of significant topics from this broader perspective. Among the issues addressed are those of class, state and ideology, state intervention in personal life, and the social control of (and sanctions against) certain groups (P. Morgan 1983:2–3). In "Ill and against the Law" the criminologist Dorie Klein argues that patterns of class and ethnicity have more to do with U.S. drug policy than the pharmacology of specific drugs. Upon examining social, political, and economic forces in historical perspective, Klein concludes that "domestic opiate policies . . . [have] come about as part of a larger state project of social control" (1983:33). This point is related to John Helmer's early thesis on the racial and class biases in drug legislation, which he traces from the early opium laws directed against Chinese immigrant workers to more recent marijuana legislation directed against Mexican farm laborers (1975; see also Reinarman 1983). Other articles in the *JDI* issue discuss relationships between drug production, distribution, and consumption; international capitalism; and political dependency (McBride; Koskikallio). In "Business as Usual," Robert McBride explains how expansionary capitalism generates heroin markets and controls drug distribution. Arguing against the popular notion that illicit drugs are a "social aberration," the author shows them to be integral features of late capitalism (1983:147–66).

Another useful piece that directs attention to an important, though neglected, aspect of drug phenomena is a contribution to a comprehensive textbook edited by two physicians (Lowintin and Ruiz:1981). In "The Social Bases of Substance Abuse," Harold Alksne explains that drug addiction is as much a social construct as it is anything else and argues that "our definition of what is substance abuse is inevitably related to who is involved in the perceived substance abuse and who makes the judgment" (1981:78–79). He describes the social-control aspects of the construct and also explains how the "abuser" comes to be conceptualized as the source of and explanation for social instability and community disintegration (1981:79).

The work of the anthropologist Jagna Sharff also includes material on the urban drug scene (1987; 1986; 1980). Her ethnographies include descriptions of and explanations for drug-related behaviors among low-income Puerto Rican residents of a New York City neighborhood. Arguing against the deviance perspective, Sharff outlines certain social and economic constraints that result in a logical pursuit of "illegal activities" by some residents. In her studies, Sharff directs her attention to the neighborhood and its residents as a whole; her unit of study is not drug users or participants in a drug network.

To broaden our understanding of drug users, we must, as the anthropologist Leith Mullings asserts, "insist on looking at the vertical links that connect the social group studied to the larger society" (1987:6). This directs us to explore the role of economic, political, and ideological forces in shaping the nature and context of drug users' lives. Within this framework, culture is understood as a mediating factor in the ongoing relationships between users and what Delmos Jones calls "higher-level urban institutions" (1972:51). Instead of a "bounded and self-perpetuating design for living," cultural forms might be, as Anthony Leeds puts it, "responses to adversity as it is structured within a particular social system" (1971:15–16).

In shaping a new framework for understanding drug users, we might also borrow from theoretical advances in the anthropology of development and underdevelopment. Adopting a perspective in which social phenomena are intertwined directs us to consider dynamic relationships between so-called marginals and mainstreamers. For example, Janice Perlman's notion of the "myth of marginality" might be applied to street addicts, who may, in fact, be significant players in the whole system (1976). Using political-economic models, we can conceptualize the nature of drug use in America as shaped by capitalist development, state-control policies, and myths and propaganda about specific drugs, drug users, and drug cultures.

The illegal-drug industry, a profit-making enterprise in a capitalist-based world economy, controls much of the availability of certain drugs, which are often targeted to consumers in particular communities. From this perspective, some persons involved in the drug scene may be viewed as participants in a viable sector of the economy. Social-science investigations of drug users tend to focus on low-level actors in this informal sector—street dealers, distributors, consumers. State drug-control policies (criminalization and medicalization), primarily developed during this century, have shaped the nature, patterns, and settings of use and therefore constitute "integral features of a society's drug problems," as Reinarman has pointed out (1983:9). Myths about drugs (legitimate drugs as miracles, illegitimate ones as "demonic") and drug users are intimately tied to class conflict. In addition, segmentation of the drug-using population by class (further differentiated by race, ethnicity, and sex) is found not only in general public opinion, the mass media, and public policy but in the scientific literature as well.

The next challenge is to connect this macrolevel context with information on the social group in question, within a more local political-economic framework. The holism of anthropology serves as my guide in providing readers with a more accurate portrait of hard-core drug users' lives. In this scientific study, "the readily apparent is questioned" and "what was before unknown is disclosed." While the directly observable "facts" about hard-core addicts include a life of pain, filth, poverty, degradation, despair, violence, and disease, I explore the ongoing surrounding conditions that give these "observable" facts their "correct" meaning. This project, in short, goes beyond a formal empiricism. As an anthropologist, I am guided by the basic principles of my discipline, although this book moves away from the strict boundaries of traditional academia. To approximate a better understanding of the subject, I borrow the tools and techniques of various disciplines—anthropological theory, anthropological and sociological research techniques, historical perspectives, psychological material, and ethnographic and literary styles of prose. Essentially, the aim of this study is to further our understanding of drug users in urban U.S. settings by using an anthropological approach to wed microphenomena with macroconstructs and explanations.

The analysis presented here rests on the assumption that class relations constitute the most compelling macroconstruct within which emerge the words, the cultural meanings, and the experiences of the people whose lives we hope to better understand. In all the aspects of life—from the most personal to the most social—the structure of class relations circumscribes behavior and thought. While social relations are opposed and negotiated, social institutions remain very powerful in reproducing the overall structure of class relations and dominant ideologies. These notions are central to the argument of this book. As the data indicate, street addicts are in intense contact with powerful social institutions. It seems reasonable to apply the theories of social reproduction to explain the nature and dynamics of the relations inherent in this contact. Reproduction theory, generally applied to educational institutions, is here developed to provide an alternative to the view of "drugs as a social problem" and the "drug abuser as a social menace," indicating along the way conditions under which these social phenomena occur (Harris and Young 1981; Bourdieu 1977; Bourdieu and Passeron 1977; Karabel and Halsey 1977; Willis 1977; Hall and Jefferson 1975). John Clarke and his colleagues present a similiar perspective in their analysis of youth cultures. Their discussion of hegemony, applied to street-addict life, helps explain the relationships described in this book:

> Gramsci used the term "hegemony" to refer to the moment when a ruling class is able, not only to *coerce* a subordinate class to conform to its interests, but to exert a "hegemony" or "total social authority" over subordinate classes. This involves the exercise of a special kind of power—the power to frame alternatives and contain opportunities, *to win and shape consent*, so that the granting of legitimacy to the dominant classes appears not only as "spontaneous" but natural and normal. The terrain on

which this hegemony is won or lost is the terrain of the su-
perstructures; the institutions of civil society and the
state. . . . The role of hegemony is to ensure that, in the
social relations between the classes, each class is continu-
ally reproduced in its existing dominant-or-subordinate
form. . . . [Hegemony] has to be *won,* worked for, reproduced, sustained. . . . Its character and content can only be
established by looking at concrete situations, at concrete
historical moments. (1975:38–41; emphasis in the original)

CHAPTER II

Homelessness and City Shelters

> It is the circumstances under which . . . disability is converted into social dispossession—not "deviance" per se—that need to be examined.
>
> KIM HOPPER
> "More than Passing Strange"

A walking tour of the Lower East Side north of Houston Street leads one through a maze of poorly maintained tenements, newly gentrified co-ops, empty lots turned into neighborhood gardens and community plazas, buildings put in various states of repair by city-approved homesteaders, abandoned structures, and large illegal squatter tents with banners that proclaim Gentry Out! The tour may also lead to the geographic periphery of the Lower East Side, where hundreds of homeless people sleep in dreary and dangerous city-owned shelters. There are striking contrasts between the center of the east side, sometimes referred to as the "East Village" and sometimes as "Loisada," and the peripheral area infamously known as "the Bowery." For one, the center is bustling with all kinds of people—young artists and poets, older Ukrainian immigrants, Latino families, refugees from the "Love Generation," street vendors selling goods ranging from trinkets to heroin—all, neighborhood residents and visitors. In contrast, the Bowery, between Houston and Third streets, is mainly congested with cars heading toward the Manhattan Bridge or FDR Drive. What with the low-rise buildings, all the empty lots, and Tompkins Square Park, the center has a breezy feel to it, and it may be one of the few remaining points from which to glimpse the open sky in Manhattan. But over by the Bowery, where several shelters line the avenue, the tall, wide buildings are drab and lackluster.

These shelters, owned and administered by the city, have become home to many of the poorest street addicts on the East Side. They are places to get "three hots and a cot," but not much more. There are plenty of East Side addicts living in abandoned buildings and various parks, including Tompkins Square, who dread living in a shelter and going through the shelter system. Wintertime is especially hard, but sometimes even then there are alternatives. A local church, for example, has been known to take in a handful of homeless people during the winter, and some squatter settlements can be "winterized." Vic stays at the church, though he has tried out the public shelter. These are his comments on the options:

> When my situation happened where I was homeless, I just moved in the men's shelter, that's all. [Then] in the summertime I slept on the street because I'd been in the [shelter]. . . . I just refused and in the park I slept wherever I could sleep—at least I knew where I was sleeping; I had a choice. Well, I stay at a church now. . . . [There are] only ten people; it's clean; there's clean sheets every day; they feed you. The people that run the church care about you; they talk to you like human beings; they concerned about what's going on; they try to ask us what happened; they don't be with an attitude like, "Well, yeah, you're home-

less," just give you a bed and that's it; you know, they talk to you about everything; it's just like going to somebody's house.

"I call myself a soldier," reflects Isaiah, who braves the cold in his makeshift home in an East Side park. Only a handful sleep the night in the park during the wintertime, though it crowds up to fifteen in the summer. Isaiah's communal home is a park gazebo, somewhat refurbished to accommodate the most basic needs. "Now you see a bunch of couches lined up there where people lays. . . . We put up cardboard [around the iron gates of the gazebo] to keep the air from coming in on our heads, and sometimes when it snows we put up plastic to keep the snow from coming in." Along with a dozen blankets and some sleeping bags, a wood fire keeps them warm. "The bottom is," declares Isaiah, "the cold weather, it's hard. I was cold but I had at least ten, fifteen blankets under me plus the sleeping bag. I worry more for other people too that was around us."

James spent many nights in the city subway system before moving into his Bowery shelter. "I was living in the trains," he recalls, "when it was cold, and then I'd sleep in the parks, in cars, and there's quite a few [shooting] galleries I used to sleep in too." When Shantall first "got caught out in the street" she virtually lived in a movie theater. As she tells it, "I would just stay in them all night movies. . . . [For] twenty-four hours you pay like five dollars or three dollars to get in, and I stayed there really for a whole month one time." Pete K. had tried some other arrangements before fixing on the shelter. He explains why he prefers the shelter, as bad as it is, to one of the other possibilities:

The difference is this. In an abandoned building you have more control over your person, but in a shelter situation you have more, how could I say it?—you feel like you belong, you know what I mean?—no, that's a wrong word, that's a bad word. You feel like, yeah, you a part of something, you know, you not just completely isolated, and like you can develop relationships, friendships and shit like that, and that's important to people, man. You know what I mean?—you can't do that in an abandoned building.

Before Shantall found refuge in the movie theater, she had been living in a Manhattan hotel with her boyfriend. "My man got busted," she explains, "and I was keeping up the rent all right, but now the hotels called him up and wanted everybody out." Eventually Shantall made her way from the movie theater to three different women's shelters run by the city. Emil, a male prostitute, has also been in and out of various shelters, a circumstance he attributes to problems private and domestic. But Kevin G. thinks something bigger is going on. "I live in the S Building—the four-million-dollar [building] for homeless men that they're gonna try and copy in all the big cities because they realize there's gonna be a depression. There's guys out there, there's a lot of them that are junkies, and that's how they ended up that way—like me—but there's goddamn insurance salesmen and stuff there now."

Isaiah attributes his situation to the city's housing crisis "after this gentrification came around, with the homes on the Lower East Side being turned over [to] the middle class, average white person, this and that, or well-to family." Ray is with Isaiah on this one. Of the East Side, he says: "This is a very, very rich area—why you think they building and shit up in here? They chasing the window wipers, building and erecting new buildings; why do you think they doing that? They not doing that just for you—they doing that, understand, because this is a rich neighborhood, man, and they building it up, and eventually just the rich will be down here; eventually, you understand, all these winos are gone, the dope fiends are gonna go, and you put them where you know where to get them." Shirley, also homeless, echoes their sentiments. "I walk by faith, not by sight, 'cause I see too many gross things. I seen this coming. I seen a vacant lot and the ones that are repairing it is the whities and they're making it so hard for us to move back where we came from. . . . [And Mayor Ed] Koch, he ain't doing shit but taking everything what we need—medical, school—and I don't like it, and homes. And half the time it's the landlords that set the shit on fire. I've been burnt out '55, '65, '75, '85, I ain't taking no more. I can't take no more."

THE SHELTERS: "THREE HOTS AND A COT"

Shirley went over to the women's shelter on Lafayette Street, just parallel to the Bowery. "I didn't even stay there a month," she says, reflecting on the experience. At the time, Shirley was quite ill, suffering seizures and becoming a frequent visitor to the hospital emergency room. "I was supposed to stay off my feet, and I come with a letter from the hospital stating that, [but] they didn't give a damn what my doctor said." Instead, Shirley was required to clean the toilets and showers in exchange for a bed to sleep in at night. "They was getting me up at six o'clock in the morning, and made me work like a dog—I used to clean the walls, everything, they never even paid me. . . . The shelter as far as I'm concerned is a racket."

Martha has been in the shelter system "going on five years now." She started out in a family shelter when she and her son were burned out of their apartment. Martha last lived in one of the women's shelters where children are not permitted, having decided to send her child elsewhere. "I didn't want him to be in no more family shelters, [so] now he's down South with his father's family." Martha knows he is doing all right there, but breaks down thinking about it. "See it's just one thing after another. I swear to God . . . it's just being I'm his mother, it's hard, you know?" Although she wishes for an apartment of her own, Martha gets no help from the shelter social worker and is pessimistic about her prospects. "In the last three years I busted my ass looking for a place, and people who's on welfare fucked up a lot of things for other people to get on it. So you get disgusted."

For women, the shelter experience includes shifting residences in the city. Both Martha and Shantall have lived in several of the women's shelters that are dispersed throughout Manhattan and the other boroughs. Shantall has lived in three of them, Manhattan, Queens, and Brooklyn, although her moves were not always by choice. "A new shelter opened up," she explains, "and the big office pick out the girls who supposed to be transferred. It was supposedly for the age group—any girls that's like thirty and up are supposed to move. The one that I'm staying in now—in Brooklyn, in Park Slope—it wasn't my own wishes to go, but my name was picked out, I guess. This was a must—'pack your stuff, you're leaving.' "

For men, a step into the Municipal Men's Shelter, known as the "muni," is the starting point for the shelter experience. It is here you first present yourself to the authorities and reveal your homeless status. But the staff there do not carp on that—

it is their job to accept your word and hand you a little card called a meal ticket. The meal ticket and a voucher entitle you to food and a bed at any number of men's shelters around the city. Just along the Bowery there are at least four of them—the muni itself and the Kenton, Palace, and Sunshine hotels. There are others around the city, too—the armories at Ward's Island and Fort Washington and the newer place at Bellevue. Each shelter has a different feel to it, and it used to be you could choose which was the one for you. More recently, it is getting so you don't have a choice; you go where there is room, or where the shelter bus lets you off. Vic describes the procedure from the beginning:

> First of all when you first come in [the muni], you got to go to window nine. When you register they'll ask you what you want from the shelters. You tell them you want to try to get yourself together, which is what everybody tells them. Then they evaluate you to figure if they want to send you to the second floor. If you go to the second floor, you get a worker. Then your worker will assign you to a hotel for usually about two weeks. You go to the hotel, and give them your ticket, and they'll assign you a bed—no sheets, nothing like that, just a bed, because, see, if you go up there and there's like dirty sheets on the bed, then you have no sheets, and it's just like that. On the day that your ticket is up [after the two weeks], you got to go back over there to your worker, and then he reviews your ticket. He could extend it or whatever. As far as I know, they always extend it, 'cause I've known people there said they been down there two years almost, going on the ticket.

The armory at Ward's Island is one of the larger shelters; all told, it can house hundreds of men. The dormitory is set up as a maze of sections, within which are smaller cubicles sleeping ten men each. The cubicles are separated by partitions that go up to your neck so you can see and talk to people in the other cubicles. There is one big bathroom for the whole building, with ten shower stalls and toilets. When you first arrive they give you a new set of clothing, and twice a week you get clean sheets.

There are several shelters on the Bowery, home also to hundreds. Among these are flophouses, like the Sunshine, Delevan and Palace hotels. At the Palace, sleeping arrangements are dormitory style, with rows of beds separated by partitions. Alongside each bed is a locker that separates one bed from the next. There is really no privacy to speak of. The closest thing to a private room are a few separate cubicles, reserved for paying customers. There is one bathroom for each floor, and clean sheets are a rarity.

The Kenton is also on the Bowery. Since it has been fixed up, it is a nicer place than the Palace. While the Palace is where they send just about anyone, the Kenton houses shelter employees and other day workers in the city. As Ernest C. puts it, "The Palace is mainly for the public, [whereas] employees from the shelter live in the Kenton." There are all types among that "public" at the Palace. Pete K. calls it the biggest shooting gallery on the East Side, as well as a place day laborers call home. "They call it the 'Snake Pit,'" remarks James; Pete is surprised that a tragic fire has not yet struck the Palace. "It's a tinderbox," he says, "and that's frightening." As in other city shelters, most of the hotel's residents are, to use Ray's words, "black and Spanish," although there are a good number of whites as well. In any shelter you find young and old alike, except at Bellevue, where the age requirement of forty-five or older is strictly enforced.

Nearby is the central intake office for women's shelters around the city. These are set up dormitory style, as at the Flushing facility, where cots are lined up on a "big, gigantic floor." While in most places bathrooms are located on the same floor as the beds, Shantall notes that those at the Park Slope shelter are "way downstairs in the basement, and everybody call them the dungeon." Each person's space is so limited that there is hardly room for the allotted bed and locker, and a sleeping "neighbor" is barely three feet away. In Shantall's view, the Bushwick shelter, a converted hospital that is old and filthy, ". . . is the nastiest fucking place you could live in." At the Flushing shelter, pigeons share living quarters with women, a condition Martha could not bear. "I mean how you gonna sleep when you wake up in the morning and you got pigeon shit all in your hair, on your forehead? The only way you get away from that shit is up on the balcony, but if you on the drill floor, you could forget it. All of them [shelters] got mice, but this is unbelievable, 'cause I cannot sleep when I hear them; I stay up all night; I don't go to sleep." Shantall lived there too, and she knows what Martha is talking about:

[There were] maybe 200, 250 beds on the floor, and they got pigeons flying. I know it startled some people, but these pigeons fly into the wind. You know, they have bars on the windows, but the pigeons go right through the bars, and they'll come and the ceiling is real high, you know; it got bars and stuff up there. Pigeons will go, just land up there, sit there for a while, and they'll drop their stuff right on people's, wherever, oh, hear what I say, on the bed, the floor. I mean, it's horrible.

Rules, Regulations, and Standard Procedure

Every shelter has rules, official ones and the ones made up by staff as they go along. In time, the rules become a matter of course. Ray, who has lived in shelters for three years, rattles them off: "No girlfriends, no fighting, no drugs, no weapons"; and, as Arthur V. notes, "There's a line for everything." Unlike the situation in the men's shelters, women must contribute to the upkeep and cleaning of their facilities. All the shelters have wake-up calls and get people moving early in the morning. At the Kenton, for example, guards wake you at seven and get you out of the hotel before seven-thirty. From there you can walk the few blocks to the muni basement for breakfast. It is more or less the same at the other shelters: "Check-out in the morning at seven-thirty, and sign-in starting at four o'clock in the afternoon." At some places, you can stay at the shelter all day, although you are forbidden to spend that time in bed or even in the sleeping quarters.

Shantall explains that the procedure at the Park Slope shelter is up and off the sleeping floor by six in the morning. The only exceptions are for those who request a "bed pass" for sick days, although these are not always granted by the clerk at the office. Stanley J. describes these procedures at the Palace: "You have to be out before eight, and you have to sign the book, if you don't sign, then you lose your bed, and then you have to get another ticket [at the muni] in order to get back in." The Palace rule prohibits people from staying indoors or entering the hotel during the day. But the way around that is to pass a buck or two to the desk clerk, who will then let you back in. James warns against trying to slip by the clerks: "If you decide to try to sneak or stay in there or sleep 'til ten o'clock and then go out, they can refuse you service when you come back; they could say, 'You don't have a bed here any longer,' and then you have to go back to the muni, and then it's very foul when you go there." Late afternoon check-in is also essential to reserve your bed for the night. If you miss check-in, you risk losing your bed. Then it's back to the muni again. And finally, most shelters close their doors at night by eleven. Once again, if you are late, "they will not let you in." Some places close even earlier. Shantall's curfew at 10:00 P.M. is a lights-out bed check. She notes that "when the lights are out, there's no way for you to turn it back on"; only the staff can do so. After a while these procedures become second nature, and it is important to know what do to. After all, as James points out, "It's not just one or two nights you need the shelter; it's a period of time—now it's weeks and months," or, as Shantall and Martha know, sometimes years.

The city's shelter system is not the place to go for help in finding an apartment, work, or a kindly ear for one's woes. Caseworkers assigned to individual residents are not in a position to do much for their "clients." At most, they can be depended on to provide a meal ticket and a shelter voucher without too much hassle or too many questions. Of the social workers and doctor at the muni, James says, "They could only do so much." Several shelters have a special work program that residents say is pushed with considerable enthusiasm by administrators. According to Ray, the Ward's Island work program is "where you make $12.50 a week; that what they call Phase I. They give you about thirty days to make up your mind. I was gonna get $12.50 a week; I didn't, I didn't do it."

In every shelter Martha has been in, the same work program has been available. Like Ray, she did not participate. "I never did go for the work program, yeah, the $12.50 a week bullshit. . . . We clean these showers, scrubbing walls, sweeping the floors . . . when the aide's getting paid ten dollars and eight dollars an hour." Shantall says the women in the Park Slope work program report to their shelter jobs after breakfast. "The girls that work $12.50 every week—but the job is not little, believe me; the job is you gotta do a whole lot of work—[the girls] are told what they have to do; this one will clean the bathroom; this one will mop and sweep the third floor." In describing the work program that operates out of the muni, James observes:

> This seems to me like forced labor. They're trying to get people on [this] program. They give you a better place to sleep, but you have to work twenty hours a week, and they give you twenty-one dollars. These people are like me—off the street—who they try to work there because now they don't have to pay me. It seems like forced labor 'cause they're doing jobs there that they don't have to pay a regular salary. People in the kitchen, for instance, the dishwashers, they're getting over one hundred dollars. They got people now doing it for $21.50 for twenty hours.

Social Life: "A Thing about Survival"

Shelters provide round-the-clock guard service. Guards are there mainly to keep order among the residents and to check for illegal possessions and activities. They are also there to keep the peace between those embroiled in bitter disputes, like, says Pete K., "the alcoholics, [who] have a tendency to fight amongst one another." In women's shelters, guards keep a log of those who do or do not fulfill their mandatory duties. "You're supposed to make your bed as soon as you get out of it," notes Shantall, "and most of the times those security guards with pads and paper are writing down all the beds that's not made, and they'll call downstairs and say this bed wasn't made up, you know—they'll call downstairs saying, 'Okay, bed twenty-two, don't feed her breakfast 'til she comes back up, make up her bed.' You gotta be fully dressed before you could eat, things like that, but they mainly rushing you off the floor."

Most places have guards search residents as they enter the shelter, checking for drugs and weapons. As in prison, these items always manage to find their way inside—sometimes because a resident cleverly gets by a conscientious guard, sometimes because a guard is not on his toes, but most often because many guards are participants in the illegal action and commerce. Arthur V. says that most guards are "drunks and dope fiends themselves." On the other hand, Ray reports changes with security, at least at Ward's Island. There, the newer guards are called the "Mod Squad" by residents because "they are very, very young and very precise—shakedown, [they] check you smoking reefer, put you out. If you smoke in the dormitory, understand, you get a day or a week suspension."

At the Park Slope women's shelter, security is pretty tight. "When you come in," reports Shantall, "they have security guards downstairs in the front, and they have to go through all of your things; they have a metal detector to check your clothes, make sure you're not carrying weapons. They go in your bag; they'll turn it inside out." Vic thinks security is only beefed up when things get tense around the shelter, like the time at the Palace after a stabbing. There were suddenly more guards at the door, although Vic insists that made no real difference. "You can come in that door with anything that you want. There's a guy known in there that comes in with a .38 every day. I come in every day with a tension knife in my bag. All I do is stick it in my umbrella, and they just never open my bag, and then say [the metal detector] goes off, I say, 'Oh, it's the rings on my bag or the umbrella.' " Even with beefed-up security, the guards are not always around. "Like this morning," recounts Vic, "I came in and there was no security, and there was like eight people, they just walked in; the thing beeped them; nobody was there."

Ray agrees with Arthur V. that guards are into drugs. He describes them as young kids who "smoke more reefer and snort more coke than Carter got liver pills." Still, adds Ray, "They'll come down on you." Similarly, Vic notes that "the staff at the hotel gets high theyself; most of them are in their twenties, and they talk about how they get high." He continues, "They come up to cop from one of the guys that are selling the coke or the dope—you see it back of the conference room, and money passing." Shantall has firsthand experience with guards making purchases. One time, she recalls, a guard even woke her up to send her out to cop dope. Shantall did it and earned thirty-five dollars for her effort. While guards will sometimes purchase drugs from residents, at other times they use extortion—"long as you give them something, they let you in with drugs." If you don't comply, there may be consequences, as Arthur recounts:

This happened to a friend of mine. A guard found a nickel bag on him, and says, "If you give me the nickel bag, I won't say nothing." So my friend Gary says, "No, fuck you; it took me all day to hustle this up, this bag of pot;

I'm not giving it up." So the guard says, "Well, we're gonna have to put you out." So he said, "Fuck it, put me out." So they put him out and they told him, "You can't come back for ninety days." He went back seven months later, and they still said that. They said he's ban[ned] for life, but if he would have given the cop the bag of smoke, nothing would have been said.

Shantall has been booted from the shelter for doing drugs inside. When she and another woman were shooting coke in the bathroom they were caught by a guard, "so that's why they moved us. Any drugs in the building, if you get caught doing anything in the bathroom, they call it a 'code three,' and [you] get put out for a week." Martha knows about code three too, but she says guards don't really care about the drugs and only act when someone else brings it to their attention. In that case, says Martha, "They tell you that you have to go; they transfer you to another shelter. They make a bullshit thing called 'code three,' which is no such thing as 'code three,' 'cause they is not supposed to put you out in the streets for seven days without no shelter. . . . [but] you could always beat the system, go back in the shelter, give them a different name, that's all."

Shirley does not feel protected by shelter guards. Reporting on problems she has had with other residents bothering her for sex, she says: "You got to watch and fight; these bulldaggers don't leave you alone—and the female guards see what these ladies are doing, they don't do shit; if anything, they bulldaggers theyself." At Shantall's shelter, the guards "mostly be getting high, and they gay too. They come in there dressed hard, with pants—butches—and they looking for a girl." Shantall reports no problems with male guards at her shelters except for the rule that they are not supposed to get "friendly or personal" with residents. Shantall says, "They not even supposed to be talking or laughing with us, but, you know, they can't stop that." Martha, on the other hand, has seen some serious abuse of residents by shelter guards. "The guards in there is fucked up," she asserts; "they beat on the girls. [One time] I seen a guard beat a girl all the way down the step. She wouldn't leave, and they wanted her put out. And he beat her, punched her all in her face, dragged her down the step."

But Martha is most offended by the snobbish attitude shelter guards seem to assume with residents. In some cases, attitude can land a guard in the hospital. Stanley J. tells about the one with a "nasty attitude" who "got his head all chiba'd and boom. It was his mouth that really got him in trouble." As Martha sees it, "The guards have a tendency of acting like they so much better—it's how they talk to you." For example, she says, if you have a question,

> they look at you like you're stupid, and that's wrong. When they came out on me with their little nasty ways, I'd let them know, being that if you let them know in the beginning where you're coming from, then they change up—"Oh, why you talking to me like this?" "Because it's the same way you talk to me"—sometimes you could just take but so much, and say, "Fuck this shelter; fuck them putting me out." I'm tired of how they treating me 'cause I'm no dog and I'm not no child, "Don't yell at me; don't scold me, baby; I'm a grown woman. You know my fucking son is almost your age."

Theft of personal property is fairly common in the shelters, although residents do not have much in the way of possessions. Shantall claims it is easy to lose a nice piece of clothing to another resident. She points out that while the shelter provides some clothes, they are not "the type that you would want to wear, you know, that look easy, that keep up with the style." So when a woman does acquire something new, or "up with the fashion," it tends to disappear in short order.

In several cases, residents have fingered shelter employees as culprits. Arthur V. recounts the time when everyone was told to evacuate the building so guards could search lockers, cubicles, and beds for a weapon reported to be inside. As he tells it, the guards kept more than the gun that they found, and residents' complaints fell on deaf ears. "Yeah, they complained, but what's the charges for this deal?" Arthur asks rhetorically. "Judge ain't gonna believe that it was staff over a resident—so, you just can't win, you know what I mean?" Vic reports that it is fairly common for staff to set up residents for a rip-off and then get a kickback in return. In one incident, he says, "I was sitting there, and the guard came over to one of the guys that did the robbing, took him to the side and said, 'Listen, you see that man right there?' and he pointed to this middle-aged white man in the line. He said, 'When we checked the pockets at the door, he had a wad of bills.' He walked away, and then they robbed him and got the money. The guy did the robbing told me that all they had to give [the guard] was twenty dollars." Shelter provisions are sometimes in short supply because staff are taking them home. Martha noticed that staff were often stingy with everything from food to tissues. She then saw that some staff would arrive at work with an empty shopping bag but leave with it stuffed. "Me and my friend Sondra, we's taxing them now, 'We find that you taking it you gotta give us some too, 'cause we will tell, that's right, [a] tax.' "

There are plenty of problems between residents, too. Fights break out often, rip-offs are common, and petty quarrels sometimes prove deadly. The way residents tell it, the most common squabbles are between young and old; blacks, Latinos, and whites; "homos" and "straights"; and all folks waiting in food lines. What might seem insignificant could trigger a bloody feud. "In the meal line," Vic warns, "you get in that line, you gotta be able to defend yourself. 'Oh, you stepped on my foot, you funky,' 'Don't blow smoke in my face,' 'That's my seat—you know, people say real stupid things; you gotta be tactful, and anyway, you gotta push because people are pushing you." Fighting is not at all uncommon, explains Shantall, and "mainly it's over food. There's over two hundred girls there [waiting to eat], and some girls just steal somebody's plate." Tensions reach the breaking point, what with all the different types of people crowded under one roof and, as Ray says, where "there is no own room."

"I get along with everybody," declares Arthur V., "I got that kind of personality." T.K. has not had trouble, either, although he has seen many fights between other residents. "It's the way I carry myself," he explains; "people look at me and seem to respect me. . . . I try to be righteous with everybody, and I like to be treated the same way." Even so, both men know that shelter life is tense, and the potential for flaring tempers is always present. In the shelters, Arthur says, "There's a lot of shit that ain't in the newspapers, I guess because they don't want to make a bad name."

In many cases, according to those who have witnessed some heavy disputes in the shelters, people take sides along color or ethnic lines. Although Arthur has "a lot of black and Spanish friends," he has seen "a lot go down" between the races. He tells of the time he "saw two Puerto Ricans and three black dudes carrying this one white guy into the bathroom and beat the shit out of him, and took all of his money. I went and reported it; nothing was done about it, that's what really made me crazy, 'cause if it was a black person, man, they'd be there in a minute, [but] 'cause it was a white guy and the staff is almost all black [nothing was done]." According to Arthur, particular kinds of white guys have the most trouble: "Some straight guys that come up from, say, Utah or Georgia, and they're not hip to running in the city, and especially the black people and the Puerto Ricans, they prey on people like this. When I say prey, you know what I mean by prey, you know? They're vultures, man, when they got to move, they move right in, and take everything."

Ray, although he "hates to say it," concurs with Arthur that the majority of residents and staff are black and Latino. "See," he observes, "white people's scared." Shantall agrees. At her shelter, there are few white women to begin with, and those that come stay for only one or two days. Pete K. says that old white men are the most vulnerable, though they sometimes have buddies who protect them. "There's a couple of guys," he points out, "that are old white dudes, and the people that live around them won't let nobody bother them, and that's good. I mean, what could you do—if you gonna take something from somebody, take it from somebody that's gonna give you a fight. Don't take something from a harmless guy that's not really gonna do nothing. Yeah, that's not sporty at all." Ray says some whites go to great pains to avoid their black and Latino roommates. Fear, he says, keeps them apart:

Even when they would eat on Third Street, you'll find white guys would come late, when eating time is almost over. When you go in to eat, man, you in the big crowd. I mean you being swamped, and a white guy bump into you, understand, one of them black guys says, "You do that again," you know what I mean; they're scared, and they got every damn reason to be scared because they will be hurt, and they have been hurt, and they [were] hurt for being white.

Ray prefers the newer shelter at Bellevue to any of the others he has lived in. "It's good, it's clean," he explains. More important, "You gotta be forty-five years of age and over to get permanent residency there." The younger fellows can be tough and difficult, so Ray seeks to avoid them. At shelters with young "street kids," as he refers to them, "old people get ripped off, and they're scared." He describes the Fort Washington shelter as a case in point. The place is filthy, with "commodes stopped up with feces, the washing bowls extremely dirty, and they have bugs, lice." Ray concludes that "the bathroom is not fit for anyone that's old." Beyond the filth, he says, are the young guys into homosexuality. At Fort Washington, "you go there to mess with faggots, and there's a lot of trouble." Ray likes "the age ruling [at Bellevue] because there's less chippies you got to deal with." For him, "Anytime a man think he a woman, they should shoot their ass."

Shantall also lives in a shelter with an "age ruling"—thirty years old and up. At her shelter, age doesn't seem to be a factor as far as rip-offs are concerned. "You always gotta be sleeping with one eye open," she warns, "because you don't know who is gonna do something." Living with the age requirement does not please Shantall as it does Ray, since she sometimes feels she lives in "an old-folks home, or a nursing home." Shantall also says that, regardless of age, "most women [in the shelters] are gay—they go in the life; they go with other women." Unlike the scene described by Ray, Shantall suggests that younger girls are more vulnerable to the sexual advances of older women in the shelters. She recalls the case of one young woman at a shelter open to women of all ages:

> They have these young girls coming in, like seventeen, eighteen. [This one girl] said she was eighteen, but she looked so young. Anyway, she didn't know too much about the gay life or nothing, but there was this girl that liked her or something, and she was forcing this [young] girl to go out with these men . . . they be taking advantage of this girl. So one day they raped the girl—other girls, like four butches raped this girl. After that raping situation, she cut her hair; she's the one that's becoming dominating now—in other words, you know, she calls herself Rambo, cut her hair real short, she got a little beebop walk to her. That's how she got into the life, by other girls forcing theirself on her.

Many residents report problems in shelters related to homosexuality. According to Ray, "Homosexuality is rampant, and the violence is rampant because of the homosexuality." Shirley has had her share of problems with "bulldaggers," and Martha facetiously refers to the Bushwick women's shelter as " 'the men's shelter,' 'cause there's nothing but aggressors in there." Martha also points out that if shelter staff "catch" two women in a love affair, they will be separated—"They'll let one stay and send the other someplace else."

Fights between residents are often sparked by jealous partners in a homosexual relationship. Pete K. explains that most shelter violence "involves faggots—young boys fighting over faggots, or young boys fighting their faggots. That's regular shit—envy: 'I want you and I can't have you, so nobody can have you,' and all that sick shit." Ray notes the same pattern: "A guy got a faggot he calls his woman. The faggot gets an interest in you, or the faggot don't like you. He go to the guy and tell the guy, 'He said something to me.' After a while it's 'Leave my woman alone'—that's his girlfriend, you know what I mean?" Warren sees differences between shelters on this score, and he notes that the Palace houses many homosexual men:

> It's mostly gays, mostly queens from around Third Street that try to get into the Palace. The perfectly gay ones make up at least 30 to 50 percent of the population. I'm not talking about the guys play off being straight and are gay. Whatever is not on dope, almost, is queens. At one point, there was so many faggots in that place it was almost unbearable. I'm talking about all kind of homos. It's like every homo from all the hotels had converged on that place, and the establishment doesn't like that because it causes too many fights—too many instances of violence that surround homosexuals in the building, so that they usually find reasons to throw them out.

When Vic lived in the Palace, he learned at first hand about these fights. He describes the time he returned home to the Palace after visiting Desmond, his lover, at Rikers Island. Before long, words passed between Vic and a fellow resident, a "queen" named Flash Man. The argument moved to the street where, Vic recalls, "I commenced to beat her ass." By the next day, he had a new reputation, laden with honor and respect:

> I had people that had never even talked to me before coming up to me and saying, "Yeah, you're all right; you bad; I

never knew you had it in you." So now I can hang out in the whole group of gays, with their husbands and be—it's like part of the family, I guess that's what you call it—you know, the security. [They] come up to me, pat me on the back, say, "Way to go." They nicknamed me "Hambone." It's like a lot of people now don't disrespect me; there's a lot of people respect me, because they know I'm a player. So once they saw that I didn't just sit back and be quiet, like I usually do, that I had it in me, that I'm not to be messed with, I've had no more quarrels since then. The gays in the shelter have what they call husbands and wives, and you cannot let another drag queen come in and call you a name like "bitch" or "faggot," because if you do, then the rest of the gays gonna say you're soft. [They] say that you're friends, we're friends, and "Oh, I love you, this and that," but when it comes down to it, you're by yourself, unless you show them you don't play shit. If two queens fight, or two gays fight, the husbands will stay back. If a straight dude comes in and wants to slap one of the gays, the gays are gonna jump in together. Is this clean?

Warren notes that each shelter is "like a total world in itself," where, in James's words, "everything goes on." According to James, "You get all classes of people—you got winos, you got dope fiends, you got older men, you got a couple of crazies, bugouts." Shantall says many women entering shelters have "something wrong with them—they're a little off," like the "nut" who showers with her clothes on and her bags by her side. Pete K. knows the people Shantall is referring to. He describes them as people "with fixations":

There's a guy that stamps his foot all the time. There's another guy that just smokes cigarette after cigarette. There's another guy that just sits around talking to himself.
There's another guy that takes books, and he's not reading them; he's just looking at them; sometimes they're upside down, sometimes they're sideways. There's another guy, he'll take the entire contents of his locker, take it out and put it back in, and do that constantly all day long. There's another guy that wants to stay in the shower for six hours.

Pete finds it difficult to group the types of people living in shelters: "They are not easily divided—whites are a minority, and usually the whites are there in two age groups, either young or very old. Young, they use drugs, old, alcoholics. The blacks and Hispanics are primarily drug users, and they're in the middle range, like in their thirties, around my age. Sixty percent of [the residents]," he continues, "get high, and the other forty percent are day workers, primarily—laborers for moving companies and stuff like that. You don't see them during the day." Warren says shelters are divided by their type of resident. Construction workers, for example, live in the Delavan, while shelter employees live at the Kenton. But Arthur V. sees "all types" in each place, and "everyone does something—either drinks, takes pills, shoots dope." And Ray notes, "When you dealing with the shelters, you do things you don't want to do. It's a thing about survival, 'cause you got some desperate people in the shelters."

Street people often liken shelter conditions to those at city jails. "It's really institutionalized," Arthur V. points out; "it's something like a jail, but knowing you can leave whenever you like." As in jail, there are many regulations—"You line up for dinner, the monitors wake you up, you gotta abide by their rules." But Arthur, who lives at the Ward's Island shelter, also finds a difference: "It's not where it's like overcrowded, like in jail, that brings out a lot of tension—it's not like that; we got a lot of room." But Pete K. disagrees. He lives at the Palace, located on the Bowery at the edge of the East Side. What with the rules, the guards, the homosexuality, violence, and "jail-talk," living there is "almost—no, it's not almost—it is exactly like jail."

In some ways, people living in shelters start behaving like prison inmates. At first, Shantall was surprised by the goings-on at the shelter. "They act like they in jail," she says; "believe me, when I first came here I couldn't get my eyes off these two girls that was in the bed ahead of me; they was in the bed together." Martha also noticed parallels between conduct in prison and things happening at the shelter. Fights break out often, usually "over little, petty shit" and "lots over women." She explains how it works: "If they feel that you alone, if you act like [you're scared], then they'll fuck with you. I mean, them gay girls around there [in the shelter], it's like girls up in Bedford [a state prison]. You hear what I'm saying; I've been in Bedford, so them bitches mean nothing to me." Arthur V. tells about an unwritten "jail" rule that shelter residents should also abide by:

> If someone just walks in and sits on my bed, I tell them, "Get the fuck off my bed, man," stuff like that, and jail's just like that. That's where I picked it up from, in jail. First of all, you ask permission if you can [come in]; we call it our "house." You ask any person in the dorm, "Can I come in your house?" and then they tell you, "Come

on in,"—you don't just walk in; a person could get hurt that way.

DISPLACEMENT AND HOMELESSNESS: WHOSE FAULT IS IT?

Manhattan's Lower East Side has long been subject to the city's overall economic, political, and social developments. From the time this study began in the summer of 1984 to the present, the area has been a center of illegal drug activity, the object of a major police crackdown (Operation Pressure Point), a quarry for landlords and real-estate investors, home to ethnically diverse poor and working-class residents, and the site of major housing battles (from the squatter settlements of the mid-1980s to the Tompkins Square "riots" of 1988–89 (Carr 1988; Aletti 1988; Salamon 1988; De-Giovanni 1987; Goldstein et al. 1987; Sharff 1987; Turner 1984). For New York City overall, important changes in the employment picture brought on by economic restructuring have resulted in chronic poverty, persistent unemployment, and a rise in the number of people now called "the working poor" (Stormes 1988; Hopper 1988; Rosenberg 1987; Susser 1986; Tobier 1984; Baxter and Hopper 1981). Moreover, the city has also seen a significant decline in and scarcity of its affordable housing stock, which Kim Hopper and Jill Hamburg (1984:6) attribute to

> developments in the private market (the redirection of investment capital to more lucrative alternatives, and growing incidence of abandonment and gentrification), the steady rise of shelter costs (especially for land, fuel, and interest), the erosion of government subsidies (for new construction, renovation, and rents), and generous tax breaks

(such as incentives for the conversion of low-rent dwellings to high-rent apartments or condominiums).

With these forces in motion, the most vulnerable of the city's residents are faced with "displacement pressure." In a 1987 housing report about the Lower East Side, Frank DeGiovanni notes the following pressures on residents: "excessive rent burden, overcrowding, deterioration (physical decline in the condition of properties), excessive rent increases, presence of suspicious fires, landlord inducements to relocate, warehousing, and tenant harassment." (1987:33–39). He comes to the "incontrovertible conclusion that a large number of lower east side residents, possibly as many as 5,853 households, have recently been exposed to substantial pressures for forced relocation" (1987:50–52).

The housing stories recounted here by street addicts point to the limited options available once they are displaced from their homes (whether on the Lower East Side or elsewhere in the city). Their most viable "choices" include shelters, abandoned buildings, local parks, or subway stations. Street people can be rather creative in finding some form of shelter, as is Shantall, who recounts her month long stint at an all-night movie theater. While East Side street addicts may live in local, communal squats or be active in the movement against neighborhood gentrification, they are more likely to be found in the shelter system.[1] In addition, some street addicts, although generally not politically active, articulate an understanding of the larger forces that help to shape their lives and circumstances, as we heard from Isaiah, Kevin G., Shirley, and Ray.

Given the housing pressures on working-class and poor families, homelessness cannot be attributed to individual failure to "make it." People who have or develop drug addictions may be even more vulnerable to housing displacement and institutionalization. When this happens, however, others often attribute the homelessness of such persons to individual weakness and personal failure, a view that turns this vulnerability to socioeconomic forces on its head. Given such a logic, other explanations for homelessness need not be examined, and little social responsibility is taken for the situation. The presence and visibility of bedraggled, homeless street addicts may, in fact, be an important ideological tool in perpetuating popular explanations. In keeping with the "obvious" facts (slovenly dope fiends hanging out on street corners) and explanations (according with an ideology of individualism), services to homeless street addicts need not be very extensive, humane, responsible, or even adequate. The experiences of street addicts living in city shelters attest to the insidious nature of shelter life, where residents ultimately feel punished for being without a home. The current social response to homelessness, purportedly addressing critical housing needs, appears instead to be a well-organized system of social control.

SOCIAL CONTROL AND THE ORGANIZATION OF SHELTER LIFE

In describing their perceptions of and experiences with state-provided shelter, homeless street addicts point to relative powerlessness as a pivotal condition for a successful system of social control. Their powerlessness is maintained in the interplay of various aspects of shelter life that operate as mechanisms of social control. These mechanisms include the use of dehumanizing and infantilizing rules, procedures, and practices within the shelters, as well as the structuring of antagonistic social relations both among shelter residents and between them and others.

For street people, entry into the system often means dealing with a bureaucratic authority indifferent to the real, complex needs of the homeless ("They didn't give a damn"). Poor treatment begins with the first step into the central administrative offices, where would-be shelter clients are expected to be undemanding and deferential. To receive "three hots and a cot," a potential client takes responsibility for his or her homeless situation ("When you register they'll ask you what you want from the shelters. You tell them you want to try to get yourself together") and is then shipped to an available shelter location, regardless of personal preference or need. According to the New York City Office of Special Services for Adults, homeless individuals may enter any shelter, but they may be sent or driven to another site if there is a lack of space or if the particular shelter is inappropriate for a particular walk-in client (personal communication 1990). Nevertheless, shelter clients seem to feel their decision-making rights are to be surrendered in exchange for "bed and board."

The quality of the "bed and board" that clients' receive represents another mechanism in the effort to contain and deprecate street people. On the Lower East Side, for example, shelters are located at the periphery of several neighborhoods, thereby discouraging integration of shelter residents into local communities. In addition, the dwellings themselves are ramshackle, dreary, and depressing. As reported by residents, most shelters afford no personal privacy, are minimally stocked, filthy, and barely habitable. Several shelters are overcrowded and some are firetraps. Taken as a whole, shelter facilities serve as a physical reminder of and actual condition for sustaining the lowly position of the people who live there.

Residents are also expected to follow official rules and regulations as established by the shelter authority. Rather than help clients make their way through the system, the rules seem designed to regulate daily activities of residents. The routines set out for shelter clients are similiar to those for prisoners, as noted by residents who have experience with both institutions. From the 6:00 A.M. wake up calls and the 10:00 P.M. curfew to the bed-pass rule for sick days, residents are not at liberty to make even the most basic decisions for themselves. In their efforts to negotiate the system, however, shelter residents often find ways to circumvent the rules. Rigid and unyielding in its design, the shelter system begs for the criminality and deceitfulness it produces. In addition, although shelters are becoming more permanent sources of housing for street people, the system is not providing the extensive services that clients desperately need (from housing placement to medical and mental-health services). As a result of these conditions, shelters will continue to breed more criminality, disease, and violence (see Chavez 1988; Barbanel 1988; Hopper et al. 1982; and Baxter and Hopper 1981, which similarly describe shelter rules, regulations, and the poor quality of life for most of those who live in shelters).

The practice of using residents as cheap labor in a special shelter work program constitutes yet another mechanism in the effort to contain and control this population. In the program, residents clean shelter facilities at very low wages, prompting James to call the program "forced labor." More than a way to get toilets and floors cleaned at little cost to the facility, the work program is important for the message it conveys: that residents are, in some way, indebted. Like the incarcerated "criminal" who has a "debt to society," the shelter resident is also obliged to make good. It is unclear, however, whether residents "owe" for public services rendered or for their homelessness. Either way, people who live in shelters are again reminded of their culpability, leaving them open to exploitation and management by others.

The quality and nature of social relations within shelters form another aspect in the manipulation and control of homeless people. In general, shelter social relations may be characterized as alienated and antagonistic, hostile and disaffected. A bureaucratic structure defines the organization of shelter life, which in turn shapes these relations. Within shelters, divisions between people are created and maintained by various means. For one, the homeless are divided into various special, separate categories. Drug addicts, for example, are distinguished from homeless people who are mentally ill, homeless "families," and the homeless "older" person. In addition, the shelter system differentiates between people by social constructions of age, gender, sexuality, race and ethnicity, workers and nonworkers, residents and shelter employees. These divisions direct anger, tension, frustration, and rage among residents, and between residents and low-level shelter employees, and they ultimately ensure institutionalized control over a rather broad spectrum of people.

Structured antagonism within shelters is apparent in the descriptions of relations between residents and guards. The latter are positioned as enforcers of rules and procedures, the keepers of "law and order." As such, their duties range from ensuring that residents clean their rooms to expelling drug users. Given such a mandate, a "them versus us" dynamic characterizes the interaction between guards and residents. Although obscured by their roles within the system, sociocultural and class ties between shelter guards and residents are rather close, and lines between shelter employees and clients are often blurred. The "authority" provided to guards by the system, however, directs tension and conflict at the level of peer interaction. While guards do monitor residents by enforcing shelter rules or by making up rules of their own, actual social control occurs higher up. At this level, both guards and shelter clients are kept in check by the logic of the relations that derive from their structured roles within the system.

Tension and conflict are also directed between various categories of shelter residents. These conflicts emerge from the combination of factors that make up the organization of life in shelters. A basic element in shelter organization is the segmenting and separating of the homeless according to acceptable social categories. There are shelters for the young and for the old, for men and for women, for singles and for families. As we heard from shelter residents, the divvying up of shelter space is also based on employment status (e.g., "workers" at the Kenton and Delavan) and sexuality (e.g., homosexuals at the Palace). This form of housing segmentation does not recognize that the categories, arbitrarily defined, may not apply to the actual identities and circumstances of the people involved. Housing segmentation, however, helps shape new boundaries for self-definition and circumstance, and it thereby becomes a significant structural constraint on behavior and choice.

The combination of paltry material conditions and housing segmentation gives rise to conflict between residents, often in the form of physical fights. With basic resources so scarce, violent interactions often occur on food lines, or over food, clothing, space, and because "there is no own room." In describing these conflicts, residents also express dominant cultural understandings, particularly those of race, gender, and sexuality. Carrying with them patterns of racial segregation from the outside, residents battle it out along color lines within the shelter walls. In addition, the language and descriptions residents use in talking about homosexuality reveal a repulsion and disgust corresponding to the larger culture's beliefs about normal/abnormal sexuality. Combined with the dominant gender ideology, these notions of sexuality help organize personal relations within the shelter, perhaps allowing for some measure of companionship and the satisfaction of sexual needs. Stereotypical male and female traits and roles (from macho stances to "husbands" and "wives") appear as significant socializing tools in the management of daily life. As such, these cultural constructions are adaptive and creative. At the same time, however, interpersonal relations are a focal point of conflict and the arena for its (often violent) expression. With the lens focused on struggles between "husbands" and "wives," gays and straights, blacks and whites, and so on, more fundamental class conflicts are obscured. Broad social inequality and external sources of oppression remain hidden behind the anger and malevolence found among class equals in the shelters.

The potential for street addicts, the homeless, the unemployed, and the indigent to organize collectively and express discontent in radical ways is foreshortened by these mechanisms of social control. While some homeless street addicts articulate an understanding of larger forces that shape their circumstances, overt resistance is generally limited to individual gestures. For shelter residents, various forces of divisiveness work to direct hostility inward, diminish individual self-esteem, inhibit collective consciousness and solidarity, and perpetuate relative powerlessness. The position of street addicts in the housing crisis is in keeping with their overall social and political roles. At first glance, they seem marginal. In fact, however, street addicts are important for the part they play in maintaining boundaries of social conflict and in shaping public misconceptions about the causes of such social problems as homelessness.

CHAPTER III

Making a Living

> The essence of capital is its ability to mobilize social labor by buying labor power and setting it to work. This requires a market in which the capacity of human beings to work can be bought and sold like any other commodity: buyers of labor power offer wages, which sellers accept in return for a commodity, their own labor. The market creates a fiction that this buying and selling is a symmetrical exchange between partners, but in fact, the market transaction underwrites an asymmetrical relationship between classes. Through that transaction, workers are paid back a portion of the product of their own labor in the form of wages, relinquishing the remainder as a surplus value to the capitalist class.
>
> ERIC R. WOLF
> *Europe and the People without History*

With but a few exceptions, the East Side's street addicts have seen little in the way of reward or satisfaction in their efforts at working "legitimate" jobs. Ralph, a local handyman, began with part-time employment as a teenager. His first work experience was through a special city program for youth—summer jobs he held for a couple of years.

Another year Ralph worked as a counterman at Schraffts, and then he became a stockboy at Whelan's drug store. Though he barely remembers those jobs, he spent more than a decade working for a glass shop on Avenue D and Fifth Street "until they closed about two–three years ago." A low-level worker, Ralph never made much of a salary and was left with no prospects when the shop closed. "I haven't worked since," he asserts. Manuel, forty-two, started hustling at an early age. In between hustles, he tried his hand at various jobs. One time he worked in a "hat-trimming place," then "for this rag place down here—in textiles, you know, garments." Altogether, Manuel has held about four or five "steady jobs," though none was to prove particularly lucrative. Fifty-year-old Tom Silver was last employed six years ago. "I was a cook," Tom reports, "and my take home pay every two weeks was about $170, [with] room and board—I worked for the Salvation Army right down the street."

Although he has not worked in six years, Tom has a long lifetime work history. A veteran, he has been renting a room in an East Side shooting gallery for the past nine years. These days, Tom supplements his veteran's pension by "working the streets." Years ago, when he was seventeen, Tom started out in the air force. After four years there, he tried his hand outside. As Tom recounts it, he held various jobs between stints in the armed forces, none of which came to much:

> I remember I was working at one of those textile places downtown. I was making forty-five dollars a week, packing clerk. I seen the ad in the paper—Lockheed was hiring. I went out there and applied for the job. I worked for [Lockheed], did menial jobs mostly. [Then] Grumman made contracts and I was one of the ones they laid off. In '62 I went back into the air force, because I had a very bad drug habit. I went back because that's the only way I was gonna clean up. I stayed clean for damn near four years. Somewhere be-

tween there I worked for the New York Public Library, off and on. I was a clerk. I [also] worked for the Department of Welfare. [At one time] I was a machinist. I was in the air force a total of twelve years.

Like Tom, Herbert C. was a military man. He spent two years in the army, having first volunteered as a teenager and later joined the air force. "At the time," Herbert recalls, "I thought perhaps I might stay in the service forever. I was in about a month; I think that I was sorry I was in—but anyway, I was stuck with a four year commitment—it was the regimentation and everything, you know; I wanted more control over my own life." Nevertheless, Herbert stayed with the air force for another eight years. Since then, he has tried his hand as a dishwasher, a methadone maintenance counselor, an off-track betting (OTB) cashier, a clerk, and a waiter. These days the fifty-five-year-old Herbert suffers severe bouts of depression. For years a heroin addict, Herbert more recently became addicted to cocaine. He is also homosexual, and his years of "high risk behaviors" have taken their toll. Worried about AIDS, Herbert has stopped shooting drugs, and he is not promiscuous in his intimate relations. He thinks that perhaps a job might help him feel better, take away the "depression moods."

While many folks recall getting a first job as a youngster or teenager, these early experiences did not necessarily lead to new opportunities or even dreams of opportunity. Jesse first started making money when he was ten years old. This was when he was sent to live in Texas with his grandmother, who had little means to provide for him or his sisters. "After school and weekends," recalls Jesse, "I'd work—selling fruits and vegetables. Then it was selling the latest jewelry, and the guy would pay ten cents on the dollar. That's how I made it, spending money, and my grandmother would buy groceries with that." As he got older, Jesse continued to be a salesman—sometimes his body, sometimes drugs. When Joseph was nineteen, he found a job as a bellhop in a Manhattan hotel. He used this opportunity to learn the system of hotel locks and security and developed a profitable scheme of stealing from guests' rooms. When Jerome landed his first job, he was just sixteen years old, still in school, and working

in the West Village, working for this landlord. I used to come home from school, [start work] at four and get off at twelve. Sometimes I ain't come home, sometime I stay at his house, on the weekend I stay at his house. Then on Saturday I go hang out. Sunday night I go back over there to his house, in the morning to school, then had to struggle home from work. My boss was like a fag, and like I was not into it at that time.

During the two years he worked for the landlord, Jerome quit school, and he eventually quit his job too. "That's when I started really hustling the streets," Jerome says. Samuel Arnold, thirty-three, lives in a flophouse and washes windows as cars stop at the red light on the corner of Houston and the Bowery. His job history includes factory work as well as day jobs. One job was at a toy-manufacturing plant where both he and his sister worked. "My sister fainted on the job; she fell out from the fumes from the paint," Samuel explains, "so I left it." For the past several years, he says, "there was no other job like I would punch clocks, you know; I worked on trucks, [they] come by, want you to do a little work, load the truck." Dennis T. has also given up on "punch the clock" type jobs. Early on, he discovered it was easier and faster to make more money on the street than in the factory. As he puts it, "In the few hours on the street, I was making more money than at the warehouse, which was good money at that time." Dennis continues, "It was 1969. I was making maybe $160 a week, but I'd make a couple of hundred in one night down here in the city, by conning, whack and beat [con games]." He blames some of his job problems on his drug use, which would make him sleepy, late, and generally not a very good worker. Still a teenager, Dennis was fired from his first two full-time jobs:

> The third job I had, working in a warehouse as an operator, same thing. I'd be up and I just kept the job for my moms 'cause it was like at the time I was nineteen—it was like the last touch of reality, really, because I had lost touch with reality in the sense that I wasn't living at home anymore, I was living in Manhattan, shooting junk, and really, in my heart, to be honest, I was still just like a little kid. You know, there I was; I wasn't home anymore; emotionally I was still like a little baby, really. But here I was, running around with a crazy crew. Sometimes I used to talk to my mother on the phone, I used to cry.

These days, Dennis is a thirty-five-year-old "dope fiend" who struggles to make a dime bag selling heroin and coke on East Side street corners.

In describing his work history, T.K. expresses disgust and frustration with his past experiences. On several occasions, he has worked as a security guard in supermarkets and other stores and at the airport. Those jobs, he says, were generally boring. He has also worked at a car wash, in a hospital, and for a bookstore. The job he describes in most detail was the one at a New York City textile company. As T.K. explains it, his bosses liked him because he was a good worker, though they also saw him as a trouble maker:

The only thing, they didn't like me to [be] getting people together, talking about the work situations, and causing, you know, an uprising. They didn't want no riots or anybody to start [a] strike or anything like that. I had an incident with one of the bosses. He started using people—he wanted people that they can use, people that was afraid to speak up because they felt if they did, they would lose their job. They only hired blacks and Puerto Ricans. When I got hired there was another black guy that was hired two days after me. He's the type of person whose very, you know, he don't think that much; he's very immature for his age. They used to tell me, "He's just like a three-year-old," you know, behind his back; "he'll do anything we tell him to do." They would use him for doing hard labor, cleaning bathrooms, sweeping up the whole place, stuff like that which wasn't supposed to be his job. After you worked there six months you supposed to get a raise. I got my raise within seven months, after I told them about it, you know, so they gave it to me. Anyway, this young fella, the one that was immature for his age, he was working there for about a year, so I had got two raises within that time, and he hasn't got his first raise yet. So I used to tell this young dude, "Well, why don't you talk to them and tell them you've been here a while, and you expect a raise." So when he talked to them about it they told him the reason why he hadn't got a raise was because he's single, he doesn't have a family. This is what they told him, and he fell for that. I told him, "Look, man, they're pulling your leg; you're supposed to get a raise regardless if you're single or you got a family or whatever, and you're supposed to get a vacation and a week's pay." So he kept talking to them and talking to them about it, and after a while they gave him a raise, but not the amount he's supposed to get. You're supposed to get twenty-five cents more [an hour], but they only gave him fifteen cents more. They was really using him, but they was just using a lot of people there as slave drivers to get the work done as much as they can, and if you didn't speak up, if you didn't know what the work was about, you just didn't know. So they got tired of me, tired of me speaking to the brothers, you know, about the situations going on with the job market. I just didn't like being used and abused that way. When you're working for people you go out with your best ability, to do your best, and they use you as a tool, you know, and I didn't like that 'cause we was all men; there was no kids there.

TO THE PRESENT: ASPECTS OF INFORMAL-SECTOR WORK

Ralph, a thirty-six-year-old heroin addict, lives with his brother and nephew in an apartment on the Lower East Side. He considers himself unemployed and is grateful to his brother, the family's main breadwinner, who has a full-time job. But Ralph does have rather steady work, though he does not consider it "employment." He does day work from time to time for a friend in the neighborhood who also happens to pay him. The way Ralph looks at it, "I just do these favors and she pays me, you know." He does a little bit of everything—moves furniture, paints rooms, plasters, runs errands. His friend pays him from a dollar or two for going to the store to sixty dollars for painting a room. Since the woman is in charge of two buildings on Third Street, there is always some "handyman" work to be done. "It's not actually a steady job," Ralph insists; "I'm not like a super or anything like that." It turns out, however, that when pressed to think about it Ralph figures he averages "two weeks out of the month" on steady projects for his friend.

"Legal" Opportunities

It is not altogether uncommon for dope addicts, street people, and other East Side residents, to take on day work. Sometimes the work is mentioned in passing, or it comes up when talking about a particular day's activities. Manuel says that although he doesn't have a job, he does work loading and unloading trucks, "[sometimes] moving furniture, or doing light boxes for forty to forty-five dollars a day." Connie also works on a truck, lifting cartons of milk, cheese, and eggs for store delivery. She has been doing this for three years, and the work is pretty steady. To add to her earnings, Connie usually steals some of the cheese and sells it to a regular customer, the owner of a local cheese shop.

Others mention clever ways to make a buck. On occasion, Don Moore earns several dollars by buying snacks, liquor, or groceries for fellow residents at their shelter. Some days he works as a mover's helper to pick up $10 here and there. One week he earned $135 in three days by unloading poultry from a truck. Mike, a former attorney, sometimes sells legal advice on the street for a couple of dollars, while Reggie often picks up work as a pallbearer at a local funeral parlor. Lloyd Robertson plays his conga drums for coins in a park, Samuel Arnold washes car windows on the Bowery, and Larry "goes canning"—redeeming empty bottles and cans for five cents each.

Nobody is getting rich this way, but the money helps pay for basics. Lou has been working as an "off the books" janitor in his building, and the landlord pays fifty to one hundred dollars, "depending on how many days I work." Isaiah took a three-week reprieve from the streets, working at a summer camp in upstate New York: "From dusk to dawn I worked, had to clean up after every meal. . . . I ended up with something like eighty dollars, including the bonus, for seventeen, eighteen days."

"I like to work," says Quentin, who gets depressed when he is not working. For the past month, he has been at one job that keeps him happy. It is straight work, no crime or dealing—"that's why I'm broke today." Quentin continues: "I service and install automatic fire systems, work with the fire department, do the whole inspection. I learned it quick; I do a whole job by myself now, got to the point where my boss tells me 'go,' and he stays in the car." For now, he isn't doing drugs, though temptation is everywhere. As Quentin tells it, staying straight is especially hard when your boss is getting high on coke and dope. Antoine understands. Off drugs and looking for work, he is determined to change the course of his life. "Since I started looking for work," Antoine says, "I don't have no luck." It's been ten weeks, he explains, and the streets are mighty tempting. "I don't even come out too much anymore; I don't hit the streets too often," Antoine points out, "which is one way to handle [temptation]." But it's hard to find a job when you're stuck inside your apartment.

Arthur V. picks up "odd jobs," as he puts it. "Every job I had since I've been on drugs, I'd hold it like a year and a half," he says. "I'd think I was pretty good. What I would do was get my fix the night before, so when I woke up, I'd get off [take the drug], I'd go to work early, I'd perform good, cause I'd be all hopped up. [Then] I'd start taking days off, start coming in late." John H., who does day work as a mover on a truck, understands about getting "all hopped up." "Coke," he explains, "makes me want to work."

Drug Work

When East Side street folks work in the drug field, they are usually at the lowest levels of the industry. As in any other good capitalist enterprise, the drug business is structured hierarchically, so that those at the bottom receive the lowest wages and hold the most vulnerable positions within the organization. Workers at this level are a dime a dozen, except during bad times, when "it's hard to get anybody out there to deal." Quentin made that comment at the height of Operation Pressure Point, when sellers were busted as quickly as they could sell a dime bag (a dime bag refers to $10 worth of product; a bundle is equal to ten bags [$100]; a package is five bundles, or fifty bags [$500]). But generally, there is always someone who is willing to sell, especially if the pay is good and if it includes a "cura" with the morning coffee.

"Cura" is a Spanish word with two meanings—a "cure" or "healing," and "priest." For street addicts, "cura" refers to a bag or two of dope given as a form of payment for work done or to be done. "Curas" are generally reserved for street sellers, the peddlers in parks and on corner sidewalks. As addicts, these sellers cannot begin their work day without first "getting straight," which the "cura" allows. Management knows that dope-sick sellers won't attract customers, who might think the strung out salesman is pawning off dummies or planning a rip-off. Trust is an important ingredient in this business.

Those who are part of a regular crew begin their work day very early—six or seven in the morning. The crew meets at a spot designated by the manager, who dispenses the first set of "curas." The sellers leave, find someplace private, shoot up, and return to the manager, who is waiting to distribute the first round of goods for them to sell. Throughout the day, sellers touch base with the manager or his representative in order to deposit the proceeds of completed sales, secure additional goods to sell, and pick up a set or two more of "curas," as well as their cash payments for the day. Salesmen average several packages daily, bringing in thousands of dollars. In addition to the two or three sets of "curas" (morning, lunchtime, and, for some, at the end of the day), sellers are paid between $100 and $150 per day, with an occasional extra $5 for lunch. On good days, when sales are up, managers may reward workers with a special bonus—usually extra dope.

"Curas" are not only important for keeping the help in ready shape for their job tasks but also for assisting managers in predicting the marketability of the day's product. The addict-seller, who has the first taste of a particular cut of dope, reports to the manager on its quality, flavor, and, therefore, its sales potential. A good or bad batch, explains Jesse, is often assessed by the seller, " 'cause we're the ones who shoot it first. They give us samples in the morning, and they ask us how it is. . . . We tell them if it's gonna sell." A bad batch is a weak product, caused by poor-quality heroin or by dope that has been cut once too often. For addict-sellers, a good product "just takes the sickness off," although other users may get "completely zonked out." Once the word gets around, a bad product means a slow, short work day, while a good product results in swift, high-volume turnover.

For many sellers, the "cura" payment system (coupled with cash) is adequate since, as Miriam points out, "it's the only way I could get straight." Quentin always liked getting paid in "curas," and says he wouldn't work under any other condition because, "Suppose I get busted; I'm gonna go to jail sick." While Jesse agrees that it keeps you supplied, he also points out the drawbacks. With selling in general, and the "cura" system in particular, you soon develop, Jesse explains, "a dealer's habit." In his view, "Doing more than your usual—being constantly turned on—just gets your habit higher and higher."

The street seller has one of the more lowly jobs in the business. Barton, who has seen many years in the industry and many sides of it, reports that street sellers are "more or less like junkies; either they're doing it for the drugs or the money." Along with their coworkers—the steerers, touters, and lookouts—street sellers are the most visible cogs in the wheel. They are their industry's public representatives, and the ones most likely to be busted. Arrest is considered a risk one takes in business, and street workers do not expect management to bail them out. On management's side, the arrest of a worker represents a potential three-tiered loss: the worker, the drugs, and the money. In general, managers do not expect busted workers to compensate them for the money and drugs confiscated by the police or lost during the confusion of an arrest. There have been exceptions, however, as several street sellers report. Miriam details her case:

> I was just selling, there were about thirty [customers] copping, the cops was coming up from behind us, so everybody was crowding me. [I was selling] thirty dime bags [$300 worth] of Destroyer [a brand name]. So the cops are running up behind us, and I put the bundles under a rock. I had told my lookout, "Keep your eyes on the stash," and he didn't, and [a customer] goes under the rock and takes

it. Now [the managers] think I'm supposed to pay for those bundles because the guy stole them. They never paid me yet—[I'm] supposed to get paid $140 plus six "curas"—I had four "curas." They say they're not paying me; they're taking it out of my pay. He says when he feels that I paid $300, when I work $300 off, then he'll start paying me again. Well, this morning I took the "curas" and I didn't do nothing, so he's out looking for me now. He'll probably hit me upside my head, that's it. I've never had nobody else I've ever worked for do that shit to me. As long as I've been in this game, I've never had to pay nothing when I took a bust.

Miriam expects the issue to blow over, and she plans to start work for someone else. Generally, however, managers do not make a fuss over losses that come with arrest, since they have devised a fairly successful system to minimize the extent of these losses. This system includes splitting job roles and duties among the street workers, as well as following some basic business principles. As noted, street workers include sellers, lookouts, steerers, and touters. While sellers deal directly with customers in carrying out the transaction, lookouts watch sellers' backs, keeping an eye out for cops and thieves. Steerers and touters are walking publicists, important in a business that relies on word-of-mouth advertisement. Touters spread the word about the product by hawking on street corners and parks and by tracking down particular customers. Similarly, steerers tell those looking to make a purchase where to find a certain seller.

The manager, sometimes called "lieutenant," plays a pivotal role in the system. He is the contact person for the street reps and mediates between them and the never-to-be-seen "big bosses." Responsible for day-to-day operations, the manager oversees workers' performance. He is also responsible for distributing and collecting the day's products and receipts. In some cases, the manager may use a trusted underling to do part of the work. For example, another position, somewhere between a street job and management, is that of the holder. Street sellers, never entrusted with large amounts of goods or cash, may meet with the holder rather than the manager to secure more product and surrender cash throughout the day. Quentin describes a typical five- to six-person crew:

> Just one guy sells. One guy [the holder] holds the package, like he'll sit on the other side of the park. You'll have two lookouts, and then you got a [steerer/touter], he'll tell people where it is—he walks around the area saying, "BT's over by the park, or over on Second Avenue," you know, like that. The holder will have a few packages on him— about three or four, no more than five—so when [the seller] runs out, the pool is right there.

The seller, Quentin explains, waits until he sells an entire package before handing the money over to the holder. The holder then gives him another package to sell and takes the cash earnings "straight to the manager." In describing a variation of the basic design, Jesse also notes that "babysitter" is another term for the holder:

> Now a babysitter is a person that looks after the packages. They'll be about four blocks away from risk, from where we're selling. I go with the manager and he'll tell the babysitter to give me a package. I'll go and sell that. Every $100 I make I give to another guy to hold onto. This way I don't have it; if I get busted, I don't have it; I have very little

cash on me, and the most they're gonna catch me with is a package. Now that babysitter, all that babysitter does is look after the packages, you know, watch, watch—he has them either stashed underneath a car or in a trash can or somewhere in an empty lot—so we never go anywhere near the house [the organization's local operating site].

This division of labor works quite well in ensuring that not too much ever gets lost—whether by worker or customer pilferage or in the event of worker arrest. "They don't care how many times you get busted," notes Jesse, facing a two- to four-year prison sentence, "I'm getting busted with such little amounts that they're not really losing because they're selling; you see, I'm selling anywhere from $5 to $15 to $20,000 in product a day, and if it's not me, it's somebody else. Now if I get busted, the most they gonna bust me with is a package, which is only $500 'cause that's the most they give you at one time."

The combination of the "cura" provision and the system for laying out the merchandise in intervals promises to hold workers in check. "They worry about me taking off with a package, but then, again, they're not," observes Jesse, "they're not losing much. You see, I have just about every stamp out there wants me to work for them as a seller because I have a good reputation of not running off with a package, of being honest. When I work for a stamp, I'm loyal, I sell as much as I can and I promote the product." Sometimes, however, workers do take off with the goods. Not all managers react to this in the same way, according to those who have done it. "It all depends," points out Quentin. "Some guy who you mess up on a bundle, which is ten bags, could have you killed; some guys who you mess up five packages [twenty-five bundles] won't do nothing. . . . It's all depending on whoever is running the show. Best thing is not to fuck up—you do right by them people, they take care of you." Isabel makes a similar point. As an individual entrepreneur, she once ran her own small street operation with four steady workers. At one point, she had two men working for her, but they "cut out on everything" (stole from her). The female workers were easier for Isabel to handle, using the same methods as other managers. "I'd give them their wake-up, plus you can control them because they become like indebted to you. They wouldn't let anything happen to you, 'cause something happen to you, they have to find somebody else to work for to support their habit. The nicer you are to your worker, then he won't even need to work for somebody else."

Quentin notes that workers can begin at the bottom of the job ladder and work their way up. "You start as a lookout," he explains, "[move] up to a seller, and then to a holder." Management positions, however, are more difficult to secure, and they are usually reserved for persons with family ties to those at higher levels of the organization. Sometimes a worker will take a step down the ladder, depending on circumstances. Fred, for example, decided to take on a less risky position after being released from jail. "I'm going shopping in the street," he hopes, "and then I'm gonna steer, you know, bring customers, or lookout, [but] I ain't gonna sell."

A common way of marketing street drugs, then, is to organize a crew who work together regularly. This is not, however, the only way workers are procured for drug sales. Another pattern, becoming more and more common, is for managers to recruit different workers for day work. When Rafael was a manager, he would come around to street corners or walk into a popular eatery during the early morning hours and ask,

"Want to work today?" In the past, he says, workers "were more permanent than now." Barton agrees: "Sometimes you never see the same person working in the same area—there is always somebody different."

When he held the important position of "main man" in an East Side racket, Rafael was also responsible for recruiting managers. In this operation, he decided who would be a manager and who would be a street seller. He explains the importance of finding workers with certain personality characteristics for the various duties they performed or roles they filled. For management positions, Rafael looked for "the butch kids in the neighborhood, stick-up kids, you know, the majority of the stick-up kids got a lot of respect in the neighborhood, so you hook them up." These tough kids, according to Rafael, would be able to keep the street sellers in line and "keep the weight off you." Once you "hook 'em up," he says, you then "hook up their friends." Tough guys are not necessary for some positions, and you look for other traits. "Some guys got a good sell," Rafael points out; "they could sell, and you just hook them up like that." In his own case, Rafael started out as a talented stick-up man until he was recruited by a boss impressed with his abilities.

On the Lower East Side, there may be as many as 100 managers operating sales of the major products, heroin and cocaine. Although such a large number of operations might trigger territorial disputes, Quentin says that "there's enough for everybody, and more."

Different operations are known by their product brand names—Outstanding, Z83, Super Talent, Allen Boys, K200, Neutron, Ninth Train Dope, Master Flash, and Solid Gold Dope, among others. Visual symbols often go along with the bag names. Miriam explains that the stamps are associated with certain operations located in specific neighborhoods, "like Dr. Smith or Destroyer, you can only find them down here [near Houston Street]. Like over by Little Italy, they got their stamps, and then down in the alphabet land, they got their stamps, and like Black Rose is over by Madison."

Managers sometimes sponsor contests for customers to keep up the catchy names on stamps. "It's like a talent show," explains Rafael; "managers will pay whoever can think of the best name for the bag—everybody thinks up names that rhyme, and that's how they get their names." Fred says that the various managers get along quite well with one another, and it is not uncommon for them to congregate on the street early in the morning before the work day begins: "Every morning at six o'clock on Delancey and Allen—that's where all the [managers] be—maybe six or seven brand names will meet at the square. All the [managers] know each other; they shake hands in the morning, say good morning to each other; they're all there for the same purpose, to sell drugs and make money."

Working cooperatively is important for running a smooth operation. Rafael recalls his days as a main man: "I tried to keep the [managers and sellers] in a tighter group. Whatever territory I had, they could work from—say from Eleventh Street and Avenue B to Third Street and Avenue B. If one worker finished, he would stay in the street 'til the next worker finished, and then they would all stay out there until the last one finished. We had a beautiful understanding." Barton also points out that territorial divisions are not marked by managers, many of whom work for the same distributor, also referred to as the "big man." According to Barton, there are approximately nine distributors on the Lower East Side. "They more or less operate with each other," he explains;

"each person has his space, territory, or area to cover, as far as distributing their product." Barton continues:

> You see, one guy will have one area, like the Village, the Village is his—he'd never come up into like the Bowery and try to distribute. That one particular area, there is only one person running it, that controls it. In other words, they have their own land; it's like a farm. A farmer only has a certain amount of land that he's allowed to work with, but as you cross over, there's another farm— that's how the distributors work—they have their own certain borderline, and after that, there's another's land, another distributor.

As far up as most workers in the business see, the distributor heads a company's organizational pyramid. The distributor, according to Barton, is "like a telephone, in a sense—he would pass the word on to the head man. The head man would go from him to the dealer [manager], and let the dealer know what he has to do." Still, as Quentin points out, "there's always somebody bigger." Figure 1 displays this hierarchical structure in which the largest number of people fill the lowest-ranking jobs and only a few fill the top positions.

According to street workers, those at the higher levels of the business tend to reserve the best positions for close friends and family members. "Drug dealing and drug distributors," says Barton, "is passed down like family heritage." Quentin notes a similar pattern. "A lot of times [they] are very close friends; they know each other from their country." In more recent times, these are Latin American countries. As Quentin puts it, "Mostly all the Ricans have all this shit [drug business] up here, you know, and they all related, and then they don't consider him brown, they don't consider him

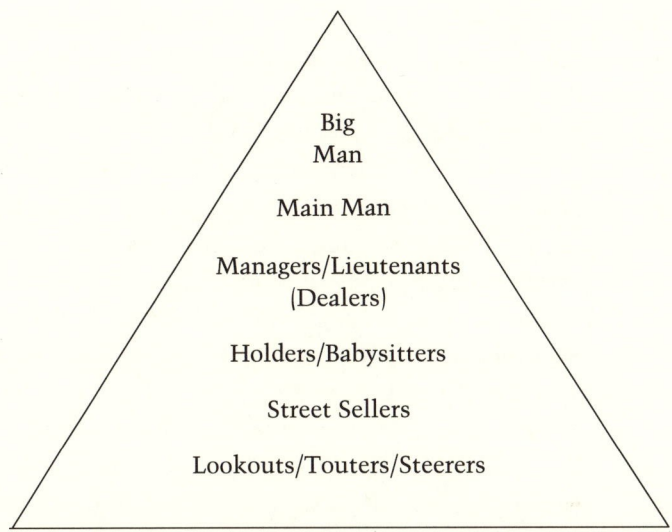

Figure 1. Hierarchy in Drug Distribution

white. Mostly all around here are Dominican and Spanish, Puerto Rican, Cubans."

Barton provides some historical background on drug distribution in New York City. He argues that Latinos have only recently become involved in drug trafficking and distribution, having moved into a well-established market:

> The mob situation is when drugs started really surfacing in New York City, back in maybe 1964, 1965—that's when cocaine and dope really started getting heavy in the city—uptown and Little Italy, certain areas of Brooklyn, Coney Island, Williamsburg, Flatbush, and a few in Jamaica (Queens), Staten Island, Jersey City. So there is a lot of involvement with the Italian mafia in the city—drugs were something like another income to them. Nowadays a lot of people thinks it's all the mob, everything to be done

with the mafia—which is wrong. There is big timers [involved with drug imports and distribution], but there is also small-time people who really need extra money. As far as bringing it into the city, we're talking about small-time gangster-like people, from uptown or somewhere upstate, mixed race. You find that predominantly nowadays it's Cubans, Dominicans, Puerto Ricans. They're Spanish but they speak English. They are mostly who is around nowadays. Out of those three, you could say more or less it's the Dominicans definitely, because everything comes from South America and that's like family. Now they may have an uncle growing cocaine in South America somewhere, they could send them the pick. Dominicans run everything here on the Lower East Side, Dominicans control it all. Further uptown you have the Italians, and, say, mid-Manhattan, you have basically half and half.

For several years, Rafael worked for an Italian "mob" family involved in many different illegal activities, including drug sales. As he remembers it, the organized-crime family he worked for began recruiting black workers in Attica and Greenhaven prisons. "They started recruiting Muslims because they were more dependable and trustworthy. [The boss] started recruiting [brothers] that were dismissed from the temple for whatever reason. We all hit the street within one year of each other . . . and they didn't like the idea of it being all black, like, in other words, his whole family had turned from Italian to black, I mean all his workers, and this is what he didn't like." Now, says Rafael, things are different, since the Cubans have taken over so much of the business. "The Cubans," he complains, "are a lot more violent. They don't have too much respect for a body, for people, and they knock off children, women, men, dogs and cats, you know, it doesn't really matter—so it's much more violent now than before. Before, like you try to use more discretion than violence."

Another important aspect of the business is preparing and packaging products for sale. This is done inside certain apartments set up as a "mill" or "factory," so named for the assembly-line system of cutting and bagging drugs. Cutters may be skilled workers and are referred to as "chemists." They have special knowledge of certain "procedures" for mixing drugs with additives. A mill needs only one or two cutters, although as many as twenty baggers may be working the production table. Baggers are responsible for weighing, bagging, and sealing drugs in little glassine bags. The whole procedure is broken down into steps so that each worker has a different task to accomplish. Baggers are often women and older men, although the table is guarded by younger men, armed with guns. They are there to make sure that workers do not steal, as well as to protect the factory from outside intruders. The concern with worker theft, however, is great. Sometimes, baggers must work the line naked except for the plastic gloves and surgical masks worn for protection. As Quentin points out, "They're afraid if they have clothes on, they'd slip some stuff in someplace."

Isabel started out in the drug business at the table, as a bagger. She was eighteen years old then and had just "ran, left home." Up to that point, Isabel was not into drugs, but that soon changed. "See, I lied; that's how I got the job. They thought I used drugs 'cause I tried to act hip, but I had never used no drugs, you know, [just] reefer, and eventually I wound up shooting drugs for real." Isabel explains that a major job-related hazard is that "you catch a habit"—from handling and breathing in the drugs. "Everybody's got their head right in the dope," adds Angel. "Eight hours of doing that, like wow . . . people falling off chairs, you know, fasten your seat belts." Isabel's first job was taking the dope that sat in front of her and placing it in the glassine bag. Most of her coworkers were women because "a man is physically stronger than a woman— a woman is more petrified—you know, like you see all these men standing around you with guns." While women are the line workers, Isabel says, "it's mostly men that oversees you." On a recent visit to a mill, Angel similarly noted several male guards with weapons, including one with a sawed-off shotgun, and "a dozen, mostly women and a couple of old men, with masks on, and white smocks, and gloves. They look like their gonna do a fucking operation or something, man, and like I says, Jesus Christ, I was amazed—they're just doing it, covering it, laying it, boom, bagging it, you know; it goes down the line."

Supervision of workers is pretty intense, making theft difficult. Besides the armed guards, the product is weighed and bags are counted once they reach the end of the assembly line. "If there is anything missing," warns Isabel, "you might not live to tell about it." Angel echoes her words. "They watch very, very carefully. This is a life-and-death situation—anybody get caught, they'd find them in the fucking river." Isabel describes another safety measure devised by supervisors, moving factory locations regularly: "Different days we wouldn't know where to go. So you ask the apartment tenant [term for factory manager], and he would tell you, 'Go to this spot today,' and it would vary."

Rafael's experience was slightly different. He was a factory supervisor, having worked his way up from a bagger. The operation worked out of one building, owned by Rafael's boss, "so usually everybody that had an apartment in the building was a worker or a lieutenant or a manager—everybody was down with the program in one way or another." Armed guards were a definite presence in this factory, but workers were not required to be naked on the job. Instead, explains Rafael,

> they were strip searched going in and coming out. You're not allowed to have nothing in your pockets going in, so there's no need to have anything in your pockets going out. [They were] very good searches—that's one thing you learn how to do, just about better than the police department—to search. It's a more extensive search we do—we go all around the shirt collar, the jacket collar, down the back, around the seams, down creases, around the pants. It's a more diligent search than the police department will conduct, and nobody has weapons except those authorized to have weapons.

Once the product is cut and bagged, it is delivered to the street for sale. The quality of the product varies, given differences in cuts at the mill. Also, lower level street workers sometimes cut the dope or coke again and rebag it before selling. Most customers are aware of this, and so depend on the word in the street for knowing what to buy and from whom. Ray says, "The word gets out that so and so dope is on so and so street, and so and so coke is on so and so street." The touter helps out on this. Ray describes how it works: "I go up to the touter, I say, 'Who got good dope?' He tell me 'so and so.' The touter steers you." Fred says you find out what is good by asking friends, and then try to cop from "whoever got the best thing that day." Tapping a familiar face is another way of getting information, although it is not wise to ask a complete stranger. As Rita points out, "[You ask] those you know from the neighborhood—the users."

Although it is rare, sometimes a product will not be cut enough—it is too pure, and people will overdose from it. Word gets around fast about that, too. Quentin explains, "Somebody OD, the first thing people ask, 'Who'd you cop from?' " A more likely scenario is that the drugs are cut with so many additives that users become sick. Miriam tells of the batch of bad cocaine that was killing people: "It ain't nothing but speed—it ain't coke, yeah, the SP coke." In describing this situation, she notes another source of new information on product quality. "They got a big sign over in Bellevue Hospital. When I went to check for AIDS, they got a big sign in there stating Don't Go Cop SP."

Most users do not expect a very pure product by the time it hits the streets. According to Quentin, "You could get something on the street 5 percent pure—it comes off the boat 98 [percent], so you can imagine how many times it's stepped on by the time it gets to those little bags." He also notes differences between product cuts by community: "Around here, a lot of people don't use quinine too much—they use that shit in Harlem." Quentin continues: "It's mostly black people that do the drugs from Harlem. They use anything to cut their drugs with—meat tenderizer, anything—that's why they always get so many abscesses and stuff. The first time I did drugs from Harlem, I thought I was gonna shit on myself; don't know what the hell they cut it with. We use baking soda."

Jesse says the product he sells is not that pure, but "it's the best thing out there." He adds, "And compared to uptown, people now coming from uptown to downtown because the dope down here is purer." Jesse explains further, "Yeah, [uptown] you get the quarters, and half quarters, which is mostly all quinine, whereas down here, there's very little in a bag, but it's much purer than uptown." As far as heroin, Rafael agrees with Quentin and Jesse on differences between the Lower East Side and Harlem. "Down here," Rafael says, "they use more purer—the way I put three cuts on it [down here], uptown they could put a six cut on it, and it will sell just as fast up there." Cocaine, however, is a different story. "Now you get the purest coke in Harlem," Rafael asserts; "within the last two years (1984–85), coke has been overpowering heroin to a degree, so like there's better cocaine uptown." Rafael points out that this is true even though there are more coke connections on the Lower East Side than in Harlem. "Down here," he insists, "they use more cut—they use a lot of chemicals—speedy stuff. For every gram of coke, you might have ten grams of some synthetic, plus a lactose."

Many street folks complain about the poor quality of drugs now available. Samuel Arnold says he uses more heroin than he did in the past because of the poor quality of the product. "It was better then, and you didn't actually need that much— one bag would've last you all day. Now it's mostly garbage— might be two out of three times might be a bummer, you know." Rafael also notes that, because the quality of the product is so poor, users must work long and hard to get enough money to make the large number of purchases necessary to keep going. In the past, he says, "we paid [worker-addicts] enough so that they could take care of the business, and they didn't have to go out and burglarize. But now, like a whole day and here's a guy making $125, and the way the product is, they damn near shoot ten bags to stay straight—so by the time the pay comes, the average one owes money. Like they tally up—he took five bags, that's fifty dollars— you're lucky if you don't come out owing."

The regular customers learn which are the better brands. Samuel Arnold insists the better-quality dope goes under the names Jordache, Top Priority, and Stingray. The names are stamped on the bag, and "you get to know the workers, too." Even with this special knowledge, regular customers still get taken, end up with a dummy product—powders and sugars passed off as drugs. "I got beat the other night with [the brand] Taboo," Samuel recounts. "We went there one time and it be all right. After we got beat, right, we went back out and did some more car windows, and the first car I did I got a twenty-dollar bill, [and I went back and bought] Jordache." Lee is now pretty cautious, having suffered his share of "beats." One time, he was buying cocaine and ended up with a bag full of dummies. "I had been buying coke from the same guy; it was a brand name. One day I said I wanted six nickel bags, so I gave him the thirty bucks, and I went to the bags, and they had no brand on them, no stamp on them; so I opened up one real quick, and held it to the light—they were dummies. [By then] the guy had already gone into the building." Having learned his lesson, Lee now follows this procedure: "I don't put money in anybody's hands, and I'm not gonna buy something that I know isn't good. It's gotta be stamped, and I have to see other people purchase it. I don't want to see it come off a pile, I don't want to see it come out of a dip in the pocket—I want to see it come out of a pouch with a whole bunch of other bags in there."

Customers often send others, known as "cop men" in the business, to make the actual purchases. While copping is a common practice, the role sometimes meshes with a con game played on the customer. Tom Silver explains how it works: "I'll talk a person into giving me their money, so I'll go buy drugs for them and never show up." The targets for these cons, however, are not folks from the neighborhood. "It's called 'thieves' honor,' understand," explains Tom, "You don't beat each other—people within your own neighborhood—[you beat] somebody that lives in Jersey, upstate, Long Island, Brooklyn." These may be less sophisticated users who are more easily taken. Quentin describes a group of sellers who work a certain East Side corner. Referred to as the "dummy crew" by neighborhood people, they sell any "brand" a customer wants. Quentin explains that they stay in business by selling to "people that come from Jersey—there's always somebody that they catch."

Barton, however, insists that distributors are concerned with the quality of their products and want to keep outside customers happy. "You'll find a lot of people who will come from Jersey down into the city to buy drugs," he points out, and while "there's drugs in Jersey, the city has better quality." Quentin thinks that those who rip off outsiders are very shortsighted. They might run off with a couple of hundred dollars on a one-time beat, but if you play it straight you can enjoy the benefits of a steady clientele. "We used to have a lot of people come down from Jersey and Philly," says Quentin, " 'cause they know I wouldn't beat them. . . . The other day I met [a guy] from Jersey—he gave me his number to call him up, and anytime he comes down I could tell him what's what."

Prostitution

There are other ways street folks earn a living, whether or not they have a drug habit. Sometimes they steal, sometimes they work day jobs in the neighborhood, sometimes they sell their bodies, or help someone else do that. Isabel once said: "When I left home there was only one or two things I could do—get a job, sell pussy, or hustle. I chose hustling 'cause I couldn't see me selling no pussy." When things got too hot for her in the drug hustle—between the busts and the rip-offs—Isabel found work as a "collector" for a pimp, bringing money from the girls back to him. This job is usually reserved for men, but as a gay, "butch" type, Isabel says she was well suited for the work. When she had her own drug business, Isabel learned how to take charge, using her fists or cunning depending on the situation:

> I'm gay, my life-style, and I'm aggressive, so I got a lot of respect from the men. More so than me being an aggressor, they had respect for me, well, they called it "heart."
> They'd say, "Oh, you got a lot of heart" cause I would do things that they seen men wouldn't even do—bold things. [For example] they'd say, "Police is right there." I would just walk to pick up all my drugs and walk right by them—'cause think about it this way, the man [cop] come, he can't search me bodily—but it impressed them. I got a lot of respect with [beating people up]; I used to carry a baseball bat, back of my car. I remember one time on Sixteenth Street, I had to chase this guy, and I can't catch no man, so I jumped in [my car]; I hit him with the baseball bat across his legs from behind first, then in the front, and I got a lot of respect for that. You can't let one person do it [owe money]; then everyone's gonna do it, especially me being a woman.

Eventually, Isabel got out of both businesses. Of the drug business she says, "It was hard for me in the drug game because I'm not a very sociable person, but for money I learned to be sociable, but basically I'm a loner." Of prostitution, she observes that "to be a pimp, you have to be like, you got to hate women to be a pimp."

The prostitutes who worked for Isabel's pimp were "damn near all" into drugs. They had to hide their habits from the pimp, who "didn't allow that [because] they mess up, couldn't be a big-time prostitute" as drug addicts. They hid their habits by being sniffers instead of shooters, since the needle tracks would be a dead giveaway. But some prostitutes only do the work to get the money they need for drugs. Kevin G., a heroin addict for fifteen years, finds prostitution one way to make fast money for a fix. As he tells it, there were times when he would go to bed with only one bag of dope in his veins, and before long, he would be awake, and dope sick:

> [I'd be] feeling very uncomfortable, and I'd have to go out. I'd turn tricks with homosexuals, and let them have oral sex. I'm not a homosexual myself, but I let them have oral intercourse with me. I used to go to these movie houses on Forty-Second Street, and let the gay people who would pay you. I would keep myself very clean shaven, and for some reason it seemed to attract them, and I would get the same amount they would pay a woman prostitute to blow them. And it was very hard because I kept thinking, I couldn't get out of my mind, that this was another man, this wasn't a woman. It just didn't fit—don't take me wrong, now, I do not knock gay people.

Shirley says more and more young people are selling themselves for money or drugs, especially now that crack is around. "I've seen these girls," she explains, who "come in my block, and go down this basement; they go down there and suck people's penis, and they smoke their crack after they suck the penis." That's called "crack for crack," according to Barton. He explains, "Okay, a lot of younger women that do crack have a tendency to prostitute, you know; if they want to smoke, you could have sex with them, just to smoke crack."

Many years ago, Tom Silver worked as a pimp. Pimping, he says, was related to his drug use since the profits he reaped from the girls helped pay for his habit. "Everything I do with my life is damn related to drugs," Tom points out, although he didn't stay with pimping for long. "Idiot women get on your nerves," he explains, "always harping 'Look what I'm doing for you.'" Arthur V. hooked up with a prostitute, and the two became a team. "She needed an ol' man to watch her back, and she was making good money." Arthur says she worked from ten in the morning to midnight, and the two of them would spend the proceeds on dope and coke. "I'm not proud of it," he notes, but "it was about me and her surviving."

In Andrea's case, drug use eventually led to prostitution. It all started, she recalls, after her baby was born. "When I had my child, I thought I had a boring life; I felt like nothing, and nobody wanted me. . . . [and then] I started shooting drugs, and it ruined my life." Now Andrea can't believe it when other young women fail to listen to her warnings, though, in them, she sees herself but a few short years ago. "Like people told me, 'You better stop while you're ahead.' I said, 'Ahh, man, dope don't control me; I control it.' Sure enough, a few months later, I agreed to an offer of selling my ass for $100— so that goes to show how much control you have; dope is the biggest pimp in the world."

Working as a prostitute is not always about drugs, though it is often about money. When Lee first left home, he was sixteen years old. He was soon approached by a man who offered him twenty-five dollars for a blow job. As Lee puts it, "Nothing like this ever happened to me before. I was scared and confused, you know, freaked out. I had nightmares over this for months." But the money was good, and he was young, with no other prospects. For two years, Lee recalls, "It was definitely constant. . . . All I did was close my eyes and think about a girl, and so I said this is an easy way to make money. Any time I needed money, I had no problem."

Connie was also introduced to prostitution as a young runaway, just thirteen years old. On her way to Catholic boarding school, she saw an opportunity to escape from a miserable, abusive home situation. Connie describes her escape: "I got off the bus at the bus station, and I met a black guy. He sounded like more fun than going to school, and he introduced me to the streets—I gave my first piece away, and sold my second. When he found out that I was thirteen, he sold me to this guy in Chicago. The original dude only kept me about a week."

Connie has many a cruel story to tell about life as a street "pro," but in the beginning she was "happy, 'cause I had somebody there I could go home to, somebody to put their arm around me, give me hugs, and that was nice. I was wanted." At the time, it didn't much matter to Connie that the love depended on how much money she earned, as long as both kept coming in. "It was easy to make money back then, you know," she notes. "I could make four, five, seven hundred dollars in like six, seven hours, so it was no hassle making money." Things changed only later, when she became older, more strung out, and less lovable. Now, says Connie, "I tell these young girls, 'I mean, damn, you gotta be crazy to come out here now, 'cause you ain't gonna make no money; you're not gonna get ahead.'"

Mario, too, started hustling on the Lower East Side at thirteen or fourteen. "I got into it," he recollects, "because I thought it was easy, and it's good money." At first he used his earnings for food and other basics, "to buy little things, like sneakers and stuff, because my family was poor and people out there—the kids—they dress up wild, and I didn't want to feel left out; somehow I wanted to be in tune with everyone." Sometimes he would get paid twenty-five dollars, sometimes ten dollars, but he was never organized about it. Now, a few years later, he hustles to help pay for his drug habit and has a system to the hustle. "Now, I time everyone," he explains; "it's more of a business." When he was younger, Mario might spend the whole night with a trick, but those days are long gone: "Now, I can do two or three during a night." The money he makes depends on the sex act performed, though he averages about two hundred dollars a night. "I've done some nasty things," remarks Mario, "but when you're an addict, these things you do, you overlook them."

Genevieve didn't start hustling because of drugs, either, although they eventually became part of her life. Her introduction to prostitution came by way of a boyfriend whose sexual interests included sadomasochism, young boys, and Genevieve on stage in a live sex show. "I let this sick man into my life," she explains. "It definitely wasn't love. I think more or less it was like a hate for myself." Genevieve recounts the steps that led to her career as a mistress in an "S&M" club, a sexual stage performer, and a peep-show star:

It started out being in my relationship . . . in my personal life . . . before I got into it as a means for a living. At that time, I just felt generally bad about my life, myself. I was in a successful band, and the band had just broken up, and my relationship had broken up, and I had lost my apartment, and I was supposedly starting out a new life, and I really didn't care to do that. I was very suicidal at the time, and I blamed everything on myself, instead of, you know . . .

Genevieve finally ran away from the "sick man" who taught her the pains and pleasures of sadomasochism, but she continued to ply her new trade. "Well, of course," she explains, "once you work in one of those places, the money everywhere else seems like nothing, 'cause that money does get to you, and I needed a job." This time, however, Genevieve went back "with my act together," creating a specialty in domination. "Since I didn't like men much anyway," she says, "I would make them my slave; I would be dominant."

Sometimes the money can't be beat, no matter how hard the trade may be. Jerome's wife ("a queen, not the mother of [my] children") works "the stroll." According to Jerome, "She ain't got it all upstairs, but when it comes to making money, I mean, the lady's a money maker." Emil, another male prostitute, agrees that turning tricks is highly lucrative, though it has its downside, too. "I'm twenty years old," he reports, "and I don't want to turn twenty-one and still be out here hustling—I'm tired." On the other hand, Emil enjoys some aspects of the life. "I like doing it; I enjoy the part being on the street and talking to the other guys I'm seeing, getting high—I don't know, it's a part of life that I adapted to." Still, Emil dreams of a "steady," who might help out with the rent and other things so that he could "stay home watching television, listen to music, and buy plants and things." And then again, Emil wouldn't want to become too dependent on his steady: "I'd love a lover . . . but I have this thing; I want to be working; I want to be secure for myself, have my own independence."

In the meantime, he works the street. A popular spot for recruiting tricks is over by the piers, around Twelfth Street. Actually, Emil works the "car" as customers cruise by and pick him up for a few minutes of pleasure. Lately, things have been tough, since "the competition is a little high," particularly for black hustlers like Emil. "Most tricks," he explains, "they don't trust blacks and Puerto Ricans or Spanish because they afraid of them." But Mario says being Puerto Rican has helped business, since white and black customers like that. "I go in speaking Latino," he remarks; "[it's] erotic for them." He also points out that these customers like any "Hispanic people, not necessarily Puerto Rican—Mexican, Dominicans, or Filipinos."

Both Mario's customers and Emil's customers come from all walks of life. Mario says most of his clients are "higher-ups, people who could afford it." Mario does not dress up in drag, and he points out that "drag queens" and the "regulars" (male prostitutes) are two different types, attracting different kinds of customers. Mario adds that the two types of hustlers "don't mix too much and they don't get along too much." He calls himself a "bangy boy—a straying punk," who is "more macho, the top man, the giver." While Mario works different hustlers' bars around the city, drag queens, he says, "work down by the pier, and they get paid better than we do."

Emil often hustles in drag, which attracts a certain kind of customer. Many of his tricks are married men who want him to do things that "their wife won't do, some things their wife probably wouldn't do." As Emil interprets it, there are customers who want him to be dressed up as a woman, yet not be a woman, because "they are married, and they could mess with no other female. It's like a fantasy that 'came attached to them over the years, something they can't do with their wife. Some men told me that they can't cheat on their wife with another woman, and so they feel that they can go out and do this, but they wouldn't do it with another woman."

OCCUPATIONAL OPPORTUNITY
AND FUTURE HOPES

The stories of past work experiences recounted here by street folks point to limitations of the labor market in terms of job stability and prospects for advancement in "straight society." In these recollections, we hear that street addicts not only found employment in various jobs but also seemed to want to work. By and large, however, available jobs were unreliable, and a lack of opportunity for long-term employment with any real potential for growth was the norm. As the descriptions illustrate, these workers held low-level jobs in factories, restaurants and wholesale and retail shops, while others joined the armed forces or worked as security guards. Subject to layoffs and low wages, and overlooked for advancement, these workers understood that the future held prospects only for further "dead-end" work. Moreover, accounts of poor conditions on the job and the relative powerlessness of workers (and, as in T.K.'s case, the frustrations of attempting to "right" injustices on the job) were also important in shaping perceptions of the work experience and feelings of despair. On the other hand, the immediate financial benefits of illegal activities appeared as an attractive alternative to an otherwise dull and unrewarding future.

WORK ALTERNATIVES IN THE INFORMAL SECTOR

Workers at the lowest levels of the informal sector—the handyman, the deliveryman, the trucker, the street seller, the prostitute—are among the city's surplus labor supply, disenfranchised by those economic developments that have excluded native (as opposed to immigrant) workers (Sassen Koob 1984 and 1980; Hart 1985). As Saskia Sassen Koob notes, the growth of the informal sector "is not only a survival strategy for the poor and unemployed. . . . Notwithstanding the appearance of marginality, its expansion is fed by key economic sectors" (1984:157). The demographics of our research sample suggests that they are among those "native" workers who have been closed out of New York City's core industries and jobs (Stafford 1985). Such a labor pool represents an important advantage to the city's expanding informal sector, which produces and distributes various goods and services. The street addicts who work as furniture movers, house painters, pallbearers, drug sellers, prostitutes, truckers, and janitors are finding income opportunities within this sector. The appearance of marginality, however, continues to obscure the relationship between economic-growth trends in the city and the economic activities of street people. Informal-sector workers often accept this cultural construction of work; thereby, they fail to see their contributions to the economy of the city.[1]

DRUG WORK

The Organization of the Labor Process in Street Selling

The drug industry has grown in a context of economic restructuring in "global cities" (Sassen Koob 1984). New York, one such "global city," has seen tremendous changes in labor conditions and income opportunities at all levels of the market over the past twenty years (Sassen Koob 1984; Tabb 1982; Hart 1973). As Hopper (1988) notes, "The net effect in cities like New York has been a pattern of polarized growth: new jobs are increasingly concentrated at either end of the wage scale, income disparities widen, residential patterns are progressively segregated, and the quality of urban life becomes ever more a question of haves and have-nots." Social scientists have noted several trends over the last two decades, among them the growth in service industries and informal economic activities ("legal" and "illegal") and the economic, political, and residential displacement of the city's poor and working-class citizens (DeGiovanni 1987; Susser 1986 and 1982; Hopper, Susser and Conover 1986; Stafford 1985; Tobier 1984; Portes 1983; Tabb 1982). These conditions, coupled with the perks of an "unregulated, untaxed, high profit" industry, mark drugs as a significant "source of private capital formation and accumulation" (Timmer 1982: 383–384; McBride 1983).

The organization of work in New York City's drug industry reflects patterns common to the informal, service-sector economy of which it is a part. According to Alejandro Portes (1983: 157–58), relationships of production in the informal sector have these characteristics:

Hiring and firing are often done verbally and under vaguely worded arrangements. Workers are not protected by labor laws concerning hours, minimum wages, accidents, illnesses, and retirement. Conditions of work and duties may change, and the amount and timing of wage payments are often unpredictable. These conditions of production are obviously advantageous to employers, since they allow the extraction of more labor for less cost with relative impunity. Perhaps more important, informal labor is far more "elastic" than that under formal contract, and this allows employers to hire during economic upswings and readily discharge workers during downturns.

The descriptions of workers' actual experiences in the drug industry are consistent with the characteristics just outlined.[2] In addition, economic decisions and activities of low-level drug workers are shown to be structured from above (i.e., they are not of their own making). Moreover, analysis of the data shows that street drug workers are subject to various mechanisms of organization and control (e.g., labor-market segmentation and manipulation of needs and wants), are prey to extreme forms of exploitation, and are dependent on their employers—relationships that follow sociological "laws" or structures of the capitalist "mode" (Wolf 1982:77–79; Zimbalist 1979; Braverman 1974; Nash 1983 and 1979; Sassen Koob 1980). Also noted is the nature of relations between workers and management, which are essentially conflictual, although there is a minimum of resistance or open expression of hostility among this sample of drug workers. On the other hand, since tensions are directed between workers, relations within the group appear highly conflictual. In sum, the relationships and experiences described here have the same political-economic roots and fall into the same categories of social interaction as those in other capitalist industries.

SURPLUS LABOR

Workers at the lowest levels of the drug industry, noted to be "a dime a dozen," constitute a supply of surplus labor. The availability of labor, however, is subject to fluctuations resulting from activities outside the market itself. For example, the "bad time" reported by Quentin refers to actions by the state, specifically the imposition of police action on drug activities in a certain neighborhood, which resulted in a relatively minor, short-term decline in worker availability. In the organization of the work day, addicts are not "shiftless and lazy," as popular opinion would suggest. To the contrary, they, like other workers, are up and at work quite early. Also like other workers, street sellers secure tidy sums for management while reaping relatively low benefits for themselves. As compared to wage opportunities generally available in the formal marketplace, however, the wages and benefits of the underground economy are better—$100 to $150 daily, plus several sets of "curas" (valued at approximately $30 to $60 per day), plus lunch money and extra rewards.

EXPLOITATION AND MECHANISMS OF LABOR CONTROL

In the organization of the labor process, management employs various means of worker control, including playing on workers' drug habits. The "cura" is a cost-effective means of keeping workers hooked to the business—it keeps them coming back, keeps them toeing the line. While management does not need to "hook" any individual worker onto drugs directly, the "cura" system is a useful tool in maintaining worker loyalty, trust, and dependability. The "cura" is good business practice, helping management create the condition whereby workers would not, by necessity, steal and consume merchandise. Otherwise, employees might be empowered with too much autonomy, allowing room for arrogance and audacity and limiting management control over workers and products. The "cura" also permits management to send presentable (i.e., not dope sick) workers to face customers.

Employees are also exploited in a most blatant way through the "cura" system, becoming guinea pigs as they taste new batches of dope about to hit the streets. Given that street drugs are not subject to regulation or routinized production, the end products of manufacture and packaging are highly variable and, at times, dangerous (e.g., if they are too pure or laced with hazardous additives). Through the morning "cura," and at some risk to themselves, workers therefore provide management with highly valuable information on product quality from which sales projections may be made. The situation is highly exploitive, particularly considering that compensation for providing the information and taking the risks comes only in the form of the taste itself. The many benefits of the "cura" to management certainly outweigh the minimal cost of a wholesale dime bag or two. Comments by workers engaged in the "cura" system, on the other hand, reveal their vulnerable positions both as addicts and as workers in the business. Taking the "cura" not only keeps an addict "straight" but also ensures against dope sickness in the event of arrest. Workers like Quentin consider the "cura" insurance against the physical and mental suffering that accompanies arrest. The addict-worker is not only fettered by worker controls but also bears a major consequence of participating in an illicit industry. This suggests that the criminal-justice system, as an ongoing threat to low-level workers, helps support management's efforts to keep them locked into the system.

The average drug-addicted worker, then, is not only at the lowest end of the industry but is also the most expendable—easily fired, easily arrested. As with the "cura" system, worker vulnerability to sanctions by social institutions (arrest and imprisonment) shows that risks taken by workers are not balanced by losses taken by management (e.g., Jesse's two- to four-year prison sentence as compared to a couple of hundred dollars lost). As street workers note, they are on their own upon arrest. Management has developed an effective system of control by occasionally and arbitrarily demanding that workers compensate for product or cash losses after their arrest. The fact is that workers would be unable to make up such losses regularly, and that such a requirement would create unreasonable expectations, leading to overt conflict between employees and owners. Ultimately, management requires just enough compensation to ensure a relatively docile work force—addict-workers are relieved that bosses do not ask for the money or drugs confiscated during arrest, and they, in turn, would not even consider requesting that bosses bail them out. This system, coupled with the special division of labor and tasks in street distribution, ensures that large amounts of cash or products are never lost.

A similar principle of "unpredictability" operates in the case of workers who "mess up." Management does not have one specific way of dealing with those who, on occasion, steal or lose merchandise. The threat of violence, coupled with the "unknown" (the infraction may or may not be ignored), are useful mechanisms of employee control. Given that these workers are not protected by labor laws, instituting the system is not difficult. Nevertheless, management must properly assess the balance between threats of violence and actual punishments in order to maximize the benefits of the technique in controlling workers. If violence becomes excessive, for example, agencies outside the industry like the police or the media may intervene; in a sense, they function as a check on management's control techniques.

The special experiences of the female manager point to the role of gender in the organization of work and the social control of labor. Isabel's difficulties in managing male workers may be attributed to the limits of female authority typical in Western culture. Moreover, her description of control techniques includes employing the ascribed female attribute of "being nice," as opposed to the more aggressive male technique of threatened violence. As Isabel makes explicit, her goal was to control workers, and she succeeded with a female crew.

SEGMENTATION AND HIERARCHY
IN THE DRUG BUSINESS

As street workers suggest, it is difficult for most to make any significant progress to higher-level positions in the drug business. Workers note that better jobs are reserved for those in a kind of "old boys' network." This indicates certain structural limitations to upward mobility in the industry. Given the history of labor market segmentation under capitalism, those at the top reserve important positions for members of their family, class, or ethnic and racial group. Such a distribution of jobs helps keep some groups out of prime positions (the exclusionary function of segmentation), saving them for the "in-group." Moreover, capitalist enterprise is so ordered that masses of producers (drug "factory" workers, street sellers) generate profit for a smaller number of those who control production and distribution. Essentially, there is limited room for street workers to move up through the ranks.

For most street workers, movement is circular, not vertical. Attached to positions at the lowest levels (e.g., steering, touting, copping, selling, holding), they hold relatively minor distinctions of status. This suggests that the division of labor not only helps minimize losses through theft or arrest, but also provides workers with the belief that moving into more profitable and prestigious positions is possible. Quentin notes that progress from lookout to seller to holder does occur. While such movement may appear significant to a street worker, it is structurally a rather insignificant move. In addition, Fred's case illustrates the circular pattern. Upon release from jail, he decided to give up selling for the presumably "less risky positions" of steerer and lookout. This case points to the role of the state (through arrest and the threat of arrest) in reproducing the drug industry's hierarchical structure and in keeping the lower-level workers in line.

LABOR RECRUITMENT

Practices for recruiting workers follow patterns typical of many informal-sector enterprises. While occasionally using "regular crews," managers often recruit employees on a daily basis. This highlights the vulnerability of workers, who are left uncertain as to whether they have a job. Their situation is compounded by the growing surplus of native workers in the city, reflected in Ralph's observation that there "were more permanent workers in the past than now." He also notes that workers are often recruited by personality traits or characteristics (e.g., tough, streetwise, etc.) and by the use of friendship networks. Ralph's emphasis on personality characteristics may, in fact, be an ideological rationale for the drug industry, which concentrates its recruitment efforts in certain neighborhoods and among certain populations (e.g., low-income, minority youth and black prisoners). In effect, this recruiting strategy reproduces the larger culture's beliefs about those unfortunates who cannot seem to keep themselves out of trouble. Moreover, labor recruitment in ghetto neighborhoods for drug jobs also helps to explain the availability of such positions to low-income youth (as well as the availability of the merchandise).

The Organization of the Labor Process in the Drug Factory

In the production and packaging end of the business, there are some patterns similar to those of street selling. While the center of activities is the "factory," as opposed to the street, workers are still subject to various mechanisms of organization and control. First, as with street selling, labor is divided by task and duty. This division helps limit worker access to the merchandise, as well as to potentially valuable information about the production process. The practice also contributes to greater efficiency in product packaging. A division of labor by sex and age, with women and older men holding the most lowly positions, reflects the vulnerability of these categories of workers to exploitation. Moreover, a manipulation of cultural constructions of gender and age is reflected in the way that young men, with weapons, stand guard over defenseless male elders and women. The presence of armed guards, coupled with the strip-search or nudity requirement for low-level workers who handle merchandise, represents worker control in its extreme forms. Literally exposed and defenseless, factory workers will more likely stay in line. Thus, the stage is set for conflict between workers whose suspicions and distrust of one another inhibit any kind of solidarity. The emphasis on conflicts between workers also disguises the more basic conflictual relations between all drug workers and their ultimate "bosses"—capitalist brokers who profit from drugs.

Marketing Techniques and Drug Distribution

The apparent variety of consumer-drug products on the street results from consumer-marketing techniques organized around New York City's neighborhoods. The correspondence between certain name brands and specific city communities (Little Italy, Loisada, etc.) suggests a clever mechanism for developing product identification and loyalty among consumers at a very local level. Among the more important marketing techniques are attractive packaging (stamps), name recognition (brand names), and consumer involvement and camaraderie around drug-consuming activities (product name contests). Moreover, product names like Outstanding, Super Talent, Master Flash, and Solid Gold, which reflect strong, positive attributes and notions of success, strength, power, excitement, and wealth, encourage consumers to make symbolic connections with these products. Since they are associated with certain geographical locales, the named products allow for an ever-increasing product familiarity and for personal connection to home and neighborhood.

These personal links are important to the spread of information about products for sale on the street. This is due in part to the illegality of drugs, which forces advertising campaigns underground. Successful distribution therefore relies on personal and neighborhood networks for word-of-mouth advertisements about where to shop and the quality of goods. Structured in this way, the distribution system puts consumers in a less favorable position vis-à-vis distributors. While the latter expend relatively little on advertising and are not accountable for product quality, consumers must actively seek sellers and have no guarantee as to the quality of their purchases. The case of a hospital warning users against a certain deadly brand of dope highlights the degree to which owners/distributors are neither accountable for their products nor concerned with consumer protection. One consequence of illegality, then, is a lack of state regulation for this consumer good. By picking up the slack, the hospital's action represents a certain acquiescence by "straight" society to the drug profiteers. While addicts may receive occasional guidance by such outside agencies, generally they must depend on their own resources for securing goods of minimal quality and reliability.

This variation in product type and quality has important, though contradictory, meanings and consequences. Street sellers, known to "cut and rebag the dope again," are showing some autonomy from their bosses by such action, albeit at the expense of fellow addicts. Also, addicts and sellers report the use of different additives in different areas of the city, expressed in terms of ethnic and racial preferences. Differences in coke and heroin are considered to mark (ethnic/racial/cultural) inferiority and superiority, a common way of viewing cultural products by members of the larger social system. In turn, sellers and experienced street addicts label different categories of customers by geography (locals versus out-of-towners), who may or may not be ripped off. These tensions between consumers and sellers are essentially the same as those among the various categories of street and factory drug workers. They are conflicts reproduced to inhibit solidarity among drug users, who are left powerless and manipulated. Their conflicts (and personal failures) become the focus of attention by various social agencies and the public. As a consequence, the social conditions that direct people to the "drug world" are left unexamined, and the drug industry continues to flourish.

CULTURE AND IDEOLOGY IN PROSTITUTION

I have emphasized a detailed description and analysis of the structural aspects of work in the discussion of the drug industry. The material on prostitution, however, also focuses on certain ideological processes and cultural understandings. I assert that these processes go hand in hand with the organizational structure of work. Such processes ultimately provide benefits to capital, as participants fail to see the structural connections between their various activities. Without knowledge of such connections, social categories and cultural notions of gender, race, self, and sexuality are highlighted, obscuring underlying social relations. At the same time, participation in various activities represents a "life management" strategy under difficult circumstances.

The political and economic forces that have spawned the drug industry have also provided street people with opportunities in prostitution, among other hustles. While there are differences among the various activities, certain underlying principles of the market, labor mobilization and control, asymmetry in social relations, and the mystification of those relations are essentially the same, emerging as they do from common roots. With increased economic pressure, street folks flow in and out of those income-generating activities to which they have access. For example, Isabel's comments on her general work options reflect an accurate perception of available income-generating activities ("get a job, sell pussy, or hustle").

Prostitution, like the drug business, is an informal-sector service industry that recruits workers from the "surplus population." As Isabel's comments on her work choices indicate, at the level of individual decision making cultural factors are significant in steering persons in one direction or another. In turn, cultural factors are also employed by people seeking to build a life under severe constraints. Isabel reveals the importance of gender as a factor in her choice of work, in defining the work experience, and in the successful fulfillment of certain work roles. For Isabel, her personal identification as a "gay, butch type" rendered prostituting out of the question. This identity, however, afforded her the opportunity to adopt certain stereotypical male characteristics (e.g., aggressiveness) and female characteristics (e.g., niceness) to advance in the tough world of street hustling (an adaptive strategy). This example illustrates the ways in which dominant ideologies (in this case, gender) may be tools of both oppression and empowerment.

Prostitution is work involving what is culturally defined as a most intimate aspect of the self—sexuality. It is not surprising, therefore, that street addicts' descriptions of prostitution are expressed in intimate terms, intertwined with self-concepts, gender identities, and personal experience. We see this in both Lee and Kevin's ambivalence as heterosexual male prostitutes, and in Connie's account of herself as a young girl seeking love and approval.

The intersection of private and public capitalist patriarchy appears in prostitution. The sex-role stereotype of male domination and female subordination is clear in the occupational roles and positions of prostitution. Such an organization of work paves the way for a system of self and peer exploitation. Street prostitutes are compelled through economic exigency to ply their trade. This may be to satisfy immediate cash needs (e.g., Kevin, Andrea, and Lee) or as the means to acquire social status and prestige goods, as in Mario's case. Mediated as it is by the concepts and language of gender, prostitution becomes a work option for those able to "identify" with it (i.e., it appears a "natural" option). An interplay between the social and the psychological occurs in the work of street prostitution, as market factors (including the recruitment of young, vulnerable, and relatively powerless workers) intersect with the sexual ideology of the dominant culture. Since their work appears to be a "natural" option, prostitutes then blame themselves for their personal failures. We hear this in Genevieve's lament on her work as a prostitute—"I think more or less it was like a hate for myself."

A significant consequence of labor segmentation by sex in the work of prostitution is the creation of conflict between different sets of workers, often articulated in terms of social categories (e.g., gender and sexuality). As Isabel notes, "To be a pimp, you have to hate women." Street folks are pitted one against the other—with pimps appropriating the labor of prostitutes. That most pimps are men who control or protect female prostitutes generates a war between the sexes within this segment of the working class. Solidarity cannot flourish if anger and hostility are directed at one another. Whether it is Tom Silver noting that "idiot women get on your nerves" or Genevieve saying that "I didn't like men much anyway . . . I would make them my slave," the conflict helps reproduce the larger social order under capitalist patriarchy.

Not all prostitutes are female, though the male prostitute may adopt stereotypical female characteristics or express attitudes and dreams in keeping with mainstream gender ideologies. For example, a core symbolic marker that distinguishes the "drag queen" from the "regular" male prostitute is traditional male and female sexuality, as conveyed by the dress, manners, and sexual roles of participants. These markers help reproduce the organization of work in male prostitution, including setting fee schedules and determining work sites. Besides the income it generates, prostitution provides some workers with a sense of belonging, as they enjoy the company of colleagues and customers. We hear this from Emil, who takes pleasure in the social aspects of his work. Nevertheless, he dreams of settling into a monogamous relationship and "keeping house," without fully giving up his autonomy. Emil is so entrenched in a culturally defined "female" identity that his words sound lifted from the latest issue of *Good Housekeeping* magazine.

As with gender, a cultural understanding of race and ethnicity is important in the work of prostitution. Customer fear of black and Latino prostitutes reflects patterns of racial discrimination and labor force segmentation under capitalism. This form of social opposition has its flip side in the exoticism of the ethnic other, as we hear in Mario's account of clients lured by his "speaking Latino." In dealing with customers from all walks of "straight" society, successful prostitutes are also professionals in managing racial, ethnic, and gender stereotypes, which helps generate customer satisfaction.

Overall, the organization of street work (prostitution and the drug trade) is fragmented by division of labor and by the segmentation of the labor force. These distinctions determine the ideological isolation of all workers (drug workers, immigrant workers, trade unionists), such that, as Castells (1975: 53) argues, street-addict workers are "separated from their class and placed in an unfavorable balance of power . . . [cutting] them off still more from the labor movement, in a sort of vicious circle which tends to reproduce the fragmentation and dislocation of the working class in advanced capitalism." As a result of this unfavorable balance of power, street addicts, like other categories of workers, alternate between accepting of and resisting "the conditions of capital" (Castells 1975:53). Among street addicts, overt resistance is most often expressed by the individual act. On the other hand, street-addict workers also develop creative adaptations in response to the constraints and burdens of their collective situation. These responses include managing social relations, manipulating cultural beliefs and ideology, and developing symbolic identity markers (e.g., clothes, the special language of the street, and the like). Cultural distinctions, however, also accentuate differences between street addicts and other workers, thereby obstructing the "common discovery of their basic identity of interests" (Castells 1975:60; Ollman 1979:3–32).

CHAPTER IV

Crime and Punishment

> The actual institutions of the state exercise a
> hostile domination over the individual. . . . It is
> simply because the communal interest is not rec-
> ognized for what it is that one class is able to dis-
> guise its special interest as the "general good" and
> to promote it through the organs of the state.
>
> BERTELL OLLMAN
> *Alienation*

Street people on the Lower East Side are al-
ways on the look-out for police. That's what you have to do,
especially if you're a known addict or prostitute, whether or
not you are doing anything illegal. Andrea says they bust her
"just for being around . . . just being a known prostitute." It's
a real problem, especially when you want to clean up your
act. Andrea explains that her new boyfriend has been helping
her get off the streets, but the cops keep getting in the way.
"Even right to this day, I'm not prostituting for over six
months, but I bet you if I walk that street alone and don't
stop, and they need to pick up one more girl, I'd bet you they
would dare to pick me up." Lou agrees. Having lived on the
Lower East Side for ten years, some of that time in a building
he calls "a cocaine connection," Lou has developed a reputation among the local police. Now, he rarely frequents the East
Side: "I don't hang out. . . . It's just I'm well known by the
authorities and I don't want to complicate my life . . . I don't
want to put my freedom in jeopardy." Hanging out in the

parks can be a problem too. Naomi tells her friends she won't meet them at the park, since that's like "waiting to be busted . . . 'cause they can bust you for nothing, just loitering."

For addicts, shooting galleries are dangerous places. Isaiah wonders why anyone would want to go there "when the police might be busting the door in a few minutes." For Isaiah, a resident squatter in a park he calls home, some police—especially young ones new to the job—are constantly harassing him and other squatters. As Isaiah tells it, "The police named the park 'sow park,' you know, 'pig's park.' " He continues, "I don't know why they think that, but they trying to get the Parks Department to close it up on us." Isaiah describes an incident with a couple of young cops illustrating the kind of harassment street people find all too common on the Lower East Side:

> They had another police come around to the park. . . . [cop says], "You're not supposed to have this fire here; why is this fire here?" I said, "I think you better get in touch with your superior, because even they come around here and try to keep warm." This police followed me all around, you know, followed me all around, and asked me about this wood, and then the female [cop] comes along, and she's just as cocky and nasty as he was, you know, and seem like they just be provoking, provoking, provoking, provoking, you know, people in the neighborhood.

Street people are also wary of police motives in making arrests. Quentin was busted at 3:00 A.M. walking toward the Hells Angels Club with a toolbox in hand. In Quentin's account, the judge immediately threw out the case as an illegal arrest, given that there were no reports of stolen tools. "They just stopped me 'cause they felt like it. . . . You know, the

cops wanted to get off the streets; [they] thought, 'We stand
around touring for the next couple of hours or we use this to
get off the street.' . . . It's one of those cases, I was just their
getaway." Sometimes it can work in favor of street people,
like the time Fred was almost arrested for selling heroin on an
East Side street corner one Sunday morning. "[The cop] let
me go because he had another half hour to work. This cop
gets done eight o'clock Sunday morning; I got caught seven-
thirty—if he locks me up, he has to keep on working 'til
twelve, one, two, three in the afternoon. He's been up all
night. . . . It's Sunday morning; he wants to be with his wife,
home, family, kids, you know, so he just gave me the money
back and joked around with me a little bit, and he kept the
dope, and I was very lucky I didn't go to jail."

But one can never be too sure, especially in the case of
street sellers, who are sometimes sacrificed by their employers to help local police satisfy quotas. One well-placed
source in the drug business notes this to be particularly true
for known drug areas. "[The bosses] pay the police, but they
gotta have a bust, you know; what's the police working a drug
neighborhood with no bust? . . . So you give up those workers,
say a poor worker [whose] money's not always right." The
jails are filling up with those Ray calls "nonuscripts"—those
at the lowest levels of the drug scene who "go off to jail with
nothing"—while those at higher levels "walk the streets,
drive their new Cadillacs; they don't care, and the cop got a
quota to make."

Those with drug or arrest histories do not expect the police
to believe or consider their versions of cases in which they
have been illegally victimized. Lee reports a violent event in
which a local merchant unjustly attacked him. Lee wouldn't
bother reporting the incident to the police, since "they

would've found out I was on methadone and next thing you know all my rights would've been lost . . . I would've been lost in the shuffle. As soon as the cops find out you're on a methadone program, you're a second-class citizen." Connie, a longtime prostitute, has many stories to tell of brutal violence at the hands of tricks, including gang rape. Reporting such incidents to the police is out of the question for women on the stroll like Connie, who remarks, "What good's it gonna do? I got a record, you know, I can't say he raped me . . . that's stupid." She continues: "Even if you take him to court, you're not gonna win, 'cause you got a record, a 'pros' record. He can't rape her, can he?—that's the court for you. I'm the one that's gonna get the time, not the trick."

The city inaugurated Operation Pressure Point in the summer of 1984 to crack down on dope sellers on the Lower East Side. Some say the intense police effort has had a significant impact; others believe it has done nothing to stem the drug trade or the more violent aspects of the business. According to Ray, Pressure Point's major effect has been to hurt local retail business by displacing "the congestion of dope fiends" from the area who had been customers of East Side stores. For Dennis T., the intensified police activity has "wiped everybody out. . . . Pressure Point pressurized the hell out of everybody." Quentin noted a similiar effect: "The cops come down, [and] nobody wants to sell—everybody's scared to sell."

But by the summer of 1985, the situation had changed somewhat. Quentin reports that by July things had calmed down quite a bit, and the "drug war" was no longer very intense. Ray, on the other hand, notes that while stepped-up police activity causes trouble for a great many people there are but minor consequences for drug trafficking in general. As he sees it, "That Pressure Point ain't nothing, ain't stopping nothing. Okay, it may send you through changes—here come the cops, you got to walk, move to a different locale, here come the cops, it's a circle." Jesse makes a similiar point, likening the situation to "playing musical chairs, [where] as soon as the police ride up on you, everybody disperses. As soon as the police leaves, they come right back." For Miriam, Operation Pressure Point represented more than a mere inconvenience. "I did a year when that was out; it's definitely over, 'cause if they were still out there ain't no way in hell I could sell. It's still hot as hell, but it's just not like it used to be, just not Pressure Point hot."

Regardless of the ways to beat Pressure Point, there have been many arrests among the street people, addicts, and prostitutes who frequent the East Side. Arrest is an unpleasant experience, to say the least, especially when the arresting officers wield power in abusive ways. Arthur V., for example, was busted while waiting for the bus to go back to a city shelter, his home. There in front of him was an open parking meter, the coin box filled with quarters, a clear invitation: "I didn't have a dime in my pocket, and to me it was like ten dollars in front of me. . . . I mean, I think a person not on drugs would've taken it, it was so inviting, you know." So he and his friend took it, "but little did I know there were four undercover cops watching us—we were set up like bowling-ball pins." The judge agreed that this was a set-up, "entrapment," as the legal-aid lawyer called it. Arthur and his friend were released, but not before the arresting officers dished out their own brand of punishment. More hurtful to Arthur than the physical beating he got from the police was when they threw away his weekend dosages of methadone, legitimately obtained in a drug program. As he tells it, "They made me take my two methadone take-homes for Saturday and Sunday and dump them into the toilet and flush it—I guess they're against drug addicts. . . . They kept insisting I was shooting cocaine, and when I showed them my arms they couldn't believe that I had no fresh tracks, and they banged me around, kept sticking the stick in my ribs and chest."

Isaiah is furious with police, especially the white ones. The way Isaiah tells it, they don't just come in, arrest you, and bring you to the precinct house; instead, they put you through paces, and it's humiliating. Isaiah was arrested in February, at a shooting gallery in an abandoned building on the East Side:

> Two racist, piggish white police . . . came in and made us strip butt naked, while they ran through the house. . . . They lined us up and kept on hitting people . . . with sticks, fists, their backs, their ribs. They hit me in my rib with a stick. They found four syringes, used ones, and [one cop] said, "If I get stuck with them I'll beat you up some more," and they kept on, this going on for two, two and a half hours; they had nothing else better to do.

The patronizing attitude really gets to Isaiah: "[The cop] kept poking me, calling me 'son', and I think I was ten years his senior, you know, said, 'Son, what's your name?' and I got very, very belligerent with him—I didn't like it at all."

Isaiah, a black man, says it's worse for the "white boys" and for women of any race. It's as if they think it's okay for a black guy to be a junkie, but nobody else. At the shooting-gallery bust, a white man got the brunt of the policemen's ire. "These two white polices are saying to the white boy, 'Hey, honkey, come here; get out of here, honkey, you no good fuck!' Man, they beat him worst for being amongst the blacks and Puerto Ricans. . . . It seems like they saying, 'Well, you know you shouldn't belong here; you don't belong here; it's all right for these spooks and these Puerto Ricans to be eating it, shooting stuff, but not you'; that's what they be saying. And I prayed, you know, thanked God there was no woman there, 'cause they might have killed one of us, if not her too." The "torment," to use Isaiah's description, included "making us lay down where there's a lot of garbage. [They] made us lie down butt naked in all this shit, where people's make a shit, piss, and what-not, lie down; they threatened us and stepped on a few of us." Isaiah knows it's their job to "catch the crook," but these cops, he says, "took the 'h' out of humanity."

T.K. is also familiar with racial comments that police toss around. He was arrested too, on the northern end of the Lower East Side. "Police told us," notes T.K., "we should've been white, you know, when we was born, cause you in Bernie Goetz's neighborhood; we gonna get all you Hispanics and blacks out of this neighborhood. They come out their mouth with racist slurs, and they supposed to be out there protecting you."

Rita's case of mistaken identity with the local police proved difficult as well. "This cop came out of nowhere," she explains, "and he just grabbed me, turned me around, and slammed me against the car, and said, 'Where is it?'" Since they were really looking for someone else, Rita honestly told them she didn't know what they were talking about. "He called me a liar," continues Rita, "and slapped me in my face." It ended when they realized she was a woman, whereas they were looking for a man. Miriam, too, was slapped in the face by a policeman looking for drugs. "'Where's the package, bitch?'" Miriam quotes the policeman as saying; then, "he backhanded me and slapped me up against his car . . . and he goes, 'You're selling it, bitch,' and started hitting me." Andrea offers a sampling of another ill-mannered man in blue: "[He said], 'If you say one word I'm gonna kick you in your c-u-n-t, so don't try anything.'" Another time, Andrea was being frisked by a policeman looking for drugs and works. As she tells it, the situation was pretty tense, since she lied by denying that she had anything on her person:

> The cop said, "Bitch, if I get stuck with a needle, I'm gonna bust your ass." It was a new set, and I really didn't think they was gonna find it, so I said, "fuck, let me take a chance"—excuse my language but that's my language— and the needle was closed, there was no way the man was gonna get pinched. . . . He pulled them [needles] out, and he said, "You son of a bitch, I should kill you," and he dragged me out, but he didn't beat me up. Thanks to God, thank the Lord, I must have had God—no, God wasn't with me, 'cause He probably was hoping I got a spanking.

Perhaps more humiliating for Andrea was the time a policeman befriended her. He would help her out sometimes, drive her around in the police car when she was dope sick, looking to make a purchase. One very cold night, when Andrea was dope sick and freezing, the policeman came by and drove her to the avenue where she bought the drugs she needed. They went to a local deli, and she went to the bathroom to shoot up. "He came in," Andrea recalls, "and asked me to suck him . . . for free . . . which I did it, I did it for a minute. . . . I couldn't believe it; he really destroyed the respect I had for him when he did that. [He said], 'Just do it, just do it quick, come on,' and he had always treated me like a daughter."

Samuel Arnold washes car windows on the Bowery for a living. This kind of work, however, leaves one open to arrest on charges of disorderly conduct, as Samuel knows. One time officers in an unmarked police car drove up, arrested him and his fellow window washers, and took their equipment and earnings for the day. According to Samuel, the policemen made the fellows buy them sodas, cigarettes, and burgers at McDonald's. While Samuel relates these events with a tone of resigned acceptance, Lennie finds it frustrating and exasperating that cops can get away with stealing his money. He says, "They beat me for forty-seven dollars, and my lawyer says forget about it because you got no receipt. . . . How could I get a receipt when the cop came in and [said] to give [him] my money?" Finally, Lennie comes to terms with the situation: "They can keep the forty-seven dollars, they need it that bad—it shows you the petty bastards that they are, you know; there's six of them. What they gonna do, split the forty-seven dollars? Good, I hope they enjoy it."

When Stanton was arrested at Washington Square Park, he didn't give up without a good fight. It had been a real nice June day. Late in the afternoon, Stanton went to the movies, and later to Cooper Square, where he shared a park bench with a guy drinking Bacardi. The two of them sat drinking and listening to a jazz band. After a while they decided to head toward Washington Square. A group soon formed, playing music, singing, drinking, carousing. "So we went on like that the rest of the night," said Stanton, until twelve o'clock, when "the cops came in, said they were closing the park." Stanton and his new friend muttered a few "fuck yous," and that's when the trouble began. Next thing you know, explained Stanton, "the cop said, 'You with the mouth, come over here.' So he brings me over to the car and starts rousting me, tossing me up against the car." In the meantime, Stanton is trying to talk his way out of the situation by mentioning his sister's boyfriend, a police sergeant, by name. But the policeman, a young "cherry" as Stanton describes him, was unimpressed and remarked, "I don't care who your sister's fucking." With that, he swung at the officer, hitting him on the temple. The policemen threw him in the squad car, and the young officer began hitting Stanton, who was now handcuffed: "He's sitting there hitting me with the palm of his hand upside my head, right in the side, boof, boof. . . . I kept trying to get away from him, and he'd lean over the seat, boof, and so I tried to bite him, tried to bite him."

After he was brought into the precinct house, Stanton spent the next three hours alternately getting beaten and resting. Throughout the ordeal, however, he fought back in his own way. During the first beating, Stanton knew the officer was trying to get a kidney shot, but kept missing as Stanton kicked back to protect himself. When the policeman threw him in the cell, Stanton snapped back, "You gotta work on those kidney shots, man." A half-hour later, the officer came back for Stanton's second beating, this time challenging him to a fight. Stanton refused. "He was like trying to test me, and I just went down into a passive resistant move, and he sat there and kicked me." Frustrated, the officer then tried to scare Stanton, warning him of what awaited him at prison. "He's sitting there," reports Stanton, "saying, 'Yeah, well, might as well give you the Vaseline now, 'cause you're gonna get fucked in the ass, fucked in the end by all these niggers.'" After his twenty-eight-hour ordeal Stanton got out, went down by Cooper Square, and he met up with a friend. "He was drinking some Bacardi; he handed me the bottle . . . we sat. He had problems, I had problems."

Talking back to police might make things worse for a guy in a jam, as Jarmin has learned. When he recalls being victimized in his past, what comes to mind are incidents with police, "what I would call police brutality," he notes, "and that's excessive use of force or intimidation tactics, harassment." Jarmin explains that his ways have changed over the years, "When I was younger, you know, police would say something, I gotta say something back to them. . . . Now that I'm older, I approach it differently." T.K., now in his thirties, started talking back to cops when he was a teenager. In their many run-ins with police, T.K. and his twin brother would speak up, since "we weren't the type that didn't talk up for ourself, we always talked back and let them know we not no chumps, or nobody you could put something on." One time, T.K. and his brother went over to visit some girlfriends at a housing project. The housing police were suspicious of them, and, as T.K. relates it, "They came up on me and my brother and tried to do us bodily harm, and we fought back, and we got arrested."

Other than talking or fighting back, it is difficult to come up with ways to take issue with the abusive ways of police. When Stanton was busted in Washington Square Park and beaten by the arresting officer, a criminal-justice representative came by his cell at three in the morning to ask if he had been abused. Stanton told him, "No, everything's cool," thinking that reporting the cop would only hurt him in the long run, "I know it's gonna fuck up my time; anytimes you had a fucking beef against the cop, you're gonna wind up doing worst time." Mario came up with a clever way to oppose the brutality he experienced. After a burglary arrest, Mario was beaten with a blackjack until his kneecaps were dislocated. From that, he "caught ill feelings towards the police," and felt "The only way I could get back at them was to actually get myself inside." He then decided to become a paid informant helping to snare drug-using officers, a position that he held for about a year. Isaiah's rage against the police prompts him to murderous thoughts: "I would kill them, you know, if I had a gun in my hand. . . . Yes, I would kill them, slowly, slowly kill them; I detest them." However, he also has a range of other ideas on how to handle the issue. First, he wistfully imagines mustering the support of the Black Liberation Army in getting the most brutal and racist police off the streets. He also considers contacting an old street buddy, a lawyer and former "dope fiend" named Kenny, who might be able to arrange some sort of taping or recording of brutality as it happens. And in passing, Isaiah also urges "everybody to pull our resources to get the creeps off the job."

COURTING THE LAW

Whether or not the police are playing fair, frequent arrest comes as no great surprise to the East Side's street people. With arrest comes the familiar "revolving door" routine that New York City's criminal-justice system is famous for. Quentin describes the pattern: "All I was doing was I came out and I wasn't home two hours and I was back in the courts, and then I would get off the Riker's Island bus, get back into New York. . . . Went out in the street, four days, that's all I did, and I woke up, I said, 'What am I doing?' "

Almost as typical as arrest is being assigned a legal-aid lawyer, although there are occasional exceptions to this pattern. For example, workers who are considered important to the drug business have found themselves represented by a private attorney sent by higher-ups. This is what happened to Quentin when he was employed by a Dominican group. Barton explains how it works: "Pushers [street sellers] are not a big-time thing. . . . If [they] get caught, that's [their] problem. Now the dealer and the runner, they're a different story. Now if [they] get caught, the distributor takes the time off to get them out of jail, goes to court. If you have any legal problems, it's okay."

For a time, Rafael was in a position to arrange bail and legal representation for arrested workers. "It wasn't a big thing," he says. "I was reimbursed [for] whatever money I'd use for a lawyer to get somebody out on bail." Quentin also points out that the easiest target for arrest is the street seller, and the street seller is usually an addict. "It's always the drug addict that's gonna need to sell drugs, to get straight," Quentin notes, and if one gets busted "there's somebody else be out there just to be in his place."

Those with private legal representation seem to be the exception. For most drug-related cases, and for many of those that are not, the representing attorney is a legal-aid lawyer. Arthur V. liked the lawyer who was appointed to defend him after his arrest for stealing from the parking meter. For one thing, the public defender explained what was going on with the arrest (i.e., entrapment), and then she believed Arthur when he told her the arresting officers threw away his methadone take-homes. Arthur was afraid that she might hold his addiction against him, like the cops did. But he found comfort in her assurances that she understood his situation and knew about addicts. Stanton, too, liked his lawyer, who, besides being "a cute little thing," dealt with him kindly and represented him well in front of the judge.

Stanton's attorney also offered to call his mother to see if she would come down and bail him out. Sometimes this gesture, perhaps helpful to the defendant, can be a problem to friends and family called upon. In Stanton's case, his mother did not consent. But when Naomi was called by a public defender for Bobby Q., her resistance was down and she agreed to come and help him out. They had only been friends, Naomi recounts, but he interpreted her act as a gesture of love and faith, getting her more involved with him than she intended. That night, Naomi recalls,

> I was really utterly alone, and somebody had been shot just outside my door, and I was very scared and lonely. . . . Right around that time I got a call from a legal-aid lawyer saying in a sweet voice [that] Bobby was off to Riker's unless he got bailed out now. At that point, I had known him a couple of months; he had never really put the moves on me. . . . I went up there with forty-seven dollars, all the cash I had, and tried to bail him out, and this is my nurturing thing or whatever, and I did it. . . . That was the beginning, because I had done something that he couldn't believe anybody would do for anybody else.

Often several days pass before a prisoner is sent before a judge. Frequently, prisoners receive a "time-served" sentence and are let go. When Samuel Arnold was arrested for washing car windows, he spent three days in jail. The judge gave him "time served" on a charge of disorderly conduct. In Arthur V.'s parking-meter case, the district attorney had complicated the situation when he found some old warrants on Arthur and gave them to the judge. The judge seemed angry and

> hollered at the DA . . . for even bringing such old warrants—one was from '74, he threw it to the side, one was from '78, he threw that to the side, and one for this year he put time served. For this entrapment charge he gave a conditional release—if [I] stay out of trouble for one year,

this charge will be dropped, off my record, but . . . if [I] get a felony charge, he made it clear I will do a year on Riker's Island.

On prostitution charges, Andrea has been given "time served" (usually three days) or fined. But she says, "I have never paid a fine yet. I have always told them, 'You're actually sending me back out to the street to make the money to pay the fine,' so the judge therefore sat back in his chair and thought about it, and said, 'You're right, no fine, case dismissed,' and that was it."

T.K. was involved in a case where the judge dismissed the charges for lack of evidence. This was after T.K. had spent four days in jail and had lost money to the arresting officers, who used it to buy themselves pizzas and sodas on the way to the precinct house. As he tells it, T.K. was hanging out with a friend who was selling methadone on Fourteenth Street: "They arrested me because I was with him, and they said I was abetting to the sale of a controlled substance. . . . They robbed me of my money and tried to make me sign papers saying this was the money for the sale. . . . I didn't sign anything because it wasn't like that." T.K. continues, "When I got to court, my legal aid read the charges, and she said it doesn't make sense why I was arrested, even the judge said it doesn't make sense, and so they just threw the case out on me."

Jesse is in one of the more difficult situations. Within just one month, he was arrested twice for prostitution and about a half dozen times for heroin possession and sale. A friend helped him out with two of the sales arrests—lending him money for a lawyer, who had the charge reduced from sale to possession. After spending five days in jail, Jesse got out on a Friday and was arrested again the following Monday. "This time," he states, "they're trying to send me upstate, get an indictment on me." Jesse, a low-level street seller, could kick himself for not being more careful. "It was a lady cop. I couldn't tell whether it was a cop or not, which I should've." Now he is facing a two- to four-year prison term. "I went to court, they offered me the two to four, and the judge told me if I didn't accept the two to four, and if I took it to trial and blew [lost], it was four and a half to nine." Jesse thinks he better go for the two to four, and explains that this particular judge has been tough ever since his daughter overdosed on drugs. "I was the last one on his calendar," he notes, "and every drug case that went before me got time." A letter from a drug-free program he had signed into did not sway the judge. According to Jesse, "[The judge] didn't want to look at it; he said, 'The man is going to prison; there's no ifs, ands, or buts about it,' he says; 'he's going to prison.'"

Lennie was also arrested for sale of a controlled substance—in this case, Valium. Although he doesn't understand it, the case was dismissed because the lab report indicated the pills were blanks. At the time of his arrest, Lennie (who has cancer) admits having the Valiums but denies he was selling them. Still, he is not convinced the pills were blanks. Instead, Lennie thinks the prosecutors wanted to "bow out of the case gracefully without looking like they have pity." As he explains it, "I'm talking about 'cause of my cancer . . . if they would give me a break, it would look soft, make people think the court was lenient. . . . So it looks like the cops did their job and it turned out that [the Valium] was a blank."

Herbert remembers the time in California when, by a stroke of good fortune, his legal troubles finally came to an end. It began when he was placed on probation for a marijuana-possession charge. During the ninety days of probation, he was given a drug called Nalline that was supposed to keep him off other drugs (e.g., heroin). Every Monday, Herbert was supposed to check in at the "Nalline station," which he describes as "very, very spooky, very Kafkaesquine":

> It was a very low building that you went in, and as you went in, you saw people all around—they were parole officers. You stopped at the desk, gave your name, and they pulled your folder and you sat down in this special section. They had a special section when you first went in, and it was a little darker in there than it was outside, and there was no smoking, and like if I was sitting here and you were sitting in that section, I couldn't talk to you. So then your name would be called and you moved to the next section, and when you sat there it was the same thing, and this would take about fifteen–twenty minutes, and then you'd be called into this other dark room, and you would sit at the side of a desk, and a doctor would be at the desk, and then just behind you, but where your peripheral vision could catch it, [was] another desk with a parole officer, and on the wall was a light, circular light, and you had to look at it, stare at it, and the doctor took a large, wide ruler and it had different holes in there, and he used it to measure your pupil, and then you had to go outside and wait for maybe fifteen more minutes, and then you came in, and he took another reading, and there had better had been a change, 'cause if there was no change, no dilation, the man in the back came and he cuffed you.

It didn't take long for Herbert to stop going to the station. "As a result," he explains, "I was a fugitive." But he was picked up several times. "I would always have to go back and lay in jail for two or three weeks, until it was time to go to court, and the judge would say, 'Reinstatement of ninety days' probation [with Nalline].' I felt like I was in the Gestapo." Although he "used heroin with a vengeance because every fix was my last one," Herbert resented others putting something like Nalline into his body. He tried to find a way out—refusing to take the medication, talking to his parole officer, writing to the judge. "The thing is," he notes, "I always got the same judge, and he was a dog; he was the only one who was giving ten years, six months at a time." At his last court appearance, his luck seemed to change:

> It just so happens there was another judge, and when he called my name, he said, "I read your letter and I was impressed by it, and a lot you said about the tests made sense to me, and what I'm going to do is release you." I was free to go, and he said, "You'll either stop using heroin or you'll die," and he let me go, but it wasn't the end of the heroin.

Sometimes when you go to court, it helps if you have some credentials. After his arrest in Washington Square Park, Stanton was finally released without bail. As he tells it, the judge made the decision after noting, "The man's a college graduate." Many years ago, Lou was a middle-class city youth raised in a nice neighborhood. Before he finished high school, he was deeply involved with drugs, heroin being his drug of choice. Still, he had plans to attend college. "In high school I always managed to pass from one year to the next; I never got left back. I didn't necessarily do poorly, but I wasn't in the top—I'd say I was in the middle academically, and that's with doing a minimum of scholastic work." His plans for college were almost sidetracked when he was arrested. "Now that summer—between graduating high school and beginning college—I was arrested for narcotics use and charged with numerous crimes, all involved with the use of narcotics." Lou did no jail time on those charges—he was given youthful-offender status and was off to college by September.

Lou made an important decision after that—to obtain the narcotics he wanted in ways that circumvented the criminal-justice system. "I tried Numorphan," he says, "and found it not only to be satisfying to my heroin need, completely replaceable for heroin, but I also found it to my advantage because I didn't have to go through these other steps—[it was] an alternative to having to go and deal with the slum-lord drug dealers in [certain] areas of New York." Lou continues: "The Numorphan was prescribed by the doctor and issued by the pharmacy. I was able to get it in a legal way where I couldn't be pursued or punished. . . . I could go around the laws in getting it, and the laws would protect me now because it was under the medical profession."

LOCKUP

Lloyd Robertson grew up believing that "a man ain't a man unless he goes to jail." "I believed it," he explains, "and was proud of the fact that I went in, and I came out showing, 'I went to jail, blah, blah, blah; I got busted,' that kind of thing." After having spent most of his life in and out of jail, Lloyd now notes ruefully, "I wouldn't tell that to my son." He also finds it annoying that some people make distinctions between "jail" and "prison" as if there is any real difference—"Everything is prison; incarceration is prison." When you're locked up, you're locked up. (For governmental definitions of "prison" and "jail," see Bureau of Justice Statistics 1983:78.)

The last time Isaiah was at Riker's, he was sent to the detoxification ward, where he met some young kids just starting on a path he knows all too well. Isaiah talked to them, urged them to change direction while they still can: "I said you're doing this just to be passing time, just to get a free high; I said it's not all about that, kid; I said I'm thirty-six years old and I said you're twenty-one; I said if you keep looking at me, you'll be seeing a revolving door of yourself and a rare reflection of a mirror."

Dennis T. says you get jailwise real quick. At the age of twenty-one, he was sent to the homicide floor at a jail called the Tombs. Although he was convicted of assaulting a police officer, Dennis thinks the judge sent him to the homicide floor to teach a young punk a lesson. "There were guys up there for two years waiting to go to trial. One of them comes up to me, he says, 'You're a cute looking guy.'" The experience gave Dennis two things—"a complex" and the smarts to protect himself. Lee shows many scars on his body from the fights he has had with other prisoners. This happened more often, he explains, "when I was young, only eighteen, and I was kinda like a pretty kid." Lloyd's first-time jail experience was similiar—"This cat says, 'Man, why don't you keep your rat next to mine,' like I'm some kind of funny bone."

Maybe Lloyd didn't understand what it was like to spend so many years behind bars. Ray, however, sees both sides. When he first went in, Ray was "a nice-looking guy, nice curly hair, a nice build." He goes on:

> You know, [I was] young, spry, and you got them men in jail for years, you know, tell you something, I did six and a half, no intermission, see, and a nice-looking person comes in there, nice-looking man who takes the form on as a woman, and this is truly what happens. . . . Well, you be in there awhile—I'm not talking about just six months or

a year—I did six and a half years, and I'm not trying to make no excuse for it, but I seen people walk in jail, I mean they look like they woman, they look like a lady, and I'm not gonna say that I didn't jam them, because I did jam them.

A homosexual transvestite, Jesse is preparing for a return to prison, having been convicted. He dreads going back, since "if the heat [from the prison radiator] don't get you, the boys will." Jesse explains, "The way I look, I am the most beautiful woman they've ever seen—I'm soft, and I'm not bad looking." He plans to choose a mate right away, someone just for protection. "Otherwise, they gonna be forming lines, just as the lights go out . . . they be forming lines with grease in hand." Jesse has been beaten and raped in prison before and now has "nightmares of that happening all over again." His feeling is that "just because I'm a punk doesn't mean I'm a punk," and he plans to defend himself against "all of them." He continues, "I don't take kindly to people demanding sex with me, you know, and I don't give in idly, even though a lot of people tell me I should just go with the flow." Jesse explains that the system offers the option of separating homosexuals from the other prisoners in special living quarters. This is not a viable alternative for him, since "protective custody is worse than being in population." As Jesse explains:

At least in population I can grab one person and say, "Listen, you want me to be with you, then you have to watch my back." You find the right person, he'll do anything for you because you one if you carry yourself like one . . . point blank, problem taken care of. With a bunch of homosexuals, you can't do that—it's everybody out for themselves. Being with a whole bunch of gay people, especially drag queens, is much worse, 'cause the majority of them are jaded, vicious, resentful. . . . With them, you constantly have to argue, whereas I know what's expected in a population of all males. You know, when you fight a man, you either whip their ass or they gonna whip your ass and it's over. With a faggot, you can't turn your back on them, because the fight's never over, and just as soon as you turn your back, they're gonna hurt you.

Connie understands Jesse's strategy. When she spent three years in a state prison, she needed a way to take care of herself. "I learned when I was a kid," she explains, "to use what you got to your advantage"; in prison, she chose to use her physical size as leverage. "I've always been big, so when I went in I always played butch—I wasn't butch, but, you know, I got over that way. . . . I'm onto those dumb girls; I said, 'You remember me on commissary day; I'll take care of you so nobody hassles you,' and life went on."

Nevertheless, things didn't always go easy for Connie in prison. "Everybody fights in jail," she remarks, "especially if you're white, 'cause you're the wrong color." Sometimes a dispute in the street drags on in jail. Rita, a young Puerto Rican from the Lower East Side, reports fighting with two black women in the park by Houston Street. The police arrested them all and "put us in the same cage," reports Rita. "I started cursing the hell out of them," she says, "and one of them told me, 'Shut up, you fucking Puerto Rican.' When she told me to shut up, fucking Puerto Rican, I just attacked her."

When Arthur V. was busted for taking the coins in the parking meter, he waited some time in the bull pen. "I had a kind of hassle with this fat guy in there," he remembers. "The guy started talking about 'Why don't you pick on yourself'; he says, 'Mark Goetz [referring to Bernie Goetz] killed my own people and I'm gonna fuck you up for it.' And I said to him, 'Look, pal,' I says, 'I don't know about Mark Goetz, I'm in here for my own problems, just like you are,' so the black guy came up to me and my friend and shook our hands and apologized to us." In describing fellow inmates, Dennis T., who is white, seems most afraid of black prisoners—"A lot of the guys were Black Panthers, you know; a lot of them were stone-cold killers." In Lee's case, too, many fights in prison involved, he says, "a racial thing."

"There were fifty-two of us in one little bull pen," reports Arthur V., "and alls they did was hand you a salami-and-cheese sandwich and these packs of sugar and hot cup of tea." Isaiah considers the floor the best spot in the pen. "Once you get in there, you have to be shoveled from one bull pen, which is a holding stall, to four different pens, and [in] each one of them you're lying on the floor, especially if you're going through changes, withdrawals, going through a lot of uncomfortable moves—so the best move and the best comfortable position is on the floor laying down." The benches are just too narrow, Isaiah explains, "and everybody in there stinking from laying in other bull pens in other precincts, some people walking around with crabs in them, and I'm trying to stay away from other people."

T.K. agrees. "You got people in bull pens not capable of holding no more than fifteen people, and be about twenty, twenty-five people in a little cell for three or four days; a lot of times you gotta sleep on the floor or sit on the floor, because the benches they got on there is not enough, you know; it's really messed up. Then they give you baloney sandwiches every, every meal, and like cold tea, and the toilet bowls and everything is all dirty." Andrea insists that "it's not regular baloney"; "they feed you baloney sandwiches every eight hours that a dog would turn away, God-honest truth, dog sandwiches." In describing a stint in the pen at the Tombs, Fred also notes the poor conditions and food. "Monday, Tuesday, Wednesday, was hell; it's like a dungeon downstairs; they feed you baloney-and-cheese sandwiches, and you gotta sleep on cement floors."

Generally, conditions in the medical wards and in regular cells seem to be better than those in the bull pens. When Isaiah was sent to detoxification at the Riker's Island infirmary, he was delighted to find vast improvements since a visit in 1980. "To my surprise, the whole place was clean and bright, because [before] it was a filthy, disgusting, low-down, dirty, filthy dungeon—I will give [that place the] 100 percent Good Housekeeping seal." It seems the Tombs doesn't have facilities to deal with addicts, so most often they get sent to the new place at Riker's. But Fred, an addict, preferred to face withdrawal at the Tombs rather than get sent to Riker's. "I just didn't want to go to Riker's. The Tombs is nicer, you know; Riker's is far away; I just rather stay here. . . . I imagine maybe I should have went to Riker's, I don't know." Fred also says the regular cells at the Tombs are a lot nicer than the holding pens. The latter are downstairs, a place he refers to as "the dungeon," while the cells upstairs are much better— "It's nice, good food, clean, everybody has their own room, you got a mirror, got your little own bed."

When Fred refused to go to the medical facilities at Riker's, the doctor at the Tombs was cooperative. Everyone sees a doctor when they get to the jail. Fred says the doctor offered him methadone, since he was feeling pretty dope sick. As he recalls the conversation: "I said, 'Doc, if you give me methadone, do I have to go to Riker's?' She said, 'Yeah, you know, think about it.'" And she didn't push it. Isaiah says the medical personnel have always treated him very well. "I got all the respect and attention from the doctors and nurses, but from the officers you was a dog, you still a dog." The doctors have to follow a lot of rules as far as detoxing an addict, and Angel knows about this. As he tells it, "kicking" in the joint

> was a mother. Now the doctor went out of his way for me, sending me something [Valium], you know; I was [dope] sick. He says, "Angel, I cannot give you any more meth, the stupid fucking laws, I just can't." They took me down in ten days. I was on a hundred milligrams, [went] to nothing in ten days. I thought I was gonna die, I was that sick. Now the doctor says, "Angel, I can't—I understand what you're going through, believe me, I had enough patients, and the laws are going to change." Now this is how petty it is. If I had gotten sixty days, they would have maintained me for the sixty days, right, so I got ninety days, so I can't. Anything sixty days or under they'll maintain you on the program, so I got three months, so [they] can't.

While detoxing in jail is a fairly common experience for street addicts, giving birth is not. But it happened to Rose, who found the officials to be less than helpful or understanding. In fact, at first they didn't believe she was pregnant, and later they didn't believe she was in labor. The only ones who believed her were some fellow inmates. It happened at the House of Detention on West Tenth Street. She was seven months' pregnant at the time of arrest, and she could have gotten out on bail had she told the baby's father where she was—"But I don't want nobody to know that I was in jail; that's why I stood there." The baby was born in an ambulance on the way to Bellevue Hospital:

> You see, my belly was so small that the doctors in jail said, "Oh, the junkies don't know—they never getting a period or nothing," but I knew I was gonna have the baby the second of August. Two days before [the birth] the doctor told me, "You due in two more months," and I told the doctor, "No, I gonna have the baby in a couple of days." She says, "You crazy, you can't know." You can't tell them nothing, because you're an inmate; they don't believe you. That day [August 2] I was screaming because I have such a pain, and this black CO [corrections officer] was telling me to shut up. I put this pillow in my mouth because [she said], "If you keep screaming, I'm gonna put you in lockup." They put me in lockup, man, with those pains, they put me in that dirty room—it was so dark and cold and I was screaming, screaming, screaming. . . . The captain from the floor came, and she said, "Well, what's wrong, why you lock her up?" and [the CO] said, "She been screaming all day, all night; I can't stand her screaming." I told one of the girls, one of the inmates, that I was ready to have the baby. . . . She believed me that I was gonna have the baby. [The inmates told me to] have the baby, don't scream, just try to hold the pain in, have the baby in the prison, in the lockup so [I] could sue the city. So the captain came, and all the police came, so they was so lucky that I had the baby in the ambulance, and the girls used to tell me, "Don't scream; try to hold the pain and keep pushing out; we'll help you, we'll help you."

CRIMINAL JUSTICE: TAKING
THE "'H' OUT OF HUMANITY"

Relations between street addicts/"criminals" and the "organs of the state" (police, jails, lawyers, and judges) are clearly hostile. The criminal-justice system, which helps to manage social conflict, considers the addict a destructive threat to American society.[1] Its representatives act accordingly, doing the dirty work in the name of heroic protection of "good" citizens (Klein 1983; Reinarman 1983; Kramer 1976).

Conflict between addicts, their lawyers, and the judges presiding over their cases appears to be less overt than those between addicts and police. In part this is because the addict/"criminal" has limited dealings with lawyers and judges. The fate of arrestees within this area of the criminal-justice system depends on the resources they can bring to bear on the situation, combined with the pressures and practices of the court. Important resources for an arrestee include ability to pay for private legal representation, family support, and personal credentials (e.g., Stanton's college degree, which helped him win favor with the judge). Legal-aid lawyers, reported by arrestees to be generally helpful, appear committed to upholding the pledges of their job and profession. Given constraints of time and resources, however, public defenders can only provide basic services, and they may be compelled to call on the meager resources of arrestees' family and friends for bail or other assistance. In the courtroom, judges are, in part, guided by the precedents and principles of the law. They are also concerned, however, with maintaining a balance between jail and prison space and with slots to fill (or not overfill). In this balancing act there emerge two "kinds" of judges—the "liberals," who allow crooks back out on the street, and the "conservatives," who throw them in the slammer. Individual futures often depend on luck—landing a tough or a soft judge, as we heard from Jesse, Herbert C., and Lennie.

For street addicts, interactions with police are more frequent, more constant, and, perhaps, more intense. On the street, law-enforcement officials are empowered by their badges and their mandates to set out upon a search for the relatively weak and powerless (yet "bad") drug addict. We hear in the words of street addicts that conflicts between them and police are particularly visible and acute, with relations marked by intense anger and hostility. Several factors contribute to the special tensions between street people and police. A certain arbitrariness in arrest is one such factor, according to street-addict reports. A person may be arrested for being "known" to police—as we heard from Andrea, Lou, and Naomi, who no longer live, "hang out," or walk in certain areas, whether or not they have violated any law. Others report that police make arrests to fill quotas, or to get themselves off a street beat and into the police station; however, if it be too inconvenient, a police officer might not make a particular arrest, as illustrated by Fred's experience. While arbitrariness engenders frustration and rage, it also provides a "loophole" for addicts who may, at times, turn it to personal benefit.

One aspect of law enforcement does not appear to be arbitrary to street addicts; that is, police efforts are consistently directed at the lowest level "criminal"—Ray's "nonuscript." Relatedly, while major police crackdowns may devastate individuals, they do not have significant consequences for the broader drug-related systems of production, distribution, and consumption. Operation Pressure Point, for example, wreaked havoc on the lives of some East Side addicts like Miriam, but it did not impair local drug trafficking. Special police efforts are at once costly and ineffective, suggesting that other factors weigh on police policy decisions. Political-economic considerations may be the hidden agenda behind official mandates to rid our streets of the drug scourge (Musto [1973] 1987; Hamid 1988). Operation Pressure Point, for example, coincided with the influx of real-estate developers on the Lower East Side. At the same time, special police efforts provide a symbolic demonstration to the general public that "action" is being taken against "criminals." Moreover, police crackdowns remind low-level, visible, and vulnerable street addicts of their powerlessness (Finder 1988; DeGiovanni 1987; Goldstein et al. 1987).

Police harassment and provocation is reported over and over again by street addicts. The tales of Isaiah, Arthur V., T.K., Rita, Miriam, Samuel Arnold, and Lennie attest to the verbal and physical abuse of addicts at their hands. According to these accounts, police use various means to control and manage misfits. They often turn social categories and dominant cultural constructions of race, gender, and personal failure against addicts. The name calling and condescending insults, racial epithets and mental abuse, and physical brutality and sexual exploitation are effective techniques of enforcement that advance antagonistic relations between addicts and police. These enforcement techniques also help create psychological distance between police and addicts. In this "making of the stranger," the "dope fiend" appears less human, more objectified to police.

This psychological process may be particularly important since addicts and police occupy social and class positions not so very distant from one another. In fact, psychological distancing, conflict, and the social roles of "cops" and "criminals" together obscure these fundamental ties. The "criminal," socially marginalized and economically disenfranchised, sees only the man or woman in blue chasing him down. Broad social-control functions of police are thus masked behind their uniforms. By granting police an important ideological role, as well as actual enforcement duties, a larger pool of working-class and poor people may thereby be managed. Those who become police are generally kept in line by fulfilling their job descriptions, while those who become criminals are, in turn, directly managed by the police. Moreover, the battle on the street between police and addict/"criminals" is particularly brutal, which helps keep conflict from spilling beyond this dyad. Class conflict is thereby deferred and obscured behind the cop-criminal conflict.

RESISTANCE AND RELATIVE POWERLESSNESS

In these workings, the criminal-justice system is powerful and effective. It is difficult to imagine that street addicts could change its course. Indeed, the system allows little room for them to change even the course of their personal fates. As individuals buck the system, resistance generally comes in the form of particular acts, usually against other persons (e.g., police). The power differential between street addicts and criminal-justice officials renders the acts of the former rather ineffectual. While street people may actively or passively manage the system by manipulation or compliance, overt confrontation is normally repressed. As Stanton's story highlights, various forms of opposition are attempted to no avail. Stanton recounts his verbal confrontation with an arresting officer, followed by a physical battle between the two. He also attempts to close the distance between himself and the officer by noting a point of commonality—his sister's boyfriend is a police officer. Ultimately, Stanton understands that his is a losing cause ("anytimes you had a fucking beef against the cop, you're gonna wind up doing worst time"). Jarmin learned to become more passive, while T.K. landed in jail for fighting with an officer. Mario, on the other hand, found a creative form of resistance, becoming an informant to get back at the police. In expressing his rage and frustration, Isaiah makes reference to various ways of finding recourse. Among these, Isaiah advises "everybody pull our resources," a potentially insightful suggestion. While these efforts reflect forms of individual resistance, they are also bounded and appropriated by the addict-police conflict.

THE NATURE OF IMPRISONMENT

The organization of jail life is defined by a bureaucratic structure that in turn shapes the nature of social relations within the confines of prison walls. Social relations among street addicts/"criminals" within the context of jail are often highly conflictual. Tensions between cellmates may reach high levels; however, they may also dissolve into ties of friendship and caring.

Structured antagonism within jails emerges from a combination of factors. As we heard in vivid detail from experienced street addicts, basic resources and physical facilities are scarce and squalid. The language of confinement (e.g., "holding stall," "bull pen") reflects the system's overall perspective on prisoners: they are like so many cattle. As compared with guards ("from them you was a dog"), prison doctors are generally seen as more empathic to inmates' needs, although constrained by prison rules and regulations. According to the New York City Department of Corrections (Office of Substance Abuse Intervention), jailed addicts may be maintained on methadone only at three facilities on Riker's Island, although there are drug-free treatment facilities at other city jails (personal communication 1990; see also Joseph et al. 1988; Joseph and Roman-Nay 1988 on Department of Corrections facilities for addicts in New York). Taken as a whole, these factors combine to dehumanize and degrade inmates, who then inflict their frustration and rancor on those most available and vulnerable—fellow prisoners.

Conflict between inmates generally appears in the form of sexual exploitation, physical violence, and racial hostility. The young and inexperienced are most vulnerable to sexual violence and exploitation (jail rape). Racial tension originating outside prison walls is often played out on the inside. Inmates do not reinvent the wheel; rather, they borrow from established social conventions and dominant cultural beliefs to channel their rage (e.g., gender ideology: "a pretty kid"; "nice-looking man who takes the form on as a woman"; "soft [like] the most beautiful woman"; and race: "if you're white, you're the wrong color"; "fucking Puerto Rican"; "a lot of guys were Black Panthers, you know, stone-cold killers").

Nevertheless, points of connection among inmates are recognized, forming a basis for cooperation during their confinement. As with conflict, cooperative interaction is often organized on the basis of dominant cultural understandings. Gender notions again come into play, as we heard in the creative adaptations of Jesse and Connie ("you find the right person, he'll do anything for you because you represent the woman"; and "I've always been big, so I always played butch"). From these examples, we see that the organizing principles of conflict and cooperation are based on rather conventional ideas. From a superficial perspective, however, inmate behavior appears unusual and exotic (the so-called prison subculture). Instead, the important factor that distinguishes inmates from others is the aberrant condition of imprisonment. For the prison system, the present form of "subcultural" social organization among prisoners may simply assist in the overall management of prisoners. Nevertheless, points of connection among inmates suggest a possible basis of collective action for change, however limited by the confines of prison.

Beyond prison, inmate experience has the potential to enlighten a new generation in the direction of broader social alternatives. Isaiah urges young prisoners to see their future in his dismal present ("keep looking at me, you'll be seeing a revolving door of yourself, and a rare reflection of a mirror"). While his words are poignant and true, the cards seem stacked against up-and-coming poor and working-class youth. As they prepare to enter the current market (characterized by poor prospects in "legitimate" industry, expanding opportunities in "illegal" enterprise, and declining availability of low- and middle-income housing), young people will fill available work roles, and some will become prisoners. An unwitting acceptance of social place appears in Lloyd's belief that "a man ain't a man unless he goes to jail." In this macho stance, he reveals the importance of cultural ideology in social reproduction. Nonetheless, Lloyd also discovers that prison experience belies a subverted cultural ideology that hurts its own members. Prisoners and their experiences can make valuable contributions to a process of "enlightened self-interest" and to the formation of a platform of broad social change. Often perceived as adversaries by law-abiding poor and working-class residents (and in an immediate sense, they are "the enemy"), prisoners/criminals would be reconceptualized as allies in the emergence of class consciousness.

CHAPTER V

Medical Solutions

> We must analyze the often contradictory de-
> mands and expectations of medicine: as a guide to
> healing and happiness, as an institution of social
> control, as a quasi-religious system of explaining
> the world.
>
> DORIE KLEIN
> "Ill and against the Law"

Many long-term, hard-core drug users have been treated for their addictions through any of a number of treatment programs. Some have entered just one type of program, but most have tried several. One addict will enter a program to kick drugs once and for all; another may just want to come down from the high dosages, dangerous and expensive, that his body has come to need. "Detox" is popular among those seeking to come down from an expensive high. The treatment involves a weaning off drugs over three weeks. In some cases, detox is helped along by other drugs used to ease the pain of withdrawal. Another program tried by many addicts is the "therapeutic community," where the addict lives a year or two getting individual, group, and behavioral therapy. There are strict regimes at the "TC," and residents must learn to obey many rules. Another common type of treatment is methadone maintenance, designed to get an addict off heroin. Since methadone blocks a heroin high, the addict substitutes a legal drug for an illegal one. Methadone users have discovered, however, that its high goes well with cocaine and alcohol.

These days, Arthur V. is back on methadone. Starting with heroin at age sixteen, he has see-sawed between street drugs (heroin, coke) and methadone for the past eleven years. At one time, he was on program methadone for four years straight. "When I first got on [methadone]," Arthur says, "I used [heroin] to see if I could get that feeling again, and no, I didn't—[the methadone] blocked it, so I started using coke." In the past several months things have gotten out of hand, what with the expenses of low-quality heroin and cocaine and the police breathing down everyone's neck. So Arthur decided to go back on a methadone program, at least for now:

Dope out there is not genuine, so I'm shooting damn near over $100 worth of dope a day, during the course of the day. In 1972, I was shooting $3 bags—one bag and I'd be kissing my feet for the whole day. Today, just to get straight you need at least $30. And I mean that's why I went back on the methadone. To me it's crazy, you know; you gotta take the chance of getting arrested; you wind up on Riker's Island; it's not worth it to me. [Several years ago] when I came off meth, tried to detox off the meth, I started shooting dope, so then I'd go back on the meth. I stayed off it for a while, but I was shooting dope and coke, dope and coke. Then I went back on methadone, and I tried to detox, but every time I'd get down to around ten milligrams [of methadone] I'd feel the dope, so I'd start shooting dope. [Now on methadone], the only thing I mess around with is alcohol and Valiums.

Ray says methadone's worse than dope. Quentin agrees and considers it his "last alternative. Once you get on it, that's it—like if you get busted or something like that, forget it, you're in trouble. Kicking methadone, you could die kicking methadone. I don't want to put myself in that situation." While most users consider methadone just another drug, it sometimes doesn't seem that way, since you can get it legally from a clinic. When talking about his drug use, Ralph lists heroin, cocaine, and methadone, but asks, "I guess you could say methadone is a drug, right?"

Lou would set Ralph straight on this point. With encyclopedic knowledge of drugs, Lou often refers to his *Physician's Desk Reference* when describing the different narcotics he has consumed over the years. In fact, Lou became so sophisticated that he avoided street drugs by securing medical prescriptions for morphine, eucodal, Pantopon, opium, Dilaudid, and Numorphan—opiates that produce heroin-like highs. Of methadone, he says,

> It is a synthetic opiate. We really don't have experiments indicating the long-range aftereffects [of the synthetics] on human beings. . . . I prefer natural opiates. This is foolproof, over thousands of years it's been tested. There was a Chinaman on a program on East Broadway where I was. He was ninety-five years old, and he was still on the highest dose of methadone, and he was still functioning quite well at ninety-five. Now this man had been used to a lifetime of opium. I'm sure that if he had used methadone for that amount of time, he would not be alive.

Samuel Arnold would also assure Ralph that methadone is certainly a drug. After all, he won't touch the stuff since his "OD" and the death of a friend that he attributes to methadone. "It was the Christmas before last," he recalls. "I was off the [methadone] program for two or three years when I decided to buy some [street methadone]. After the program I thought my system could still handle it. I took forty milligrams, woke up in the hospital with all kinds of needles in my arms." Samuel continues, "I don't mess with methadone. . . . I had bad experiences with people that's close to me died on the methadone program."

Not everyone shares that opinion of the drug. Lloyd Robertson found methadone very helpful when he needed to cut down on his costly heroin consumption. "It was a thing where I had to slow down," he explains. "Number one, you have to understand that at that time methadone lasted for two days with me. See, when you don't use methadone, it'll keep you high for two days. Not only will it cut the urge [for heroin], but it keeps you high. In fact, that's why a lot of people go to methadone, because not only does it stop draining your pocket of the money that you would spend for heroin but it also keeps you high, until the drug absorbs you, you know; your system adjusts." Lloyd's description matches James's experience. He used methadone "to get straight; it kept me straight more than a day, it lasted a lot longer than dope, and I got nice on it." After trying street methadone, which "took the urge for me to shoot dope away," James then joined a regular program, " 'cause I was getting a little tired chasing the bag." For Kevin G., methadone was great until he found that cocaine mixed very well with it, creating a "speedball" effect—a combination high too pleasurable to give up. But before discovering this new temptation, Kevin considered the methadone program a logical step in maintaining his drug consumption:

I found it [methadone] to be very similiar to heroin except that the high lasted way a whole lot longer than an injection of heroin or Dilaudid. Since it was legally obtainable by being on a program, I finally got on a program. [Before], I was a fool to be spending anywhere from $80 to $100 for garbage when I could go to a methadone program and get the real thing for free, keep myself straight, and I wouldn't have to commit crimes.

Though Lloyd sees the benefits of methadone, he knows its dangers, having discovered Valium at the methadone maintenance program. "I wasn't really into pills," he notes; "I got introduced when I got on this program." That's the kind of thing Samuel is talking about. While Lloyd found pills and Kevin discovered coke, Samuel "started drinking more when I got on the program."

James has many years of experience with different kinds of drugs—heroin, coke, methadone. In his opinion, methadone is something "the government put out; now they have control over a problem, licked, you know what I mean?" It is also "cheaper to have, it's another drug habit, and by far it's a lot worse for you [than other drugs], and it's a lot worse to kick, but [you] don't have to go out and do the things [you] have to do [to get illegal drugs]." James thinks it important to assess "the good and the bad aspects" of methadone compared to what the other drugs involve. For him, methadone meant that it took "six months to go to the bathroom. I have arthritis in my left leg now, behind methadone. It messed me up some, a couple of teeth. My teeth are in pretty bad shape. It does harm your body, but you weighing that against your going out there and chasing the bacon."

In his experience with methadone maintenance programs, James notes problems of treatment costs. He entered his first program in 1972, and was in and out of different ones for the next eight years. In 1985, James got on another program, this time a privately operated clinic with a weekly charge. As he explains it, the overcrowded city programs provide free services to clients, while the private ones "are out to make a profit." New clients are evaluated for ability to pay and given a sliding fee schedule. "Say, for instance, when a person just comes on a program," explains James, "they tell them, like in my situation, I have nowhere to live, I'm living at the men's shelter, I have no visible means of support. They say, 'You still need ten dollars for the blood work, and seven dollars a week.' Now I have seen people on the program, they've been on the program a year, they're working, they have very good jobs, they got a lot together, but now they're being charged forty-five dollars because they're on a different bracket, you know, mentally, financially." It seems those are the preferred clients, the ones who can pay. Soon after joining the program, James found he was unable to make the weekly payments. The program counselors advised the necessity of "detoxing" him from methadone. After he was unable to pay for a couple of weeks, James was given this stern warning:

> "Well, listen, you not gonna pay; we're gonna detox you; you're a burden to us now because you're getting free, you know; we're not making it. We're giving it to you, and we're not getting anything from you." That's exactly what they said; that's exactly the way it came out. "Unless you come with the money, we don't care how you get it, just as long as we get our money, we give you your methadone." It's just like any business, it's not a program; it's a business.

T.K. reports a similar problem. As a welfare recipient, he had been able to pay for his methadone. Though it is not clear whether he is referring to a public or private program, T.K. explains, "I got off my methadone program because I had lost my welfare and my Medicaid, so they wanted me to start paying money."

Lou particularly resents the methadone clinics and their personnel for the hold they have over their clients. "They just feel that complete control," he asserts, "and control is a corrupting factor." In Lou's analysis, "The methadone program takes advantage of the addict through the addict's ignorance. The program is greedy—and the people who run methadone programs are only people. They feel this control over the addicts, and that gives them a certain pleasure. It's disgusting. It really is disgusting."

Jacob's poignant tale of the Hurricane Gloria riot on the Lower East Side illustrates Lou's point. In September 1985 the city and metropolitan region braced for the great hurricane. As people boarded up storefront panes and stocked their homes with the basics, some methadone addicts found their shop door closed. Regulations of the Division of Substance Abuse Services (DSAS) require administrators to receive special permission to close a methadone clinic during any emergency such as this (Lower East Side Service Center, personal communication, 1990). Nevertheless, as Jacob recounts events, Lou's view takes on a true cast:

I'm a client of Division A. Their normal hours of medication are 9:45 A.M. until 1:15 P.M. I had a feeling when I heard about the weather that it would be a good idea to get over there early. The staff at the methadone program decided to close the program at 10:30 in the morning, which is the time by which seldom 10 percent of the clientele has arrived. So when I arrived, I was told by a number of friends they were really glad to see me, that I made it. They said they had been calling me, trying to tell me to get over, that they [staff] had announced that at 10:30 they would stop medicating. Actually they had first said they were going to medicate until 11, and then they moved it back to 10:30, so that everybody who was inside the door as of 10:30 were the lucky ones, and everyone else was fucked. Then what happened was because of the rain and the conditions outside, everyone who was medicated stayed inside as long as they could get away with it, and of course, at some point, the people who were arriving at the door were being told that they couldn't come in. I received no notification and I'm sure no one else did either. I was lucky that I made it. It was a terrifically disorganized, spur-of-the-moment, stupid decision, made by the assistant administrator and the administrator for their own well-being, to close early, and not reopen, and of course, besides my opinion of something like that, the facts are that that's gonna leave a lot of people very ill, and which can give way to crime, and lots of trouble at home, and just a lot of trouble, period. Potentially it could have meant [people not being medicated Friday, Saturday, and Sunday]. They wound up reopening the unit sometime later Friday afternoon, but by that time, most of the people who had been turned away had gone up to either buy methadone or shoot dope.

So the way the riot happened was that people were waiting outside to get in and people who were on the inside were eager to get out. . . . The bright side of the coin for me was the fact that they gave me my Saturday bottle too. There were a lot of people in there who were walking out of there with, you know, four or five, even six bottles [of methadone], who were really worried about walking into this crowd—not so much me, but some, you know, some of the women on the program, and some of the smaller women on the program. So, there's a herd of dope addicts, or let's say methadone addicts, out on the street, being told that they're not gonna receive their medication that day, and it got to the point that there was a lot of physical violence—somebody tried to bust through the window. I don't know what they figured they would do once they got inside the window, but I think that, that it just illustrates how important that methadone is to them—they would have gone to any extent almost.

However, the administrator was telling the people outside that she was sending away, that if you miss one twenty-four-hour period without your medication, the withdrawal is all in your mind. I don't know whether or not that's accurate. It's immaterial, because if you're gonna be sick, you're gonna be sick whether it's psychosomatic or biological. I definitely would [be sick], and I'm willing to believe that it's in my head, but it don't matter; you could hang that on the wall, and it still makes no difference. You know as well as I do that none of these people were gonna just go back home and sit out the next twenty-four hours, and not do anything about it. These are the people whose very souls feed off of this narcotic addiction.

You have to envision one door through which people who have been medicated are trying to get out, and there are people straining, pushing their way in from the other side, who haven't been medicated, so, you know, there wasn't so many intentional acts of violence, but there was a potential trampling situation. They were pushing pretty hard to get in. Somebody who's facing opiate withdrawal is apt to be twice their normal strength and real mad. There was one guy who was a client who looks like a linebacker, and he was trying to keep the peace, and it was about all he could do to hold back this one rather small guy.

I thought to myself, it was a very irresponsible decision, and had they known [about the weather], as everyone else did the day before, they might have anticipated it, and given everyone their Friday medication on Thursday.

There's a lot of yelling and screaming going on today. For one thing, the fact was that they did reopen the program, as it turned into the gorgeous day that it turned out to be—blue sky and all—they made no effort to get in touch with those that they had sent away, which I thought was really pushing it. They should have at least made a few phone calls. Here's another factor—while they were sending people away, every counselor, every staff member, was given explicit instructions not to answer the phone. Impressive?

I would have screamed bloody murder, but I think most of these people had hung it up and taken another route, you know. It's easy for me to say, without any doubt, that a lot of bad shit went down. It probably will just blow over, because the average patient there is not gonna go through the trouble of instituting a lawsuit or whatever. I definitely would have gotten my revenge somehow—I would have bombed the place, if I didn't think it would give me nowhere to go the next day.

These days it seems more difficult for an addict to get into treatment, especially detox programs. Arthur V. heard that you can only get into detox with a methadone program referral, and Jesse says you need a medical referral before any detox center will take you in. It seems there is always some requirement. When Arthur first tried to enter detox, he was turned away for being underage. "I was nineteen," he says, and "you had to be twenty-one. I had fucked up a coke dealer's coke . . . him and three other Ricans broke my jaw. I went to the [detox center], and they told me you had to be twenty-one years of age or older, or you needed a parent's signature, which I wasn't talking to my people at the time." Nowadays, overcrowding seems to be a big problem, and there are long waiting lists of addicts wanting treatment. "I've been trying for a year," Jesse says; "there was always something getting in my way—like, I didn't have identification, then I didn't have a place to have my identification mailed to." Finally, Jesse was admitted to a city detox center where they treated him for eight days, taking him through a process that usually takes twenty-one days. He believes that they let him go "to get me out of the way."

Eventually, Jesse was placed in a new, drug-free program, where he felt an unfamiliar sense of hope. He spoke excitedly about the help and support he received from the program's counselors and clients, his new "family." Jesse showed great patience in waiting so long for a slot; not all drug addicts can persevere to this extent. For example, in describing her hasty decision to enter a program, Rita also shows just how quickly the idea is abandoned:

> I said to myself, I ain't gonna do no more of this. I went to a drug-free program 'cause I don't need it [dope]; I'm not sweating, I'm not sick, so before I get into any trouble or any more fights, I said, let me go off the streets. I went to S [program], but they took my urine and said, "Monday."

They gave me the runaround, they saw me so desperate. "Oh, don't worry, I call up Monday," they told me. "Don't have no beds, have to do the blood, wait for five more days." I told them, "What the fuck, I'm gonna drop dead by the time that blood test comes. Put me in isolation, stick me somewhere in the back, on the bed, but lock me up." "No, we can't do that," they told me. "Are you gonna come to the blood test?" I said, "Listen, fuck you, hell, fuck you, and as bad as I feel, forget it."

MEDICAL CARE

It is not unusual for street addicts to find themselves in the hands of doctors, nurses, or other medical personnel. Street addicts are generally not the picture of health—their bodies show the strains of too many cold nights, too much bad food, and far too many narcotics. Their ailments range from endocarditis (an inflammation of the heart caused by a bacterial infection and associated with needle sharing) to abscesses (pus-filled skin infections caused by dirty needles). Certain strains of hepatitis have long plagued drug addicts and, nowadays, AIDS has left many users dead or dying.

Take Gerald, for example. A homosexual heroin and cocaine addict, he is HIV positive, with symptoms—swollen lymph nodes, pneumonia, diarrhea, weight loss. Two years passed from the time he noticed the lumps on his neck until he made a doctor's appointment. He was terrified, "being in the hospital, and them doing tests on me for AIDS every day, and telling me that they felt that I definitely was a candidate for AIDS—that was what scared me." In and out of hospitals for a year, Gerald has met with "good and bad vibes" from hospital staff. "Most people have been nice to me," he says, although some

back up and say, "you caused this yourself." A couple of times there was doctors I've gotten that acted like this is your own fault, and I didn't want to go back because when they give me that attitude I feel like they don't really give a shit about me, and don't want to help me, but that wasn't necessarily true. A lot of times they were doing that to make me realize, you know, and get myself together. Now I can see that. But also there was a lot of helpful doctors. I mean this one doctor, Dr. M., she's a female. She was very good with me—positive, and when I would go into fits, I mean actually fits, fighting her and screaming and crying hysterically, she'd be very soothing and she'd not leave me after she got the blood. She would sit with me for a long time and discuss with me the possibilities that I might live a normal life, you know, but everybody has to worry about dying tomorrow—doesn't have to worry about dying tomorrow, but there's a very possible chance that anyone could die today, tomorrow, anytime, so why worry about it, but the things you can control, control and take care of, the things you can't control, try not to even think about.

Doctors and nurses get mixed reviews by other addicts as well. Hospitalized following a mugging, Arthur V. was refused pain treatment after the doctors realized he was on methadone. "I begged them," he recalls, "please give me something with no drug in it, [but] they wouldn't give me anything—they figured the eighty milligrams worth of methadone's enough for your pain for the whole day, but that's not true."

(See Brown, Pinkert, and Ludford [1983] on medical issues related to pain and analgesia.) Arthur says doctors see it this way—"Once you're on meth, you're a junkie, you're no good." But he is quick to point out that not everyone treats a junkie so harshly. "I had one Philippine nurse and one Spanish nurse, beautiful people," notes Arthur; "they knew I was in pain. I'd be up almost the whole night in pain. So before they started handing out the medication, when everyone was still sleeping, before the doctors came in to see me, she'd come in with a cup. 'Here, Mr. V.' She'd give me my meth."

It's a touch-and-go situation. When Quentin was hospitalized, he didn't feel ostracized by the medical staff for his drug addiction. "They treat you just like a person, yeah," he says; "they treat me just like a person." When Quentin first arrived at the hospital, for example, he described his symptoms to the admitting nurse, and told her, "I use heroin and coke. She just asked me, 'How much?' and that was it, you know." Quentin's major complaint was being constantly left in the dark about his condition—"They haven't told me anything. I keep hearing people talking about endocarditis, maybe pneumonia." Still, things could be worse. When Isaiah was sent to the infirmary at Riker's, he noted a big difference between the doctors and the cops. From the doctors and nurses, Isaiah says, "I got all the respect and all the attention—but from the officers you was a dog, you still a dog."

TREATMENT AND THE SOCIAL CONTROL OF ADDICTS

I have presented here portraits of streets addicts as patient-clients, and described their experiences in drug-treatment programs and other medical facilities. As with the criminal-justice system, the drug-treatment system follows a set of policy mandates and practices that are guided by a set of ideological beliefs intrinsic to the "medical model." This model defines the addict as sick, and addiction as an illness (Klein 1983; Conrad and Schneider 1980). Representatives of the drug-treatment system are expected to act accordingly, providing services to addicts that heal and nurture. The hierarchical ordering of relations between patients and healers locates addicts in a relatively powerless position vis-à-vis their caregivers. The resulting social interaction reflects structured conflict between the addict-patient and the state (Magura et al. 1988). In turn, this conflict is reinforced and mediated by the paternalism that characterizes relations between addict-patients and their healers.

Addicts describe their expectations and uses of drug treatment, which do not necessarily correspond with specific mandates or purposes of drug programs (for program and client descriptions, including regulations and procedures, see New York State Division of Substance Abuse Services 1988; New York State Division of Substance Abuse Services et al. 1984; Joseph and Roman-Nay 1988; DeLeon and Ziegenfuss 1986; Allison, Hubbard, and Rachal 1985; Cooper 1983; Hubbard et al. 1983; Brook and Whitehead 1980). "Detox," for example, is commonly used by addicts to come down from an expensive high, rather than to stop using drugs, the official purpose of the programs (Lipton and Miranda 1983). This lack of fit points to the creativity of addict-clients in subverting the treatment system for their own purposes. Also reflected in this disjuncture are addict concerns with the broader social and legal-political context of drug use. The intended purpose of methadone, for example, is to wean addicts off heroin, thereby providing a first step out of "the life" (the street-addict subculture). Arthur V., James, and Kevin G., however, chose to hook up with legal methadone because of their concern with "costs and cops." In these cases, the methadone program was not a first step toward life without drugs, but a relatively inexpensive and safe source of them. It should thus come as no surprise that many methadone maintenance clients also consume other drugs, from alcohol to cocaine (Preble and Miller 1977; Johnson and Preble 1978; Preble 1981; Allison, Hubbard, and Rachal 1985).

These cases also indicate that official mission statements, used to justify programs' existence, may rest on shaky ground. This, in turn, implies other motivating factors behind the drug-treatment system. As James suggests, the system is an industry in itself. As such, it requires personnel to consider factors other than the well-being of clients in decisions about a specific course of treatment. In addition, organizing principles for treatment procedures may also be based on funding guidelines or ethical postures rather than on the actual needs of clients. This point is illustrated in Arthur's claim that he was denied methadone treatment because he was underage. Indeed, according to the supervisor of the Outpatient Unit of the Lower East Side Service Center, methadone programs may not serve minors under the age of eighteen; such persons may only be treated, with parental consent, at adolescent facilities (Stuart, personal communication 1990). In its disregard for the facts of the case, the bureaucratic rule reflects the dominant social practice of locating responsibility with the privatized family. Moreover, as Klein notes, the health-care system as a whole is an institution of social control, a point suggested by street addicts' descriptions of their experiences in treatment (1983; see also Reinarman 1983; Arella, Deren, and Randell 1987; Brewington et al. 1987).

An evaluation of dominant cultural understandings about drugs reveals ways in which treatment operates as an instrument of social control. The drug-treatment system abides by the "medical model," a doctrine in which addicts are considered sick and addiction is seen as an illness. This doctrine combines with a dualistic cultural construction of drugs, which the treatment system has helped to generate. Addicts in treatment are designated as patient-clients, which qualifies them for a set of services associated with various treatment modes (e.g., methadone maintenance, therapeutic communities, detoxification). Those outside the treatment system, however, fall into a cultural category that leaves them subject to a range of other consequences as drug users. As such, a significant aspect of institutionalized drug treatment is its contribution to an entrenched cultural construction of drugs and to making the addict a "captive."

In practice, drug users consume both "legal" and "illegal" substances—alcohol and program Valium and methadone (legal); heroin, cocaine, and marijuana (illegal). With the aid of legally dispensed substances, a distinction emerges between "good" and "bad" drugs. From this core distinction, a set of correlated, oppositional pairs may be charted:

Drugs

Good	Bad
Legal	Illegal
Medical Prescription	Self-Administration
Methadone	Heroin
Patient-Client	Dope Fiend

So entrenched and powerful are the correlations among items in each category that Ralph could ask, "I guess you could say methadone is a drug, right?" On the other hand, by recognizing the implications and systemic workings of dominant beliefs and practices around drugs, Lou devised a way to circumvent the system. In essence, he escaped the dualistic model by securing "bad" drugs as a "patient" (legally, medically prescribed) in order to self-administer (i.e., to get high).

In revealing the heavy load of ideology, the structural scheme presented here raises questions about inherent risks of particular drugs. This issue is also raised by several street addicts, who point out certain negative physiological consequences of long-term methadone use. Moreover, there is questionable logic in prescribing one drug (methadone) to inhibit a certain kind of high (i.e., from heroin) while the same drug enhances other kinds of highs. The logic behind these apparent inconsistencies lies with the social-control functions of treatment institutions, which direct their efforts primarily at a largely minority, and relatively powerless and poor, population of addicts. As Lou points out, and as Jacob's Hurricane Gloria anecdote illustrates, addicts in treatment are held captive by the system, subject to its rules and regulations, as well as what appear to some of them as arbitrary decisions by treatment officials. Beyond those addicts in specific programs, however, the drug-treatment system holds sway over all street addicts by constituting cultural definitions of good drugs/good people. People left out of drug treatment—by choice, circumstance, or lack of available services—therefore engage in activities that have been defined as illegal and immoral. (On program availability and addicts' reluctance to enter treatment, see Bureau of Chemotherapy Services 1988; Joseph and Roman-Nay 1988; Johnson et al. 1985.) These addicts are then subject to a range of possible consequences for their illicit behavior.

One possible consequence of engaging in intravenous drug use within the context of current social and legal-political parameters is to become physically sick. Street addicts are subject to a range of illnesses, with AIDS the most striking and deadly of them. In describing their medical treatment, addicts appear to appreciate the kindnesses of some health-care personnel. The more humane, albeit paternalistic, approach of medical personnel follows the pledge of their profession. Focused on the "patient," health-care workers may be less concerned with an individual as a "dope fiend." For street addicts, however, this translates into interactions marked by great benevolence and goodwill, traits they rarely see in their everyday encounters.

CHAPTER VI

Lovers and
Other Strangers

The main relationships which cultural forms help to reproduce are those of its members to the basic class groupings of society and with the productive process. [However], social agents . . . view, inhabit, and construct their own world in a way which is recognizably human and not theoretically reductive. It can only be lived because it is internally authentic and self made. It is felt, subjectively, as a profound process of learning: it is the organization of the self in terms of the future.

PAUL WILLIS
Learning to Labor

Ralph grew up on the Lower East Side—in the public-housing projects on Avenue D and Third Street. Born in 1949, he says, "The thing I could remember about growing up there is fun, good times. I had a good time when I was growing up." As Ralph tells it, the early years were the best. He remembers "playing games, and going out with Moms and Pops and, you know, being together. It was, you know, it was only me and my older brother—he's a year older than me—so it was like the four of us. We used to go out to dinner all the time, have a good time, the beach, whatever."

As Ralph recounts the family history, things didn't continue happily. His father, an army man, had worked as a typist in a government office after returning from service during the war. "Where'd he do his time?" Ralph was asked. "I don't know," he answered; "the only place I know he did his time is Sing Sing." In the early 1950s, Ralph's father "got hooked up—strung out, into drugs." After that, he lost his job, spent years in and out of prison. Meantime, the family continued to grow—seven children altogether, and a stepfather, "this little creep." Ralph's mother was helped along by his grandmother, welfare, and whiskey until her death from liver disease. As Ralph tells it, his mother kept the family together and raised the kids, " 'cause he [father] was seldom home—he was out most of the time anyway. I mean when he was living with us, he wasn't home most of the time—he was at his girlfriend's house. When we did see him, he'd come in like a big shot with candy and all of this, and, you know, the welfare was supporting us then."

Ralph describes himself as having been a shy child who avoided fights with other children. "I was kinda quiet and used to be by myself most of the time," he remembers. "I usually stayed by myself in the house, so you know, [other kids] used to call me a momma's boy." Ralph still tends to stay close to home. He lives with his older brother, a school guidance counselor, who also has custody of their nephew, a victim of parental child abuse. Of the seven siblings in Ralph's family, three are custodians for the board of education, one is a housewife, one is a guidance counselor, and two are junkies.

Like Ralph, Manuel is a black man born in the 1940s, though he grew up in the Brownsville section of Brooklyn. Now a shelter resident and a hustler by profession, he recalls a troubled childhood, dreary jobs in New York's garment industry, drugs, drink, and several visits to the state penitentiary. Manuel's past is tinged with sweetness and sadness, in part because his father was a "Dr. Jekyll and Mr. Hyde" type:

> When I think about the bad things he done, [I feel] real bad; when I think about the good things he's done I feel good about him. You know what I mean—he kicked my ass real bad one year, [so] naturally I'm not gonna feel that I love him, right? Then if he take me fishing, then I like him. He'd tell a joke, and we were in good spirits, then he kicks me in the ass. . . . He could flare off in one second.

Charlie also describes his father as a Jekyll-and-Hyde character. "I had a good home," he recalls of growing up in the 1950s in a black working-class suburb on Long Island; "I didn't want for nothing; I never had to wear hand-me-down clothes or nothing; I always had." As in Manuel's case, Charlie was one of five brothers. "Mom looked out for us," he explains:

> Moms, you could always sit down and talk to her; even if she couldn't give you the solution to your problems, she would sit down and talk to you. But Pops—altogether a different story—he's like the Jekyll and Hyde shit; one minute you could talk to him, the next minute he wants to kick your ass. Oh, man, me and my pops wasn't all that cool. A lot of times I wanted to kill him.

Charlie remembers his rage at a father who frequently beat him and did not always treat Charlie's mother too kindly either. "Damn near every weekend I got an ass whipping for one thing or another. I never had to go to the hospital, but I mean I had my ribs all fucked up, eyes swole, lips." On other occasions, Charlie's mother felt the brunt of her husband's fist when he'd "come in high, wanting to fight, smack her around and shit." Sadly, Charlie also recalls following his father's example at an early age. He was just twelve years old when he "knocked out a girl's eye, [hitting her with] a lock in a sock [because] she didn't want to pass off, she didn't want to do no petting." Later, Charlie joined a teenage gang whose activities included "stealing, fighting other gangs, and pulling trains on the bitches"; he explains the last as when "you get a bum broad, and it's maybe five other people, and she fuck one, she fuck everybody; that's a train."

"We was a close-knit family," says T.K. of his mother, two sisters, and twin brother. Raised in a predominantly black housing project in the Manhattan suburb of Mount Vernon, T.K. recalls a hardworking mother, sisters who watched out for their younger brothers, and two teenaged boys who discovered drugs. "Me and my brother got into the Boy's Club sports, and became good basketball players, you know, and we got a lot of trophies, we could've became pros, but start messing up with the drugs. We was very good, name used to be in the paper every time, all the time. I got a lot of trophies, you know, and I introduced [my brother] to drugs, you know; I'm the black sheep in the family; I consider myself that." His sisters, though, "never messed around"—they were "good, mostly home type of girls" who did "the right thing," and "now they still doing the right thing."

As he recalls his 1950s childhood, T.K. notes that he was a "shy type of person," and in the next breath:

My father used to yell at me, and he always looked like he was mad about something—expression on his face, you know. Now one time I had trouble in school with my arithmetic, and I was getting bad grades in math class. So he used to have me and my brother come over to his house, he would like tutor us, and my brother was a little faster than I was in the books, so he caught on fast—me, I was a little slow, and so I just couldn't understand it at that time, the multiplication and stuff like that, and I wasn't thinking at the time. . . . My brother would help me, but sometimes my father comes to check our papers and, "You got this wrong; you got this wrong," and, "You stupid," call me names and stuff, and my brother would come over and try to help me out, give me the answers, but I said, "No, I'm gonna do it my way 'cause that's the only way I could learn," you know. When I get bad, you know, wrong answer, he would hit me with the belt buckle, and one time he hit me across the face with it, the part of the belt buckle on the belt, and I had a big ol' welt under my eye and stuff, then he got mad and told me to get out the house and kept my brother in there.

After that beating, T.K.'s mother intervened, warning their father never to touch the children like that again. But his parents had their own problems, as T.K. so vividly recalls:

And sometimes I would hear him and my mother argue, all the time. I was five or six years old. He would go out and mess with different women; they argued; he'd take us in his car, driving around, buddies drinking—and he would give us liquor, too. I always thought he was a mean type of person. To this day, I never really, we really never had a relationship, you know, where I could go call him, and [say] "Hi, Dad, how you doing?" and have a really decent conversation—up to this day I can't do that with him.

Things have been tough for T.K. Besides his problems with drugs, he has not been lucky in love or in work. Not one to let an injustice slip by, T.K. says he has long struggled against those more powerful—unfair bosses, racist cops, and anyone who "messed with me or my family." But these have been losing battles, and T.K. is disappointed. "I always wanted a family," he asserts, "my kids to grow up with me and my wife and kid, you know, a family to grow up together. I always wanted that when I was coming up; I always said that when I had a family, I never wanted to go through what my mother and father went through, my friend's family went through."

For T.K., just thirty-three years old, things turned out quite different from his dream. After a divorce from his first wife, his second child was born to his new common-law wife. Far from the idyllic family life he hoped for, T.K. describes his first marriage as a battleground. One time, he reports, "We argued about her staying home, taking care of the baby, and not drinking—she would lie about being with her mother and [really] being someplace else. I slapped her and she stabbed me, and I covered up for her, I had seventy-eight stitches—after that things were never the same. She never was a proper woman, and after that, she would always grab a knife for me." T.K. recalls the end of his second marriage, when his wife died of a seizure after leaving a methadone clinic. "She was my heart," he says; "I loved her; she was a good woman. . . . I could not get her to stop [using drugs] because I was doing it myself."

So T.K. has two children. His mother adopted the oldest after the child had spent several years in a foster home, while the little one is still moving between households. "I just found out," T.K. says, "that my daughter was taken from my mother-in-law by some cousins of my dead common-law wife—it was felt that my mother-in-law wasn't taking care of her—she had suffered two bad burns when she was two years old, and now there's another burn on her arm." T.K. insists that he is trying to make some changes. Although he lives in the Sunshine, an East Side shelter, and has no steady work, T.K. has sworn off drugs and has enrolled in a computer-programming school: "See, my daughter, the youngest, she wants to be with me so bad; she says every time I come up there to take her out, she always saying, 'Daddy, when you gonna get the place? I want to come stay with you, live with you, this and that.' I always telling her a story, telling her it's gonna be soon—that's why I got into the school."

James makes no bones about his childhood—he was lonely, unhappy. "I wanted more freedom, and I couldn't have it," he explains. "I didn't have the freedom with a father, with a father to go camping, go fishing, do things the way I saw my other friends go with their fathers and do things; that used to hurt me." Although he isn't quite sure what really happened, James believes his father was an air-force man whose only contribution was his name on the child's baptismal certificate "so I would have a name, you know what I mean? One of those deals." Raised by his mother and grandmother, James was a self-described terror, "loud, rowdy, a little brat, a bully," who knew the two women couldn't control him. By his early teens, James was into drugs, messing with girls, truancy, and it's been this way ever since. "I never knew my father," he says by way of explanation; "I had no father to look up to; I had no male to be on my side. I needed."

James remembers that his mother worked a lot. "She had to—she had a day job, and then on weekends she worked in a catering hall." This meant James was often left to his own devices; by seventh grade, he "was smoking a lot of reefer and eating amphetamines." Sadly, he felt "I had no family, nobody to talk to, nobody to confront issues with, you know what I mean? When there was something really bothering me, or when I needed somebody to sit down and really rap to, there was nobody ever there. So I would choose my own form to escape."

Lee also took refuge in drugs. As far as his childhood went, he says, "First of all, my parents should never have had any children—both of them should have been sterilized." Lee, a white man in his thirties, explains that his mother didn't want her kids, and his father was an alcoholic. "They totally freaked me out when I was a kid, so as soon as I got into drugs I found an escape." In the end, four of the five brothers "got drug dependent," while the fifth one died playing football. Now there are just three brothers left, since Barry died of an overdose. Lee thinks his father makes a funny distinction between his habit and those of his sons. "See," Lee points out, "my father's an alcoholic. I could sit and drink a quart of vodka every day, and a case of beer, and everything would be great, everything would be rosy—but smoke one joint, and you're no good, you're a dope fiend, lazy fuck, know what I mean?"

Arthur V., a young white man, is familiar with that tune. It was the same in his family—his father drank too much, but calls Arthur a no-good junkie. Arthur says alcoholism runs in his family, and since he, his father, and his brother are all "addicted" it must be hereditary. For Arthur, alcohol wasn't enough to help him get through the day—what with the step-mother he hated and a difficult father. He has overdosed on drugs twelve times, not always accidentally. Says Arthur, "I would get so depressed at times that I would eat so many pills . . . I guess it was more or less sympathy . . . like, 'Please love me,' you know?" From a working-class background, Arthur managed to work for his father's boss in New Jersey for a while. The situation didn't last, and now his father won't even talk to him, although Arthur believes he is making an effort to change, now that he is on a methadone program. According to Arthur, "My father's ignorant to methadone—he thinks if I take methadone every day that I get high, and I'm not, you know. [He thinks] 'You're a junkie, I don't want to know you until you get off this shit.' " Now in his late twenties, Arthur is trying to keep his act together, living in a shelter, staying on methadone.

Although he grew up in Manhattan, Carl shares some background traits with Arthur. Also from a white, working-class family, he remembers some good times, some bad times. The best part was growing up in the Fort Washington section of the city, which was "beautiful. It was a clean area, most of the people were white, Spanish, and Greek, and as a child there really were no problems." The difficulties, Carl recalls, were in the family, where "I wasn't physically beaten down, but verbally." As a result, he explains, "I became very much introverted and shy and generally uptight . . . and I was a walking time bomb, and anyone who pushed me the wrong way, I would just pop and there would be a fight, and there were many fights." According to Carl's self-analysis, "My parents were never there for me. . . . There was no communication between me and my father, he never called me 'son,' I lost a lot . . . and everything I learned, I learned on the street." Before long, Carl found himself with a certain crowd of kids, "not the people who were seeking to achieve good marks or good jobs," and when he discovered heroin in high school "it completely tranquilized me, and I found my euphoria."

Lloyd Robertson's memoir of childhood is a story of ambivalence, love, and humiliation. As he recounts his early years as a black child growing up in the 1950s, Lloyd describes a caring and loving mother who tended to her children: "My mother treated all of us in a considerate and caring way, as a large bird would treat its chicks with its wings over, like that, as a covering, making sure everything was in its proper place and everything like that. We were never neglected by her, never."

The story goes on with bits of information on the average ups and downs of a childhood, pranks and all. Lloyd is enthusiastic in telling his story, which may have prompted a confession. "Let me tell you a secret," he says. "I used to wet the bed up until the age of eleven or twelve, so I got beatings like every morning, whenever my bed used to be wet." He goes on:

> I'd say my father's from the old school. He figured if he beats you enough, that it'll stop you. It never did. Normally [I would be beaten] seven times a week, because it used to be normally every night. If it was a good week, it'd be five times, five mornings I'd get a beating. I used to plot to kill my father many times, you don't know. My mother would be in the room watching me get beat, and say, "Look at you; yeah, you know what happened if your friends would hear that you pissed the bed." They'd embarrass me and beat me. You know, I felt like a piece of trash a lot. It's a bad feeling, I'd tell you that. Those feelings I'll never get away from 'cause I know how, I can still relate to the way, to that feeling. I felt cornered, and cheap and stupid and less than everybody else was. Another thing, when I think of it, I think it might have a little thing to play with sex on me today. The fact that it was my sexual organ malfunctioning, and you see the tie-in I'm trying to say? The fact that I was pissing the bed up to

a certain amount of age when it wasn't normal, and I'm getting beaten, it might have inhibited me later on in life, you understand what I'm saying?

I used to hate to go on the Boy Scout trips, overnight campings or whatnot. Every summer for three summers I had to go away to Massachusetts, Cape Cod, and they used to call me "the midnight sailor." You know what that means? That means you wet the bed. And they used to hang my sheets and my blanket out in the wind and everybody would see it. They figured that'd make you stop. And then they made me stop drinking water after three o'clock in the afternoon.

[The bed-wetting] didn't just stop. It got to the point where it would be once a week, or once every two weeks, or once a month, or once every third month. That's how it began to stop. And then I was able to hide it and not get into trouble; I could sneak it into the wash. That's how I learned how to get sneaky, so nobody would find out. They just—it was like being ostracized, just like I am now. I was always ostracized. I'm sorry, I was, always— that's the truth. [When it stopped], I said to myself, "Well, now I'm gonna be a man; I'll do up my own thing. I'll be grown; I don't need to hang on nobody's apron string; I'll be a man, like God intended me to be."

[Another time] I played trumpet in school, and I had lost it. It must have cost a hundred and sixty-something dollars; it was made in France, and it was all brass, a beautiful instrument. My mother and father had chipped in and bought it for me, and wanted me to be a musician, and I lost it. I always used to stop off at the candy store and come home from school, and then I was going to school the next day and I realized I didn't have it, and I got a beating for that. I was in the fifth grade, and the beating was so bad I couldn't go to school that day with the welt. Normally, I don't get welts up here, but I think the belt caught me on the side of the cheeks, and it swole up so my mother and father made me stay home.

The first thing I sold when I got hooked up [on drugs] was my trumpet—that's the first thing that went. [Later] I went back to playing music—conga in Jefferson Park, on 112th and 1st, every summer—I got natural rhythm.

I had found the trumpet. The candy store. It was Saturday and Sunday. My father was telling me how he was gonna whip my ass, and he slapped me around. That whole Saturday and Sunday he was slapping me around, every time he'd see me he'd say, "Look here, boy, you go and leave that room I'll tear your hiney off," and he'd slap me in my face, and he'd go like that. Every time I'd walk by him, he'd look at me, and I'd jerk back and walk around him, and then I went up to my room and you know what I was doing? I was drawing the three crosses of Calvary where Christ died on the hill, and my mother and father were walking past and they saw me doing this and she busted out laughing. But you know what my father said? My father said, "Shut up, woman; leave the boy alone; at least he got religion." That made me feel so good. When he said that, he took up for me. And guess what happened next, the very next day in the candy store? Jack had held it for me—it was right behind the water sprouting place, and he held it for me.

Lloyd says that the last beating he got—or took—from his father was when he was fifteen years old. Sometimes there was friction in the house, especially when his father was drinking. In general, though, things weren't too bad until Lloyd was busted on the New Jersey Turnpike for heroin possession. He was fifteen, and his father was furious. "When he got me in the house," Lloyd recounts, "he hit me about four, five times." He made sure that this would be the very last beating. "When I got up, I stood there and looked at him like [in his] eye, and he didn't do nothing. Normally, for me to do that to him, he'd jump right back at me and commence to whipping me, but he knew the way I looked at him that if he tried that again that me and him would fight that day. He didn't hit me—he just turned away. I was tired of being the baby, like being treated as a kid. I wouldn't have killed him or nothing; I just wanted him to understand that I needed respect now."

Dennis T., in his thirties, remembers the last few fights he had with his father. At the time, Dennis was in his early teens, but he and his father had always had some problems. The last couple of fights were real blowouts, and Dennis recalls them vividly:

I had a fight with him when I was drinking, and I grabbed him. I got him on the ground, and it was, it was a weight . . . that I pulled off, you know, that thing that keeps on the weights, the little steel shank . . . something like that, and my mother was standing there watching, and I wanted to let her know how angry I was at him; I'll never forget this. . . . There was always a lot of pepped-up anger. I don't want to sound like, you know, like I had a poppa who's always beating on me, this and that, but I just—we didn't get along, you know. He whacked me once and awhile for no reason whatever.

So anyway, one time I accidentally got kicked in the nuts playing a basketball game, and not too long after that

I went to the hospital. One of my testicles [was] out like a big orange. I was delivering newspapers at the time, [and] I had to get somebody to deliver the newspapers for me. Right about ten days after that happened, about three days after I started walking around again, [my father] pulled a T-shirt over my head and he kicked me in the balls. So about three months later—I was about fourteen and a half—he went to hit me again, and I grabbed him, and like I said, we just wound up on the ground. There was a weight set there, and I wanted him to know how pissed off [I was]. While I was on him, I unscrewed the weight thing and I picked it up, and I, you know, I was on top of him, and I held it up in the air like I was gonna hit him. I wanted [my mother] to come over, you know, and grab it out of my hand, and I kept holding it up, holding it up, holding it up, like I was gonna hit him, and she's standing there, you know, and to this day, he, he just, he died last year, to this day I, I always wonder—she never came, she, she never wanted to grab it out of my hand. I literally held that sucker up for about three minutes, it had to be a good two or three minutes, I held it up there—that's a long time to make like you're gonna hit somebody. And if I'd come down and hit him, that was three or four pounds of solid steel, you know, I would've fractured his skull with it; and she just didn't come over and pull it out of my hands. I always used to wonder why, why didn't she grab it out of my hands. Even as I'm telling you right now, I really don't know the answer, why she didn't grab it out of my hands.

While Lloyd and Dennis stayed and battled it out with their fathers, Connie ran away. She, Lloyd, and the others share a sadness in their childhood stories, though their tales differ in other ways. For example, Lloyd, whose family came from the West Indies, grew up in New Jersey, while Connie was an "all American" farm girl from Wisconsin. These days, they also share drug habits and some of the daily difficulties of street-addict life. For Connie, running away from her father at age thirteen seemed like the smart thing to do, although she never got far from the abuse. It all began when her mother died in childbirth:

> I was two minutes old. See, that's what my father held against me, 'cause he said he would have his wife and my sister would have her mother. It wasn't really my fault, but then it was my fault, 'cause like he said, if he didn't have me, he would have had her, and like when she was in her seventh month they said that they should terminate the pregnancy, but she wouldn't do it. He never touched another woman after my mother died; he was in his thirties, and he never touched another woman. I guess he really loved her; that's what I've been told. My father would say it—that he didn't have his wife, that my sister didn't have a mother, you know. . . . That's what he believed; he went to his grave believing that. . . . And then it hurts hard; that's how it went. So once I got of age to know, I knew he was sick. I never held it against him like some people would have, would have hated for the rest of their life, but I didn't. I love my dad; I still do. I left home when I was thirteen; then I called up when I was twenty-one. I seen him when I was twenty-four. All I wanted from him was to say that "I love you"; he never, ever, ever said it. He just wouldn't love me and I couldn't understand. When I left home, I hated him, but as I got older I could understand, you know, he really loved my mom.

When I was a kid, I had to work hard; I used to farm. He had eleven farms; my father had some money. I used to work all summer long—baling hay, making hay, oats, corn, the works. I'd give my good all day, and then all of a sudden my dad would just snap; then he'd go back to bitterness.

I was supposed to go to a Catholic school in Milwaukee. I was going in the summer to check it out. I was on the bus, and I got off the bus. In the bus station I met a black guy. He sounded like more fun than going to school, and he introduced me to the streets—I gave my first piece away, and sold my second. He sold me—he found out I was thirteen and he sold me to this guy in Chicago. The original dude only kept me about a week.

[The second guy] introduced me to prostitution and junk. [Since] I made money, he came kind, he treated me with affection. I didn't know how to accept the affection at first; it scared me. Then he was nice to me and it went from there. I was happy [because] I was wanted. I had somebody there I could go home to, somebody who used to yell at me, and put their arm around me and give me hugs, that was nice.

It was easy to make money back then. I could make four, five, seven hundred dollars in like six, seven hours, so it was no hassle making money. It was all in having someone say, "I love you"; that's all I wanted—it's the only thing that's true. All I wanted was somebody to say, "I love you," you know? But I didn't realize that the only reason he loved me was 'cause I could support his habit. You know he really didn't love me, but to me it was love because he was there.

When my father died, I said, "Dad, just do me a favor; please tell me 'I love you'; tell me it was a mistake." I

said, "I'm here to give you time to say 'I love you,'" and
he said, "No, I can't." And that really hurts, you know,
but I don't hate him—it's like a monster when you learn
to hate your father, and the man was sick, you know. And
like I'm just not a hateful person; I get hurt, I shouldn't.
. . . I guess that's why I never had any kids; I'm probably
scared. Well, I had a little girl when I was fourteen, but I
gave her to a lady. I was working the street; it was a white
baby. [The lady] had been married fourteen years, and she
wanted a baby so bad. When she took her from me she
said, "I could take you." That made me feel so good,
'cause that was the first time that anybody ever really
wanted me for me—I don't mean to cry, sorry—even on
his dying bed he wouldn't do it, and I asked him; I think I
asked him about eighty-three times.

Sandy, an East Side prostitute, also ran away from home
when she was fourteen. The situation was unbearable, and
she saw no other recourse. "I had a bad home life," explains
Sandy, who was sexually abused by her stepfather for two
years. A big drinker, he would wait until he was alone in the
house with her. It started when Sandy was twelve years old:

I hate him because of what he did to me sexually. Every
time my mother wasn't home and he was drunk, he'd sexually use me, and beat me. He did everything—rape, bj's,
touching. He'd hit me because I be fighting back.

I told my mother but she didn't believe me; that's why I
left home at fourteen. I didn't go to the police or anything—I was too embarrassed to talk to anyone about it. I
figured if my mother didn't believe me, nobody else
would. She didn't want to know what was going on be-

cause she was afraid of a divorce—she married him when I was nine years old.

Finally, I just had to leave home. I was going to kill him, so I figured leaving home is better than going to jail. I felt as if I was going to have a nervous breakdown because no one would believe me.

Now twenty-five, Sandy, like Connie, has a heroin habit, although these days she has taken up cocaine freebasing. But because of her stepfather, she never touches alcohol: "I got a thing about drinking—it just turns me off—even if I smell it on somebody's breath, I want to get away from them."

Samuel Arnold's parents were divorced. He has two sisters—one is a registered nurse, the other works in a doctor's office; Samuel is a heroin addict who washes car windows on the Bowery. He talks affectionately about his sister and mother. The younger sister, he says, is "my heart." Samuel loves his older sister too, but she was more foreign to him, having grown up in Georgia. "I never knew I had a second sister, understand," he explains, " 'til she came up one time from down South here. I know that she talked real funny, you know." Their mother, Samuel says, treated her children with "tender loving care." All the years he was growing up in the Brownsville section of Brooklyn, his mother worked "in people's house, cleaning people's house," and Samuel was often left to his own devices. The streets became his second home, and Samuel often found himself embroiled in fights after school. "It's hard to get along," he points out. "[There were fights over] different things—people trying to take something from you, find somebody trying to break into your house, disrespected by [someone] saying ugly things . . ." Later, Samuel joined a street gang, and his fighting days continued. They were the Buccaneers, and the all-male group would "go around to the grocery store to scare them, play handball in the park, mess with girls—you know, show off in front of them; and we had rumbles," Samuel continues, "with the Marcy Avenue Chaplains. We didn't have to have a reason for a rumble; you just was another gang and your war counsel was going through their territory and take everybody garbage can and throw it in the middle of the street, and they would come back and fight because you dirtied up their streets." The girls, Samuel notes, had their own gang, the "Lady Buccaneers," but "they was like a joke."

The Brooklyn gangs made quite an impression on Samuel, especially when he first arrived in the area that was to become his turf. "When I first moved on the block," he recalls, "I looked out the window and I see all these people on the street fighting; I never saw a gang fight before, garbage cans flying, and a guy got killed; I saw the guy get stabbed for the first time." In those days, Samuel explains, he was just a "baby Buccaneer—these were the older guys fighting, and I was just getting into it." For Samuel, it hardly seemed real that somebody actually died:

> He was running down the street, and like I said, a Buccaneer was chasing Chaplains, and he was in Chaplains; and he had a sword in his pants, so that made it difficult for him to run, and he tripped and there was about ten Buccaneers all over with knives and the sounds of punches— clack, clack, clack—all over in his head and his chest and there was blood everywhere, and then the ambulance came, and this was when John Glenn went to the moon, and he said, "Don't put John Glenn on the front page, put me on the front page," and he died.

Ray regrets all the fights he had with his brother. "I knocked the shit out of him," he recalls, "but when I was young, my brother used to knock the shit out of me." Now his brother is dead, and Ray misses him a lot. The fights were never over anything to remember. "Much ado about nothing, really," Ray says. "I guess he thought I was somebody to beat on." But when push came to shove, the brothers loved each other:

I didn't realize how much I loved him until he passed away; and like my brother saved me one time, jumped in front of a .45—we was fighting these Italian guys in Park Slope once, and they came around the neighborhood, and my mother made me go down and empty the garbage, and when I emptied the garbage, they surrounded my stoop— but my brother and my brother's friend happened to be on the stoop, and this guy "Crazy Boy" pulled that .45 and my brother jumped in between that .45, understand, and said, "You ain't gonna shoot him because you ain't gonna do nothing to my brother," and approached him and there was five guys on that stoop—if they would've started any-thing around that neighborhood it would have been all over. But I realized my brother loved me and he had al-ways loved me.

Tom Silver is a fifty-year-old Bowery resident who grew up in Harlem. Life on 112th Street was "fun—went to school, played ball, went fishing, chased girls, it was nice." He lived with both his parents, his two sisters, and one brother. Tom describes himself as an obedient young child who was shy, serious, and studious. "I got very few whippings because I was too damn intelligent . . . [I] would do what I was told to do." He recalls his parents as being fair and just in meting out physical punishment. "My mother or father never touched us unless you did something wrong." Punishment came in the form of a "whipping, with an iron cord." While Tom received a few whippings from his mother, there was only one from his father. "I never messed with Dad, because Dad hit me one time, and I swore he would never do it again." Although it was so long ago, Tom vividly remembers what happened: "He whipped me because he was beating my brother, and I was standing there laughing, and he knocked me clean across the room. Yeah, I learned. He slapped the hell out of me, and I learned from that—that you mind your own business when somebody else is getting punished."

Fighting wasn't a big thing to Tom, who preferred to stay home and study. "At the time growing up," he remembers, "I used to be a very dynamic person. I could meet with people—even the older people—and I guess I used to have more intelligence than the average person. I could talk very well, and I was well-read, because we had an extensive library at home, and I liked to read, [especially] psychology and medical science."

Tom managed to pursue his interests for a while and studied college psychology for one year. But by 1976, as he entered his forties, Tom was in deep trouble, much of it due to his drug and alcohol habits. He began drinking at age twelve and, by his early twenties, was into heroin. In 1976, he says, "My wife put me out, and I had no place to go." He hardly knows what happened to his family. "I really don't have any idea how old my brother was when he died," Tom says. "To put it to you truthfully on this here, I don't know the year [my mother] died; I don't know the month she died or the reason for it. All I know is that my sister told me she died, and my brother died a week later, and my father died two to three years later."

Lou considers his a "privileged upbringing." His father was an officer in the Customs Bureau, who raised the family in the Forest Hills section of Queens. Lou knows very little about his siblings, though, since they were born after he left home. As Lou explains it, "I was my mother's first child—she was about fifteen or sixteen; I left the house very young, and later on she had other children." Lou knows he has two sisters, but "I don't remember their names." He has a better memory for the Dominican nuns who cajoled him into learning with their wooden rulers on his knuckles. Those days his father was not around much, and Lou says, "I grew up alone, more or less." With little parental supervision, he discovered heroin in high school. "I had a lot of time to be out in the street," Lou explains; "from the age of fifteen I had the liberties or freedoms to spend days at a time out, unaccounted for, without having to account for them." There was one time, he remembers, when he did have to answer for his actions:

> I was about twelve or thirteen. I remember [my father]
> spanked me by taking his belt off and beating me across
> the back. And the time he did this was when I put a
> swastika on the wall, hung it up. One of my friends had
> one—he was from a German family, and he had a black
> and white and red flag, a real one, and I put it on the wall
> of the basement. . . . I never saw that flag again.

Although they are both "Hispanic," Lou and Jesse couldn't be more different. Lou, a born and bred New Yorker, spent years in North Africa and Spain, ducking various state regulations to support his drug habits. Rather intellectual, Lou prides himself on his knowledge of an array of topics—including the medical classifications of many drugs. He has been fairly crafty in devising ways to buy drugs and keep out of jail for any substantial time. In contrast, Jesse, who also considers himself "Hispanic" (since his mother is Mexican, although his father is Irish), was born in New Jersey, but reared in Texas by his grandmother. Jesse is a homosexual transvestite who goes by his own dead sister's name because "I always wanted to be like her." Between busts for low-level street selling and problems on the stroll, Jesse tries to shack up in city shelters. Sometimes it is difficult for him to get in, since he looks and acts just like a woman. Unlike Lou, Jesse hardly fits in, and each day is a struggle. Trying to stay off dope, Jesse is hoping to get into a special prison program for drug abusers when he starts his upcoming two- to four-year sentence.

Jesse's problems started early. His mother sent him and two siblings to live with her mother when he was five years old. Her marriage had ended several years earlier—Jesse's father kicked her out of the house and moved his new girlfriend in. Jesse's mother rounded up her kids and managed to keep them together—until she moved in with her new boyfriend and had a baby with him. It was then that she sent Jesse and his two sisters to Texas, staying in New Jersey with her new, smaller family.

Even before he went to Texas, Jesse "always felt lonely." He now attributes this to his sexual identity, which caused him great suffering from an early age. The move didn't help him feel part of anything, especially since his grandmother was often brutal. Though memories of his mother are fond, Jesse believes she "tried not to show favoritism—but she showed it when she had to send three of us away." He remembers staying to himself often, although he enjoyed a special, close relationship with two of his sisters. Still, he insists, "I never fit into anything . . . I didn't feel like I belonged . . . I always felt like I was by myself," and what he really wanted was to "see my mother, stay very close to her, just hang out in the kitchen and be near her."

Texas was hard. His grandmother was very strict and often used physical force to keep the kids in line. "When she found out I was gay," says Jesse, "she beat me unmercifully." That was when he was ten years old—two years after his first sexual experience. "It was an older boy; actually it was a man, 'cause he was about twenty-two, twenty-three. He worked in a gas station near where I lived." Jesse soon discovered several "gay hangouts," places he would visit each day after finishing his homework at the library. He was nine years old, and remembers feeling more comfortable with the gay men at the hangouts than at home. "I actually dreaded going home," Jesse recalls, "I was very frightened of my grandmother." At ten, Jesse tried to run away, but all that did was start his enduring relationship with the police. When the cops picked up the young runaway at the bus terminal, "They took me to some jail—some children's center with cells," where it was "about four months before my mother sent for me."

Isaiah dreams about going home to his mother, although he is ashamed to do so. A thirty-seven-year-old squatter resident in an East Side park, Isaiah says "God bless the child who has his own" and wishes he could "just go home to mother, stay there a while, but I really don't want her to see me the way I am 'cause she wouldn't even know me; I've changed a lot. So I just gotta deal with it." He remembers her as a hardworking woman—a corrections officer—who struggled to raise her family. Isaiah says he was no help, since he was a "jealous child, a terror" who started getting into trouble at age seven. "I was an aggravation toward my mother," he acknowledges, "and she was the only one bringing us up—there was six of us. She was both the mother and the father." Sometimes his mother got help with the kids from other family members. One sister, for example, lived much of the time with their grandmother, while his brother often stayed at their aunt's place. Later, when his aunt had her son, the little boy was raised by Isaiah's mother. "I have no regrets," Isaiah says of his upbringing; "at least she brought us up—except for not being that hard on me—she should have been more hard on me, you know, [but] she was a woman." Isaiah considers himself the bad apple, and recounts the kind of hurt he inflicted on his family:

> All six of us . . . bought her a diamond ring for her birthday—you're the first person I'm telling this to—and I took the diamond ring and sold it, and I sold that diamond ring. After looking at the birthday pictures on her fiftieth birthday, the tears want to come, but they just don't come out. I feel hurt behind that, you know, but I stayed away from my mother for a long time. I didn't see my mother no more until I was behind bars. She was hasty, I mean she hurried to get to me, you know, and I was facing something like fifteen years, and she got there; she stuck with me, she stuck with me. So that's the type of mother that I have. She know I did it [took the ring]. She ain't never told the rest of them, you know, she never told the rest of them.

THE HEARTS OF MEN AND WOMEN

Isaiah thinks about starting over with a new girlfriend. He has been married before, and has a few kids, but those relationships never worked out. Lately he has struck up a "platonic relationship" with this woman who wants him to get on a methadone program. Although he is thinking about it, nothing is definite. Isaiah rambles on about the possibilities: "I'm await to see her—it probably won't be until next Thursday that I do get on a program because that's when this particular program sees people—until then, it's all up to this other girl who, you know, me and her are trying to have a more intimate relationship."

It wasn't so long ago that Isaiah and his wife separated—maybe five months. They have one son together, but his other two children are "from another contact—two other ladies." Isaiah and his wife always seemed to be fighting over something, until he felt "pushed out of love." By the end of their marriage, Isaiah says, "I was like Mahatma Gandhi to her, celibacy, 'cause I didn't want to touch her—when she did something wrong to me, that's it." Although Isaiah is an on-again, off-again heroin user, drugs didn't play a major role in their problems. She was "a nut," he says by way of explanation for the fights that became physical. "I didn't beat her up," Isaiah insists; "maybe I smacked her head there, you know. She'd get a pot of something and throw it at me. I got my head cracked—like that one time I had to have five stitches, and got arrested on the operating table." That particular fight occurred after the couple had separated; Isaiah didn't like how her new boyfriend "was talking to her nor my son."

Like Isaiah, and T.K., who always dreamt about a "family to grow up together," Dennis T. has struggled to find some close relationship. Estranged from his parents and siblings, he finds it painful to be so alone. "[It] really hurts; what do you have if you don't have a wife, mother, your brother and your sisters?" But Dennis has lost them all.

He blames this estrangement on his drug use and the life-style that goes with it. "It pushed people away from me," Dennis explains, "the way I was abusing [drugs]; more or less what you do is killing yourself a little bit at a time, and people who care about you, watching you doing that—they can't keep watching you hurt yourself—they got to close themselves off emotionally after a while. . . . After a while, people just get tired."

Drugs also got between Joseph and his wife, eventually pushing them completely apart. As he recalls:

It's not that she don't want any part of me; it's just that she didn't want any part of that [drugs] for me. We reconciled two or three times. In fact, a couple of times it was after I came home from jail—I was like fresh, clean, and I wasn't really thinking about getting involved [in drugs]. I was thinking about more positive things. She considered that, told me, "Come back to bed." But as time went on, I started going right back to it.

As Joseph describes his marriage, other issues surface that seem to have little to do with his drug habits. For example, he tells of the "totally embarrassing" situation when his wife and girlfriend were pregnant with his children at the same time. Joseph explains that the women were pretty "jealous," leading to a big fight that he could only break up by hitting them both:

It wasn't their fault; it was mine. See, my wife was pregnant with my son, and my woman was pregnant with my daughter at the same time, and I guess they was more jealous of each other because they both knew it. We lived right across the street from each other. In fact, we went all the way to court, and I'm standing in front of these two people, right, and the judge says, "Wait a minute, I don't even want to hear this; take this stuff to the marriage counselor, and if you all can't get your heads together, I'm gonna lock all three of you all up." So we had to settle, and I was faced with a horrible decision, because I was supposed to decide which one that I wanted to be with, and I selected my wife. I thought it was the right decision— now I'm a little doubtful because I'm not with her.

Before they went to court to settle the case, the three of them had it out. Joseph says, "[The two women] went into physical combat," which he stopped with some slaps of his own. In pointing out that the fight occurred inside "my woman's house," where his wife had come to confront the couple, he notes, "I could never [hit a woman] in the street— would you allow me to do that to you in the street?"

Rafael, a longtime heroin addict, notes proudly that his wife never touches drugs; "She never used; she don't even smoke reefer." As he sees it, to gain respect men and women have to show different faces. His wife, for example, would "go around and take the children shopping, make sure the rent was paid, so she has a lot of respect in the neighborhood—she can walk anywhere down here [on the Lower East Side]—don't nobody bother her." A man, on the other hand, has to "build respect in the street or else you can't last—if you don't have a reputation like of hurting somebody, then they'll run over you."

When Rodney was married, his wife didn't do drugs either. "I never let her take dope," he says, " 'Never no drugs for you.' " Rodney continues, "I kept her clean—everybody else's old lady, they already had them hooking." Later, when he found out a dealer was turning her on to dope, he figured, "Now I can justify sticking up [the dealers]." Eventually, Rodney explains, he had to leave her anyway, because "I was sticking up so many people that they were chasing me, shooting at me, taking shots at me when I was with the kid in the stroller, breaking the fucking door down every fucking other day, and 'Where's your husband? Where's your husband? I'm a kill him.' "

Unlike Rafael, Lloyd Robertson is not proud of his wife. Now separated, Lloyd says of her:

Most only person I really hate right now on this planet is my wife. My father said to me, "How could you be so stupid—take a common whore to raise your children?" I broke down and cried because he was right. That's what she is. Turns out, just about everybody in the projects had her. The only reason she latched onto me was because I was a good-looking guy, kinda green, and my parents had their own home, and she figured eventually that she'd have her own home, too—that's just what it was, nothing more, nothing less. For the first four years I swore it was beautiful—she turned out to be a good mother and everything, a good mother and wife—in a way, I enjoyed it. Then, all of a sudden, she just started having men call her, and that's when I left—so I take care of my babies, and I hope to God they give me enough brains and strength where I can get a job and away from this, and get them away from her. I'm only a man that loves my family. Is that so much? Is that being greedy? Excuse me.

Lee has a new girlfriend that he likes, but he "might get rid of her" because of drugs. "I'm trying to get out of drugs now," he points out, and "now she's getting into drugs more." Recently hired as a lifeguard at the local pool, Lee is annoyed by her frequent phone calls to him at work. For him, this girlfriend may be too big a burden while he tries to "become like a straight person."

Kevin G.'s work, on the other hand, might have been interfering with his relationship with Rosie. As Kevin explains it, "I turn tricks with homosexuals—but I'm not a homosexual myself." In the meantime, he had become "infatuated with this Spanish girl" who lives on the Lower East Side. They would hang out together and snort a little coke, and they both signed up at the same methadone program. "One day in the middle of the week," Kevin remembers, "she said, 'I want to ask you something—Are you gay?' And I said, 'No.' And she said, 'Well, I'm always coming and sitting beside you and talking to you, and I've gave you money a couple of times to buy breakfast with, and I've asked you to come by my apartment, and you never did.' And I said, 'Rosie, your parents might not like the idea of a blanco coming over.' And she said, 'No, they're not prejudiced.'" With that, Kevin sums up, "We eventually ended up getting a hotel," and Rosie became his girlfriend.

Many times a lover or wife will try to help a fellow off drugs. James recalls the girlfriend who helped him get off coke " 'cause she saw what it was doing to me." Isaiah says his longest drug-free period was when he was married. When Owen married, he tried changing some of his bad habits under his "ol' lady's" influence. And Antoine, still struggling to keep off the street and off drugs, attributes his success to the strength and support of his wife. Although he feels the pull of the street and his friends, his wife helps ground his efforts to stay straight:

My wife works, and she gives me a couple of dollars to do what I have to do—going out looking for work, and stuff like that. Every Friday, she [gives me] the same amount of money—twenty-five dollars to get my clothes out of the cleaners and look for work. After that, I'm on my own. I don't blame her—we have three sons to take care of.

I got one thing in mind—that's supporting myself and my family. . . . I don't hit the streets too often. I like to stay home. As a matter of fact, I said to my wife this morning, "You know, one of my friends out there said to me"—well, I thought he was my friend—he said, "Man, all you got to do is get high." I didn't answer him because I know he's tasting and getting drunk, and carrying on every day, but that's his business—he's still a good friend of mines in my heart. And my wife says, "Don't even come out that much—don't even go out."

It's hard to articulate certain problems to a person that only knows you from one side of life—"Let's get high." I mean, they know about your family and the rest of your bit, but when it comes to getting high, all of that's out the window. And I find myself trying to be respected from all my past relationships and friends . . . but my wife just told me, "You know something, if you don't like a person, you don't even speak to them."

Andrea's new lover has also been a great source of support to her. "He got me to see reality," she explains, "He got me off the streets, on welfare, he made me do things—reinstate my life for my child." Before he convinced her to get on a methadone program, he shared his dosage with her. For Andrea, such generosity showed great devotion and affection: "When you consider a man who is taking 100 milligrams every day—not having to give to anybody—and he catches a girl like me, and then he's got to give up 40 [milligrams] almost every day, plus on weekends. It hurt him, I know, 'cause

I would never want to do that—so I know he really loved me; he really does love me."

Even so, there are times when they have their private difficulties, and Andrea wishes others would keep out of their business. A few months ago, they had a "matrimony fight," as Andrea calls it, and the police were summoned. The woman cop who showed up would just make things worse for Andrea. "I said, 'Listen, it's better don't get involved, please, 'cause I'm gonna get hurt more. If he gets hurt by any cops, I'm gonna get killed.' " The policewoman refused, saying she wanted to protect Andrea. Unconvinced, Andrea reasons that the cop was "jealous 'cause I was white and he was Puerto Rican, and what was I doing with a Puerto Rican."

With a stake in her neighborhood, Cherise worries when things at home get too heated up or complicated. A longtime resident of the Lower East Side, she is the mother of a nineteen-year-old son. The shopkeepers and the grocer know her well, and some have extended credit to her for more than fifteen years. Cherise's longtime boyfriend, Bill, has a hot temper, and sometimes their drug friends cause them trouble, too. Beatings from Bill are fairly common, and some have sent Cherise to the hospital. On one such trip, she met a young fellow who became the cause of a major domestic dispute. "I got beat up by Bill," Cherise reports, "and they put me in the psychiatric ward for a couple of days." There she met Larry, who "seemed sincere" and had no place to go. Cherise invited him to stay at her apartment so he wouldn't have to live in a shelter, and, besides, "Larry is not a street person—you could see that when I was in the hospital." At home, she says, "I was helping him, and he was doing pretty good."

At the time, Bill was in jail. When he returned, the situation was uncomfortable, to say the least. Bill made it quite clear that he didn't like the new visitor. When he told Larry to leave, Cherise took a stand: "I wasn't gonna let Bill boss me around when I told this person he could stay there." Before long, Larry started stealing drugs and money from the couple and caused some trouble in the neighborhood. With each incident, Bill became more angry, until he had a brutal fight with Larry on the street. But before that, Bill had been taking out his frustrations on Cherise:

> Larry had some pills, and he gave me a couple. Bill didn't get any. Then they had a big fight. Okay, I got my teeth knocked out and black-eyed— me, because Larry wouldn't give Bill a couple of pills. Larry intervened, like he said, "Don't hurt her—you want to fight a guy, fight me," and then they broke out into a fight. Bill won the fight. Right, but then I made them make up, and stop it. . . . Bill was getting madder and madder. It came out on me, and then it went to Larry—came out on me, then went to him, and then came back to me.

Later, when Bill got Larry in the street, he hurt him pretty bad. Cherise shrugs it off—"You know, nobody wants to hurt anybody, but it's street law; that's what happened." She also notes her preference for dealing with her domestic disputes without people like Larry interfering. Accustomed to Bill "doing a number on me," Cherise says, "I always accepted it. I always accepted it all these years with nobody jumping in; you stay away because I know how to work this situation that I've been in."

In another variation of the lovers' triangle, Naomi recounts the trials of managing two men in her life. The men ended up in a violent encounter—a rumble with a switchblade and a metal pipe. Naomi insists that her main interest is Rene, but Bobby Q. thinks she's his, since he met her first. "There's a machismo thing," Naomi explains, "where whoever meets the woman first, gets her." Her relationship with Bobby, Naomi says, was a mistake from the beginning, and she got involved for all the wrong reasons:

> I was at a very lonely time. My best friend had died, my boyfriend for many years had left me for a married woman, and then I had another boyfriend—it didn't work out, and I was really kind of battered down. I had been with men mainly who told me I was stupid.
>
> Then all of a sudden I met this guy. My family left—I'm godmother to two children, and they moved. These kids and their parents were my friends. I was just like kinda very lonely without them. So I was lost without these kids, and I looked for somebody like that, and my maternal instincts. I wasn't cutting up, I wasn't shooting up, so I had to do something else, right?

The turning point came when Bobby was arrested and Naomi bailed him out. That gesture represented a special link between them, at least in Bobby's mind. She tried to break up with him, but he managed many strategies to prevent that from really happening. She believes Bobby does not really love her, "But he's obsessed with me; it's not Naomi, it's not me, it's a white woman with college—he always refers to 'My woman's never been a whore; she's been an artist, a show woman.' " Once she told him, "You can tell people that you broke up with me if you want to save face. I give you permission—you could say whatever you want about that." In response, Bobby would either cry and beg her to stay or threaten

to kill her—sometimes in the same breath. According to
Naomi, he would tell her,

> "Please no; that'll kill me, please," and he cried, cried,
> cried, cried, but all the time in the middle threatening me,
> telling me someday he's gonna explode like the guy in
> Texas who killed everybody in McDonald's. [He would
> say], "Baby, I'm tired. I just could put my arm around you,
> just like this, look you in the eye, and say I love you,
> good-bye, and I'll pull the trigger, and you'll know what
> hit you then, okay my darling?"

FRIENDS AND ASSOCIATES
ON THE STREET

Connie shares her apartment with Joe, a friend
of twelve years. It seems this is the best relationship she has
ever had—just friends, not lovers. "If I wouldn't have Joe,"
says Connie, "I'd be dead by now." In fact, Joe has helped her so
many times and in so many ways that she really relies on him:

> I don't know what I'd do without him—it scares me. No
> matter what I do or what I've done, Joe always protects
> me. And it's nice. Like yesterday, he loaned me money to
> cook [buy drugs]. Last night I said, "Well, I'm not gonna
> have no cash until tomorrow afternoon," and he says, "I'll
> go get [my] check cashed, and I'll give you money in the
> morning," he says, 'cause he didn't want me to go out last
> night—he drove into the city last night to buy me two
> bags so I wouldn't have to hit the streets. See, he cares and
> it's really fabulous, and like he doesn't try to change me—
> he'd like me to get on a program, he always brings it up,
> but he doesn't say, "Listen, this and that and or else." I
> take people over [to the apartment] with me—you know,

girls that don't have a place to stay in the cold—and he treats them [well].

Though Connie credits Joe with all the kindness, she also has been known to help a friend or two in a bind. Sometimes she puts her two cents in where others don't want it—especially the younger girls. Just recently, Connie brought home a young, pregnant friend. "I seen her on the street corner—I picked her up and brought her home—cleaned her up and fed her." Connie is angry with her young friend, who refuses to have the abortion Connie is encouraging. "My girlfriend said she loves her baby and wouldn't give it up," explains Connie, "though she is taking drugs and pills and alcohol, and she has a gynecological infection—she doesn't even love herself; how can she love that baby?" Connie reports that she was so frustrated with this girl that she slapped her. Some time ago, the same girl had a baby boy. Connie took care of the girl and the baby during his first six months. The girl then sold the baby to a lawyer for ten thousand dollars. As Connie tells the story, her friend just came home one day with money and drugs—she hadn't told Connie what she was doing until it was too late. "She didn't even cry about it; all she cared about was counting her money." Connie, on the other hand, cried over the baby for two months. "I really loved that boy," she says. Now that the girl is pregnant again, Connie is very upset. Although her friend refuses, Connie has offered to take care of her during and after the abortion, "keep her fed, clean and high, but just have the abortion."

When you're on the street, friends are very important—though you mustn't be too trusting. But friends can tell you where to "cop a bed" for the night and who's selling what, and help out in the case of some serious trouble. In describing his drug activities, Jarmin, for example, talks about "touting" for a street seller—not for pay, "just as a friendly thing." Most shelter residents report hearing about the facilities through street buddies who advise them where to go, how to get a bed and some food. Needle sharing has a long history among street addicts, although some are now a little nervous about the practice because of AIDS. Arthur V. says he is terrified of getting the disease, so he no longer shares as much as he used to. Much of the sharing goes on in shooting galleries, private places where groups of addicts do drugs. Jarmin explains how the process works: "It's like public property almost. I mean the house owns the works, but different people come in— they use the house works. I'll come in an hour after you've been there using whatever, and I'll use the same set, and then all through the day."

Arthur refuses to go to galleries any longer and even hesitates to share works with his best friends. In the past, he didn't mind sharing needles with "a close friend or my cousins, a relative, [because] they'd be clean—they are totally clean people, and even though I did use it after they'd use it, I would clean it real good—take a tissue and wipe it." Sharing was a "reciprocal thing," Arthur explains. "If I didn't have the money to buy a set for myself, I had to use whoever had it. . . . [Sometimes] they would have no money to buy a set." Owen no longer wants to share needles either, but AIDS has nothing to do with it. As far as the disease is concerned, he says, "I feel like if I'm gonna get it, I guess I'm gonna get it. So what? Fuck it." Owen doesn't like to share, because with each use needles "get too dull too fast," making it hard for him to get a shot. Owen explains that his knuckles are the last place left on his body to get off in, and knuckles require especially sharp needles. Even so, Owen will share with others in need.

It's "lack of availability, you know—somebody come along and beg you to use their works or something. When I share, it's usually feeling sorry for someone else, and I let them use it."

Ray is not afraid of getting AIDS either, since he believes "it's just a propaganda play." When he shares his works, however, it is not just out of the goodness of his heart. As Ray puts it, "The majority of the time that I share works, I share it for profit—dollars."

Herbert C. expresses more concern about AIDS. With a history of homosexual relations and intravenous drug use, he is "very concerned" about AIDS. These days, Herbert "wouldn't think of being promiscuous or going out with somebody," and "I would never consider [sharing a needle] with anybody else [but] a good friend of mine." In Herbert's circle of friends, people are more "discerning. [Like] this guy I met the other day said, 'Yeah, you can come to my house, but you gotta have your own stuff; you can't use mine'—a year or so ago, you didn't hear that." Gerald is also concerned about AIDS—he's been diagnosed as HIV positive and is showing some symptoms of the disease. Although Gerald has a history of needle sharing, he believes "my homosexuality was more a cause than needle use." As he describes the past few years, Gerald tells of increased needle sharing, mixed with fear of getting AIDS through sexual contact:

> I had a lover who was two-timing me, and I was reading about AIDS, and the worry I had was sexual—not through needles—sexual, because my lover was a two-timer, and I was worried he would bring it home. This was in 1982; at that time, I was just about to get into drugs again because of the two-timing, it was hurting me. I was just about to really get into shooting heroin again. I had heard about

AIDS, and at that time they didn't talk about intravenous drug users, they only talked about homosexuals. I mean they had that thing about H's (hemophiliac patients, heroin users, homosexuals) which they didn't say coke—they just said heroin users and homosexuals, but homosexuals was the biggest thing. So I didn't want to be a homosexual, number one, and I felt, when I did drugs, I didn't want to have sex, so I would go back to using coke. It was when I got on methadone that I started sharing needles. In '83 I got on a methadone program, I stopped shooting heroin, but it was worse because then I got involved with coke. Then I really shared needles. . . . From using coke every day, I'd have to go to a friend's house . . . I shared needles with him, and plus I think he ran a gallery.

While sharing needles may be a deadly gesture of friendship, it is important in getting along on the street. One law of the street orders that when someone has drugs but needs a place to administer them, he shares the drugs with the buddy who provides the place. According to Lou, this kind of sharing helped him become addicted to coke, since friends would always come over to his apartment to use:

I moved into an apartment without the prior knowledge that cocaine was being sold on the second floor. Now, my apartment was on the second floor facing the staircase where the cocaine dealers would sit at night after six o'clock—until 4:00 A.M. every night—and sell five-dollar bags of cocaine. Now that's where I began seeing all my old friends—these friends, or acquaintances of mine, would buy enough cocaine for themselves and for me, and then knock on my door, offer me cocaine (which I could not resist), and then they'd come into my house, use the cocaine, and then I would use the cocaine that they gave me as a gift or as a price for payment for letting them use my house to administer the cocaine to them.

There are times when folks don't follow the rules, for which there may be unpleasant consequences. At the very least, the person is not highly regarded; consistent antisocial behavior may lead to major retribution. A recent stabbing at an East Side shelter resulted from the "greediness" of one fellow unwilling to reciprocate favors. Warren reports what happened between Jesse and his visitor: "The guy used to use Jesse's room to get high in, but he was never willing to give Jesse enough to even get a bag of dope with—after he scrambled like one hundred to two hundred dollars getting high in Jesse's room." According to Warren, arguments ensued, Jesse knifed the guy, and then Jesse was evicted from the shelter. "The guy that was stabbed was not exactly one of the favorites of anybody in there anyway," notes Warren; "but it put the stabber in a very bad position, because Jesse don't have anywhere to go now."

Money and drugs are always in short supply, so there's a fine line between being smart or just being greedy. Quentin says greedy is when you take more than you really need, leaving nothing for the others—like the guy who was beaten because "he didn't want half of it; he wanted it all." According to Quentin, "The guy deserved to get his ass whipped, because he couldn't shoot all that shit; he was just greedy." On the other hand, Lou recalls his early days as a heroin addict, when he had little money for drugs. "I didn't like the idea of jail, and I didn't like the idea of stealing," says Lou, who devised a system to supply himself with drugs. "I got people together that had the same cause, the same need," he explains,

> and in most of the cases the people were older than me. I spoke Spanish, and these people didn't, so they didn't have access to the connections that I had. So here I was, a younger guy copping, obtaining the stuff, procuring the stuff for people older than myself who had more money. They would put in the money and, just for getting it for them, I would have my supply. That's how I supplied myself for years.

On the street, it's like an endless balancing act. One time, Lee was annoyed at his girlfriend for "falling asleep in a lion's den," when she nodded out in a room full of addicts, leaving herself vulnerable to theft, or worse. On the other hand, Jarmin says to expect help from your fellow users if you overdose. In exchange for that help, however, expect also to awaken with empty pockets. He explains how it goes:

> It's like the code of the street. When you go out [overdose], and you wake up and whatever money you had is gone, that's understood, as long as whoever was with you bring you back, you ain't dead—you feel they're entitled to whatever money you may have had. As long as they don't leave—they could call an ambulance, or long as they do whatever they could do to help, [then] whatever you got they're entitled to, you dig. If they just take you and dump you somewhere, and take whatever you got, now that's a no-no, that's bad.

If you've been in a neighborhood long enough, you get tight with a regular crew. If a time comes when one wants out, everyone gets uncomfortable. Antoine's recollection of friendship on the Lower East Side tells of change greeted with expectation and ambivalence:

> I seen partners of mines that were in the game, tougher than I was, and they stopped; now they working to get them some jobs. I said, "Damn, I could"—who they think they are—they cool now, I mean they speak to you, if you come in the street, "Yeow, what's happening, man," but they don't give that same talk. I had to realize that it's not that they don't respect me in the same frame that it was before, but they're trying to do something for themselves, and plus, they are showing me, see, it's possible. I had to realize that. So once they showed me that it was possible, I do it for myself. And I'm doing it for myself.
>
> A very few get a little jealous. I attribute that to the fact that they want to get out, and at this point are mad at themselves for not getting out. They see you moving, and they still in the same spot. They see me as a threat to their own personal feelings. They all want to step out of it, but when one takes the initiative—makes the move on his own—they get distance from you. A few of them don't even want to speak to me anymore. . . . I think it's mostly that they think you're looking down at them—I'm not looking down, 'cause I was there, matter of fact, I'm not but a step from them—any day, any second, any hour, I could fall right back into the same old trap. I've had plenty of my friends say to me—matter of fact, a friend said to me yesterday—"You shouldn't even be involved with this mess, man, because this not your station, this ain't you." You get encouragement from them. Matter of fact, sometimes you get more encouragement from them, after they realize you real about it, than you get from what we call

the straight segment of life or society. They give you more than they would in the straight life because they seen it all. You could walk up and down these blocks all day long and you see people—alcoholics, winos, dope fiends—they give you more encouragement, those that are still in the game, than those that are out. They're happy for me, but it's still a little hard for them to trust me because of two things: They want me to succeed, but they don't want me to betray them; plus, they're hoping that I'm the same person that I was when we was down together that I am when I get out. Nobody wants to stay in the game, and nobody plans to get trapped. It all starts off just to be high travelers, smoking reefer, drinking alcohol, the whole bit; it's just, "Hey, man, blow off a little steam." We get trapped, and then games start being played, and it just snowballs into things that sometimes we can't handle, and I thank God that I got a grip on some of it—and I say "some of it" because I'm not completely through.

COMING OF AGE

The drug users presented here grew up between World War II and the 1970s. This era saw a decline of industry in urban centers, an increase in economic pressure on working-class families, and a deepening of political differentiation along ethnic and racial lines. (Block et al, 1987; Susser 1986 and 1982; Smith 1984; Tabb 1982; Tabb and Sawers 1978; Sassen Koob 1984; Herbstein 1983; Schiller 1977). It was also a time of important political activity (e.g., the civil-rights and women's movements), as well as the time of the Vietnam War and opposition to it (Martinez 1989; Dickstein 1989; Gitlin 1987; Albert and Albert 1984). Moreover, beginning in the 1950s, this period saw an influx of drugs—from marijuana to heroin, methadone, and cocaine—into poor and working-class neighborhoods (Johnson et al. 1985; Waldorf 1973; Preble and Casey 1969; Fiddle 1967; Mills 1965). Many of today's street addicts came of age amid these economic, political, and cultural changes. Many of them, moreover, felt and experienced the consequences of these conditions within the privatized family, which remains a significant feature of contemporary capitalism.

CAPITALIST PATRIARCHY
AND THE FAMILY

The privatized family refers to a social unit that is physically isolated and relatively self-contained, yet responsible for a range of activities, relationships, and performances in social reproduction. Claude Meillassoux (1975:141) notes that the working-class family "remains the locus of the production and reproduction of labour power . . . and lives according to an ethical pattern imposed by the ruling class [wherein] birth, nurture and education of children take place thanks to the largely unpaid labour of parents, particularly the mother." Moreover, as Rayna Rapp (1978:281) argues, the family is a "socially necessary illusion which simultaneously expresses and masks recruitment to relations of production, reproduction, and consumption . . . [and] absorbs the conflicts, contradictions and tensions that are actually generated by material, class-structured relations in advanced capitalism." These are significant social mandates that help shape the nature and quality of interactions between family members. The family relations recounted here by street addicts point to ways members "operate within [this] institutional order, and comply with the rules of the game" in the accomplishment of social reproduction (Ortner and Whitehead 1981:5).

In describing their early childhoods and family lives, street addicts point to diverse household forms—nuclear families, single-parent households, extended families, and fictive kin. Within some households, membership composition changes over time. Regardless of household form and membership composition, the model of the patriarchal family dominates (Rapp 1987 and 1978; Boris and Bardaglio 1983; Thorne and Yalom 1982; Weinbaum 1983; Rubin 1976). Descriptions of street addicts' family relations are consistent with ideological aspects of the patriarchal model, which guides some of the action and organizes some of the attitude. This is most evident in terms of the hierarchical ordering of power and authority (often maintained by paternal violence against children and wives) and of gender differentiation (expressed through notions of ideal male and female roles, duties, attributes, and concerns), as addicts vividly describe. Moreover, notions of personal and interpersonal "success" or "failure" remain tied to the ideology of the family, never escaping the patriarchal arena.

These themes are illustrated in the memories of street people as they recall early experiences. Ralph, for example, tells of an arrogant, two-timing father who *fails* to fulfill his family obligations. We can only guess the particular pressures felt by Ralph's father as he exchanged his labor power for the basic resources required by a growing household. Considering factors of racial discrimination and the relatively low wages of office workers, these pressures may have been rather great. As Ralph tells the story, however, both parent and child seem to attribute family "breakdown" to the personal failures of a father who compensates by "coming in like a big shot with candy, [while] the welfare was supporting us." Nevertheless, this purportedly "dysfunctional" family is highly successful in meeting the labor needs under advanced capitalism. Ralph's family generated several wage workers (three custodians formally employed in service industries), some "stagnant surplus" (the two "junkies" as reserve labor or marginally employed), a wageless worker (the housewife), and an upwardly mobile wage worker (the guidance counselor) whose "success" helps reinforce belief in the "American dream."

Other stories reveal the often painful results of contradictions engendered by patriarchal beliefs and practices. Reflecting an interpretation of appropriate paternal behavior, fathers described as "Jekyll and Hyde" types are at once providing and imperious. In helping his son with homework, for example, T.K.'s father would yell, spank, and beat the child. This behavior, consistent with patriarchal principles, ensures parental authority by use of physical force. Fathers who beat and humiliate their children are merely exercising their entitlements and conforming to the expectations of their parental role. In the context of this male-dominated hierarchy, wives may also be subject to physical violence at the hands of husbands. Such was the case in Charlie's household, where his father would frequently beat him and his mother. The son, having learned important lessons about men, women, and power, engages in sexual violence that starts at an early age.

Families patterned on the patriarchal model manifest rather rigid conceptualizations of appropriate male and female behavior. "Good" girls are "home types," while a quiet boy who "keeps near the house" is a "momma's boy." In fact, T.K., determined not to make the mistakes of his family, is unable to construct an alternative dynamic in his intimate relationships. While objecting to his father's stereotypical "male" behavior (hard drinking, womanizing, toughness, and, often, physical violence), T.K. blames his own failed marriage on a wife who does not live up to her sex-specific role ("She never was a proper woman . . . staying home, taking care of the baby").

"Worlds of pain," to borrow a phrase from Lilian Rubin (1976), appear over and again as people remain tied to beliefs and practices impossible to satisfy under conditions of economic deprivation, relative powerlessness, and inadequate alternative social supports. T.K.'s suffering derives from his sense of failure to provide for his children, who are dispersed throughout the city in relatives' homes. James, raised by his mother and grandmother, feels cheated and deprived of a father. While James holds dear a father image steeped in fantasy, his feelings of devastation and failure are quite real. In keeping with conventional beliefs, he locates his mental-health problems (i.e., "drug abuse") in "the monolithic family"; that is, a missing father and a working mother (Thorne and Yalom 1982:1). In fact, both James and T.K. suffer from the thought of failing to experience or live up to the family ideal.

Lee, Arthur V., Carl, and Lloyd Robertson, on the other hand, were raised in two-parent households. The structuring of their parent-child relations conforms to traditional patriarchal lines of power, with "women and children last." From Lee, who concludes, "My parents should never have had any children," we hear of childhood experiences that challenge the sanctity of the nuclear family. As Arthur tells of his painful, yet pointless, search for "love," the family as a "haven in a heartless world" (Lasch 1977) is brought into question. In Lloyd Robertson's tale we hear contradictory portraits of a mother at once nurturing ("[like] a large bird . . . with its wings over her chicks") and abusive. In fact, his mother conforms with behavioral expectations according to the sexual division of labor and the hierarchical power structure of their domestic arrangement. In Lloyd's moving account, we also hear of conflicts in the emergence of his gender-specific identity. For one, he could only "become a man" when his chronic bed-wetting ended, a belief that caused him great distress. Later, by using the threat of physical force, Lloyd commanded new "respect" from his father. The power differential between father and son then narrowed, allowing the teenaged boy entry into the province of male domination. In this case, violence was a necessary condition for a special "rite of passage," a private ritual of symbolic arrival at manhood.

Dennis T. also tells of a particularly intense physical battle with his father. The "tangle of love and domination" portrayed by an embittered child emerges as a consequence of family structure organized around age and gender (Thorne and Yalom 1982:12). With father at the helm, basic power inequities are sustained as he directs psychological and physical violence against those most vulnerable. All members of Dennis's family are victims of a socially sanctioned and sanctified arrangement that often draws people into confusing, cruel, and tragic relations with one another. In keeping with "womanly concerns," Connie expresses a steadfast belief in and quest for the "love relationship" that has brought tragic disappointment. On the other hand, both Tom Silver and Lou seem the model of cool masculinity, divorced as they are from emotional attachments. In contrast to the highly conformist gender identities of many street addicts, Jesse's homosexuality seems tied to his effort to be and remain emotionally connected to others. In all, the stories of Dennis T., Connie, Tom Silver, Lou, and Sandy, who was sexually abused by her stepfather, raise questions about the naturalness or wholesomeness of the "family."

These accounts also point to the glaring lack of institutionalized child-rearing and child-care alternatives outside the family. Connie, for example, might have made a very wise decision to run away from an abusive situation—had there been someplace for her to go. Instead, she found herself grateful to fall into the arms of a pimp. In Samuel Arnold's case, the streets became a "second home" during the hours his mother was away at work. For Isaiah, his mother was at once a hardworking woman who struggled to raise a family of six and, inevitably, the cause of her children's present and future difficulties. As the bearer of blame, Isaiah's mother is faulted for a "natural" weakness ("she should have been more hard on me, [but] she was a woman"). As long as social practice sustains gender ideologies and the myth of the family, public and political support for extensive, quality child care as an alternative to the street scene for the young will not be forthcoming. Instead, relatively small, self-contained social units remain responsible for these activities, and they then shoulder the blame for the very outcomes they are expected to produce!

GENDER IN SOCIAL REPRODUCTION

Street addicts' descriptions of their intimate adult relations reveal an adherence to patriarchal philosophy, particularly the legitimacy of male violence and notions of sexual private property. Isaiah, for example, considers "smacking [his wife's] head" different from "beating her up." The former is justifiable according to male privilege, while the latter steps beyond some acceptable boundary. Isaiah, in explaining one fight with his former wife (prompted by his dislike of how her new boyfriend talked to her and to his son), reveals a rather conventional concept of spousal rights, duties, and privileges.

In the name of defending her honor and his reputation, he assumes the position of protector, which in turn usurps her autonomy and right to self-determination. When Isaiah's wife apparently resists this interference, it prompts the use of physical force in an effort to secure control. Joseph also describes using violence to maintain power over "his women," who were getting out of hand. Like Isaiah, he holds dear a belief in his inalienable rights, while expressing a notion of boundaries or limitations to male privilege. Considering dominant cultural constructions of private and public domains, particularly as these relate to the separation of "home" and "workplace" and the "sex/gender system," it follows that Joseph places the boundary at the juncture between "inside" and "outside" the domestic dwelling. Inside, "male strength and physical aggressiveness are plausible factors in the power of men over individual women" (Quinn 1977:190; Thorne and Yalom 1982:8–10).

Conventional notions of sexuality, gender, and family are indicated by male street addicts as they talk about other aspects of their "private lives." We hear it in Dennis T's lament at missing out on marriage and family, without which, he says, "What do you have?" Rafael articulates a rigid concept of gender differentiation in his assertion that "men and women have to show different faces." His depiction of those "faces" conforms to the most stereotypical male and female characteristics. As Rafael explains it, respect and reputation are tied to such gender-specific traits as nurturance and mothering among women and physical violence among men. Similarly, Rodney, Lloyd Robertson, and Lee also refer to "their women" in gender-specific terms and attitudes. In these cases, one man "prohibits" his wife from using drugs, while another dumps his girlfriend for doing so. On the other hand, women often help their spouses or boyfriends get off drugs, as we heard from James, Isaiah, Owen, and Antoine.

As women speak of their intimate relations with men, we find similar patterns of gender differentiation in their perspectives and experiences. In Andrea's case, a boyfriend who helps her get on methadone may be unusual, but her analysis of his motivation follows conventional female wisdom—it must be "love." In keeping with feminine character, Cherise goes to the trouble of bringing home and caring for a young man with "no place else to go." Both Andrea and Cherise have been victims of domestic violence, and each has found a way to manage her own situation. Respecting the boundaries of the "private" domain, these women do not expect outside intervention. At those arbitrary times when others attempt to mediate, the women consider such "help" disruptive, interfering, and difficult to incorporate into their customary strategies. As a tactic in her efforts to deal with intimate relations, Naomi reflects on gender codes and psychological motivations, which then help guide her actions. For example, since she understands Bobby's possessiveness as deriving from a "machismo thing," Naomi allows him a graceful, public exit from the relationship (e.g., "You can tell people that you broke up with me"). Naomi's coaxing and cajoling, however, is no match for Bobby's threats, which have psychologically and physically terrorized her.

FRIENDSHIP AND THE STREET "SUBCULTURE"

As is true outside the "street scene," addicts' friends may be important confidants, companions, sources of support, or members of an exchange network. The particular hardships of street-addict life, including poverty and the unremitting quest for drugs, place special demands on friendship obligations. As such, the immediacy of daily crises is important in the formation of friendships or connections among "associates." Despite popular, exoticized conceptions of friendships within the "drug subculture," they are not so different from those outside it. Among street addicts, some people develop deep attachments, while others remain more distantly connected. It is the circumstances of street-addict life that create a sense of the unusual; actual relations conform to conventional friendship patterns (e.g., Connie and her friends, Joe and the pregnant woman).

Friends and associates respond to a range of special street-addict circumstances—from destitution to homelessness, hunger, and addiction. On the street, acquaintances share information and resources, including needles for injecting drugs. Thus, the organization of friendship is based on reciprocal exchanges in the management of daily exigencies. As the example of needle sharing shows, individuals may have different motivations for participating in the exchange (some for the "reciprocal thing," some for money). The bottom line with needles is the difficulty of securing an outlawed, and therefore scarce, good. Needle sharing in private shooting galleries is thus a logical outcome of the social and legal-political context within which street drug use occurs. While the AIDS crisis has prompted some street addicts to alter their needle-sharing behavior, needles remain an illegal, scarce commodity. Until that changes, street addicts will be pressed to engage in the practice, despite the large numbers of dead and dying around them.

Broad cultural and legal constructions of street drug use (i.e., as immoral and illicit), coupled with the general political and economic plight of the city's poor and working class (which includes street addicts), have set the stage for a range of behaviors and activities played out on the street. The separate codes, rules, and laws developed by associates as they exchange goods and favors represent strategic responses to ongoing adverse conditions. For example, the descriptions by Quentin, Lou, and Jarmin of addicts seeking to satisfy needs and wants reflect creative adaptation under trying circumstances. At the same time, the potential for collective activism and empowerment is thwarted, as creativity, energy, and effort are directed at satisfying more immediate needs. While the solidarity and collective consciousness that emerges on the street could provide a foundation for producing resistance and alternative outcomes, the street "culture" is actually appropriated by the larger social order. In this way, individual addicts and their so-called subculture (consumed as they are by drugs) are highly accommodating to the needs and interests of the dominant society. Indeed, traditional social-science research, most often focused on the "drug subculture," helps mystify ways "deviant" groups conform to dominant cultural values and behavioral expectations. In the closing quotation, Antoine touches on these themes as he vividly depicts the experience of entrapment ("Nobody wants to stay in the game; nobody plans to get trapped") and the core wishes of his street friends ("They want me to succeed, but they don't want me to betray them"). Antoine may well be correct when he says that his street friends "give you more encouragement [to get out of 'the game'] than you get from what we call the straight segment of life or society."

CHAPTER VII

Drugs, Culture, and Society

It is a wonder to consider all the difficulties with which street addicts contend. No one wakes up one day and decides to become a doper—especially a street junkie. Different drugs have their special appeal, and many addicts use a variety of them. A beginner doesn't expect to become addicted, although some users say they knew from the start that they'd never pull away. Herbert C., for example, an old-time addict now in his fifties, started mainlining as a teen-ager. In those days, he and a friend would hang around some local musicians, "And we saw the musicians high, and we knew it wasn't from drink because they weren't at the bars drinking, and we got interested and wanted to see what it was all about." Herbert soon discovered that they were getting high on heroin, and the novice wanted to learn more about it. In those days, Kent explains, it was more difficult to buy drugs than it is today, but he managed to find someone to sell him his first bag:

And I had the first fix of heroin—mainlining—and I liked it immediately, and I knew that I would use it again. I didn't have any more for like three or four days, and it went on like that for the summer. By the end of the summer, I had a little chippie—not a real habit. I went on for a long time that way [mainlining every three to four days]—for like two years. And then I got into it heavy—by the time I was almost twenty, I had what you would say, a habit.

Lloyd Robertson also started using as a teenager—once a month for about a year. Unlike Herbert, he began by sniffing heroin, then skinpopping, and, finally, mainlining. As Lloyd describes it, "I started slowly, and then it finally did catch me." Kevin G. has a similar story. Intoxicated by the euphoric effects of the drug, "like an orgasm except that it lasted five or six minutes," Kevin insisted he would not become addicted. "I believed I was stronger than the drug," he remembers:

> I swore I would never become an addict. I was a weekend
> junkie, a weekend warrior, and then weekends started
> going into Mondays and Tuesdays and Wednesdays, 'til
> one summer, in '73—I'll never forget it—it was June, July,
> I woke up one morning, and after about an hour, I started
> feeling like I was freezing, like I was inside of an icebox,
> and my arms and legs started aching all over, and I
> thought I was coming down with the flu. I called a friend
> of mine, and he said, "You got your Jones coming down on
> you"—and I realized, from that day on, I was a dope fiend,
> a certified dope fiend.

James says he was addicted to heroin by the time he was sixteen years old. "In the beginning," he recalls, "it was just experimental—everybody was doing it. Then I started liking it more and more until it was too late—I just caught a habit." Andrea, who says that drugs ruined her life, calls dope "the biggest pimp in the world." Now it pains her to see others repeating her mistakes. One friend, Andrea says, "thinks that she's been there and back, but she's just started." Shooting heroin and doing a little freebasing, the friend has begun stealing from her mother. "It's just a shame," Andrea says in frustration, "because I know what's gonna happen to her. She thinks she's gonna stop her problem—but she's at the beginning of a long, hard, ugly road—she's gonna lose her life, her family, everything that matters."

The thing about drugs is that they seem to do so much for you all at once. When James first started using, he not only enjoyed the high but thought he was "cool" and "hip" and was thrilled with "the excitement of the cop." That was with heroin. For a while, he was into smoking and shooting opium, a different kind of pleasure. A Chinese girlfriend introduced him to the world of opium, which James found exciting, exotic:

> Smoking opium is different [from heroin]. You get the
> same dope high, but it's like acid, too—you dream, hallu-
> cinate, and it lasts a lot longer. And then, you're in a dif-
> ferent setting, because they bring you into the dens. As
> soon as you walk in the place they have this big, bald guy
> tattooed across his body, saying, "You want young boy,
> young girl, man, woman; how many do you want; do you
> want a drink; you want a smoke?" You could get anything
> and everything there. I could've had a seven-year-old kid,
> or a thirty-year-old woman, or a sixteen-year-old woman,
> or fifteen-year-old boy, whatever I wanted—that's how
> they run the opium dens.

Sex and drugs often go together. Mario, a male prostitute, says some drugs are particularly enjoyed with certain sexual acts. "Amyl nitrate—poppers—sort of like enhances the feeling, and it gives [users] an 'I don't care' attitude, and it's a rush." Cocaine, he explains, is "mainly used in prostitution," since it acts both as an aphrodisiac and "brings down that paranoia." But the synthetic drug called Ecstasy is the absolute best, according to Mario, since "you get engaged sexually with someone [so that] you don't give a shit what's going on around you—you're transcendental." Similarly described is crack, the cocaine derivative, which Barton says is "like going to heaven and coming back."

Owen has a long history of "polydrug use," as the scientists and doctors call it. He has abused heroin, cocaine, Valium, LSD, PCP, and speed. Owen, an American Indian, has also taken peyote, but only as part of specific cultural rituals. "Whenever I've used peyote—I've never abused it or used it as a drug to get wasted on—I did it only in ceremony, and strictly by the book, so to speak, as directed by the medicine man at the time."

On the other hand, Owen has used heroin for twenty-six years "because it is my means of escaping from hurt—I mean, I want to be loved. I am to the point where I question whether I am able to really love, because things that I love I can relinquish completely, and forget almost immediately—or at least I have built a mechanism to make it blockable with my mind." Carl expresses similar thoughts on the psychological functions of drugs. "The whole idea of me using," he explains, "was to get away from my problems and the difficulties, not to look for more." As the years progressed, however, Carl's drug use created more trouble for him, although he still enjoys the euphoria that only comes from getting high. He began using as a teenager—smoking joints—but in a short time "progressed to pills, LSD, dope." Carl explains that some drugs allowed him to express a range of emotions otherwise repressed, while other drugs helped him remove himself from those emotions:

When I took LSD, I couldn't really relax, but I could laugh and have belly laughs, and really, when I was crying, it was such an emotional relief . . . that I liked it. I didn't like pills, because I felt too vulnerable when I took them— I felt like I couldn't defend myself physically or verbally— so it just came to selling the pills, not taking them. But the heroin just tranquilized me . . . and I found my euphoria.

Carl makes the point that when drinking liquor he would find himself out looking for a fight. "I was willing, able, and ready to fight anyone. . . . I felt powerful, and I wouldn't allow anyone to put a damper on that." But once he discovered "tranquilizer, narcotic-type drugs," Carl's violence ended, and he "was back in the womb—warm, protected—and numb to the world emotionally." Kevin G. similarly describes the pleasure that comes with a narcotic high, though he also warns of the dangers:

My father and my brother had died almost back to back, and I found that the issue didn't bother me as much when I used narcotics. It was a block-out thing for me—it killed all emotion, nobody could hurt me anymore. I felt secure with my needle and spoon. I was safe—it was like being inside the womb—like you're a baby. After the fix, you're comfortable, you're warm. You know, I believe that the reason heroin is so insidious and addictive is the fact that it gives a person the feeling of being in their mother's womb; they're back safe again; there's nothing—no external pressure put on you. . . . Heroin can only expand your consciousness to the point of addiction—it's insidious. It's so good that it just overpowers everything—it's such a good, euphoric feeling—instant euphoria, and it's very hard to just try it once and then never go back to the cooker again.

Whatever the reasons for using, the difficulties eventually catch up with you. But just as drugs create problems, they can stave them off, too, making it harder and harder to stop. As Ray points out, "If you shoot dope or coke, it's a thing like a red badge of courage. You don't care; your attitude is one of 'I don't care,' you know; you don't care about the cops, you don't care about me, you don't care about you—or, if you're in the way, I'll stick you. The objective is to remove the obstacle. It's do what you got to do; you live or you die."

James insists there are big differences between coke and heroin. He has given up on cocaine, since "it ruined me physically, and I burnt a lot of bridges behind me, as far as friendships, because people do worse things for cocaine than they would for heroin or everything else. People do more for what they call the genie in the pipe than any other drug." Shirley agrees. A veteran heroin addict, she says there is "greediness" behind cocaine and crack, where users argue over who had more. "I hear them saying," she reports, " 'You done slayed me'—that means you done swallowed more than what you were supposed to." People on cocaine, Shirley insists, are different from the heroin addicts. "See, with heroin," she explains, "I kept my Frigidaire full."

Ray has only heard about the paranoia behind coke and stories about "people getting hallucinations—feeling like bugs are crawling on them." In his own case, cocaine just makes "my sex drive more intense." The same thing happens to Jarmin; "I find it hits me like this all the time, that horny thing—every time I get high on coke, now I want some sex."

But Jarmin also knows the special dangers behind coke, far worse than those involved with heroin. While he has overdosed on heroin about fifteen times, Jarmin says, "You don't come back from a cocaine overdose—more likely it'll be lethal." He explains: "One [cocaine] speeds your heart up, the other [heroin] slows your heart down—you go out on coke, your heart busts, whereas heroin, you just be out, knocked out, you dig?" (For drug pharmacology and folklore, see Griffith 1988; New York State Division of Substance Abuse Services et al. 1984; Goldsmith et al. 1984.)

For Isaiah, the problem with cocaine is that it's "a rich man's high, and a poor man's dilemma." Now that he has the "mental desire" for the drug, Isaiah says, "Getting the money together—that's the thing that nearly drives me crazy." Samuel Arnold prefers heroin over cocaine "since I caught endocarditis [a bacterial heart infection] doing the 'C.' " He also avoids pills, because, as Samuel explains, "I never trusted them." Like Samuel, Lloyd Robertson was introduced to pills (tranquilizers) through a drug program and, similarly, shied away from them:

> In a black society, pills are something that's not normally taken—unless you're involved in a detox type of thing— because you don't have many doctors. See, like you're white, your father might be a doctor, whereas you would have knowledge of what so and so pill could do—it's beneficial towards the human body and brain. In a black society, in a black environment, to find out what a pill can and cannot do is damn near impossible to find out. To be quite frank, that's why most blacks don't use pills—because there's no information on it.

DRUGS: RICH MAN'S HIGH, POOR MAN'S DILEMMA

Regardless of the personal reasons for doing drugs or the cultural preferences for some drugs over others, street addicts of all kinds, colors, and ages ultimately struggle to satisfy their habits just about every day. Against all odds, they seem to persevere. Although it's often hard to think about anything besides getting through the day, some street addicts suspect a setup by straight society. As Antoine points out, it is sometimes difficult to see how straights are tied to dopers, since the hustle takes up so much time and seems so peculiar:

> When you go out there in the world, and you're playing, and you're getting high, and you're juggling, and you're stealing, and you're steering—that's a whole different world; a lot of people don't even know about it. And those that do know about it really don't understand that it's a microcosm of the world as it is. That goes for people who feel that they're in positions where they can control the drug flow or any crime flow; that goes for those that feel that they're beyond the drug flow—but everybody's involved. They're all involved, because each facet fits the puzzle to make what goes on in those streets. This is a life-and-death game, and it's still a microcosm of society as a whole. It's the same thing, because it all runs down the same line. We throw a whole lot of money into "Let's stop this, let's stop that," but that same money that we're trying to use to stop it circulates the crime that makes things work.

Kevin G. thinks it no accident that drugs are so readily available in the poorest neighborhoods of the city. "I know for a fact that certain parts of the government want heroin," asserts this white southerner. "How come heroin is only in Harlem and the Lower East Side? It was meant intentionally as a way to keep politically—Harlem could be a very active, political thing, but people don't mind living in a building where the steps smell like urine, living in a little closet, and their welfare check, because they have heroin or methadone to deal with it. I just basically want to sum it up with, 'Don't ever try it,' because once you try it, you generally end up married to it." In summarizing his understanding of the drug situation, Kevin quotes William Burroughs, the Beat generation author and junkie: "Paregoric babies of the world unite; we have nothing to lose but our pushers."

In line with Kevin, Lou, an old-timer when it comes to drugs, states his view on the social position and functions of the average narcotics addict:

The ordinary street addict in New York is taken advantage of by the "marketeers, the merchants of death," as commonly called in the political jargon . . . the merchants of death of heroin and narcotics. But it shouldn't be that way; this should be legal, this should be put, I mean, this should be legal to people like myself. I should be able to go into a hospital, or into a pharmacy, and buy it. I should be able to go into a methadone program and get what I'm supposed to get, not get something concocted for me that the program is pushing. When the program takes advantage of the addict through the addict's ignorance, the program is greedy, because money is the root of all evil, and money will force people, and the people who run methadone programs are only people, and money is their number-one objective in life, and even if it means cheating the addict of what he's supposed to get—it's still, to them, it's still logical, and it's still acceptable, because the addict is the lowest organism of the human structure, the human social ladder; the drug addict is, is, is the vermin; the drug addict is the worm crawling under the ground of society, and this is disgusting to the average citizen. This is worse than a fly, or a cockroach. A drug addict to the average citizen is worse than a cockroach or a rat or a mouse. The average citizen knows of the drug addict, and sees the drug addicts, and you can see it in the person's expression— something more abhorrent than, than if it were to see a mouse in its house, or if it were to see a rat, or if it were to see cockroaches climbing around its refrigerator. To see a drug addict on the street is far worse than to see any of those other creatures, you know; the drug addict is simply the worst on the rung of the social ladder. . . . I'm sure if I were a senator, or a member of the House, I could obtain my narcotics quite easily, and you know, still function as a member of society.

DRUGS, CULTURE, AND SOCIETY

The social sciences only stand to lose by ignoring how the oppressed analyze their own condition. Indeed, the dominated usually understand the dominant better than the reverse. In coping with their daily lives, they simply must.

RENATE ROSALDO
Culture and Truth

Capitalist freedoms are potentially real freedoms and capitalism takes the wager, which is the essence of reproduction, that the freedoms will be used for self-damnation. The dominant class could never batten down the hatch on these freedoms without help from below. And if these freedoms are not used at this time for their full subversive, oppositional or independent purposes, capitalism will not take the blame. It makes its own wager on uncertainty, others can make theirs.

PAUL WILLIS
Learning to Labor

These last pages of ethnographic description point to various cultural contexts of drug initiation, use, and addiction. As street addicts recount their early experiences with various psychoactive drugs, we begin to understand the physiological and psychological lure of these substances. Addicts also reveal an array of beliefs and attitudes about different drugs that emerge from differences of individual experience, cultural ideology, and social context of drug use. Cultural factors (e.g., Owen's differentiation between peyote and other psychoactive drugs, and Lloyd's distrust of drugs in pill form) and variation in the social context of drug taking (e.g., to enhance sexual pleasure and for sociability) may be important in shaping diversity among a population ultimately compelled by larger forces toward actual or symbolic homogeneity. It is these larger forces, however, that have been largely ignored by those seeking to understand the nature of addict life on our city streets.

In keeping with the social critique presented by several street addicts in this chapter, my study also considers broader factors as crucial to the analysis of street-addict experiences. I have drawn on Marxist approaches to place anthropological subjects (in this case, street drug addicts in Manhattan) within larger political, economic, cultural, and historical workings to better understand the ways power structures affect this population. I have also attempted to describe and explain activities and experiences of a particular behavioral group among the city's working class in terms of constraint, resistance, inequality, conflict, social control, dependency, accommodation, dominant cultural values and practices, together with local cultural perspectives, creative response, and management. As such, I have "stressed the unity of structure and agency . . . [considering] the activity of human subjects [which includes recollections and perspectives] . . . [while providing] theoretical reflection on the structures and systems within which people act" (Roseberry 1988:171–72). I believe that this approach allows a more precise understanding of street-addict behavior and more accurately reflects the causes and consequences of drug addiction among the working poor and the working class. Moreover, the approach suggests a more satisfactory explanation for the paradox that such unstable lives would or could persist so strongly over time.

THE CASE OF THE MYTHIC DOPE FIEND

The "drug scene" as depicted here is best understood as a feature of late capitalism. Aspects of street-addict life, and the nature of their relations and interactions, reflect processes of capitalist social reproduction while pointing to ways street addicts are (or may become more effective) social agents. The major conclusions I draw from this study center on these themes. One important finding is that certain feelings, acts, and attitudes of defiance on the part of street addicts are ultimately subverted by the larger social order; thus, what may appear to be (or, perhaps, could be) a basis of resistance becomes, in fact, a "culture of accommodation." Relatedly, certain ideological, political, and economic roles of street addicts are indicated by the data and discussions on addict experiences.

Considering the systemic workings and logical outcomes of structural constraints on and determinants of street-addict activities, it is important to consider the social benefits of this phenomenon. Although interwoven in complex ways toward a common purpose, the ideological, economic, and political roles of street addicts are discussed separately. Taken together, functional aspects shed light on some insidious and powerful mechanisms in the social reproduction of capitalist relations: particularly, the use of cultural myths, the diversion of threat, and the denial of state responsibility to basic needs of the majority public for the benefit of capital.

The economic roles of street addicts for capital accumulation center on the social construction of addicts as a distinct category, as well as on their everyday economic activities. As a special category, addicts are politically weak and disconnected from organized labor, thereby becoming a source of cheap, easily expendable labor. Moreover, the costs of daily reproduction are absorbed by addict-workers themselves. The conditions of their reproduction are quite poor and occur at barely minimal levels. The inferior position of addict-workers stems not only from their social and legal status as lawbreakers (as drug consumers and as workers in illegal industries) but also from the "invisibility" of informal-sector enterprises generally, whether or not they are "illegal." Relatedly, street addicts are a significant consumer market for unloading goods produced by the international drug trade (heroin, cocaine, marijuana, etc.). Street addicts therefore serve various economic uses—as low-wage, vulnerable, and disorganized workers (with roles in production, distribution, and services), as bearers of costs in their daily reproduction, and as consumers.

The most important ideological role of street addicts, and of the symbolic images of deviance and decadence they provoke, is in providing what Castells (1975:33) calls "the bogy scapegoat of the bourgeoisie, always ready to feed the fires of xenophobia and racism." Frequently drawn from the city's poorer neighborhoods, which are largely inhabited by racial and ethnic minorities, drug users are easily blamed for their individual bad habits and the destructive results of drug use. Their feelings of despair and so-called anomie are readily attributed to the physiological effects of drug consumption. As a popular credo now goes, anyone with enough willpower and a strong set of values can Just Say No to Drugs. Clearly, there may be certain negative physiological effects associated with drug use; however, to focus on this one aspect of street-addict life is to obscure the deeper roots of alienation and the larger forces at work in determining or shaping conflict, poverty, racism, sexism, homelessness (or near homelessness), the lack of meaningful work, and limited future aspirations. Yet because of the destruction to home, neighborhood, community, and country caused by the mythic, dark dope fiend of the street, attention to deeper issues is diverted and the fact that addicts are "human casualties of capitalist development" is masked from view (Klein 1983:52).

Given the conditions within which poor, drug-addicted people must secure their illegal potions, they often do threaten home, neighborhood, and local community. As we have seen, however, these threats rarely extend beyond the boundaries of working-class and working-poor homes and communities; therefore, they have not become an organized danger to the dominant social order. Moreover, the general, capitalistic interests that shape conditions of working-class life are also significant in shaping conditions of illegal drug use. Under the present, specific conditions of the use of illegal drugs, addicts are required to spend a great deal of time and energy in "drug-related" activities (copping, using, selling, dealing, getting arrested, going to jail, stealing, seeking drug treatment or other drug-related health care, and so on). As a result, drug use appears as the only significant organizing principle that shapes addicts' daily lives. As this study has shown, however, this empirically true "fact" is necessary for masking underlying capitalist social relations, and it must therefore be understood as part and parcel of the myth-making process in social reproduction. For individual addicts, processes in the psychological construction and reconstruction of the (mythical) self have also been shaped by lifelong experiences within various settings and arenas that are themselves largely formed by political-economic forces. Regardless of these homogenizing pressures, people attain more than one social and psychological identity, which, in terms of producing alternative political outcomes, is both a blessing and a burden.

This last point relates to certain political roles of street addicts as a social group. In their present form, such persons are a captive entity, separated from their class by mandates and practices in the state management of "deviants." The street-addict phenomenon, therefore, contributes to reproducing class, racial, and gender inequalities, to maintaining conditions of unequal access to power, and to inhibiting the articulation of class conflict. This occurs as street addicts, fashioned into a discrete group and ideologically separated, act as a divisive tool within their class, ensuring that conflict will not spill over between the classes. It also occurs as particular social, cultural, and psychological identities (i.e., other than as street addicts) are manipulated by the policies and practices of the various institutional settings within which they are found (differential treatment by sex, age, race/ethnicity, sexuality, and so forth). As illustrated throughout this book, differences are accentuated, creating cleavages and conflicts between men and women, blacks, whites, and Latinos, homosexuals and heterosexuals, users and sellers, various categories of workers, young and old, parents and children, the police and lawbreakers, and so on. Tensions between these "groups" are reinforced and defused within controlled settings (for example, the family, the neighborhood, the workplace, the police precinct).

The data presented on these pages suggest that this aspect of social reproduction is ongoing and occurs in complex ways. In some cases, for example, close associations are made between certain cultural constructs and social categories (e.g., the dope-fiend image and racial or ethnic minorities), or they may appear far apart (e.g., patterns of family interaction and gender differentiation in public institutions and the marketplace). Throughout the diversity of settings, however, mechanisms of social control and social reproduction are operating.

Street addicts are not, however, merely victims of oppressive conditions. They are also feeling and thinking human beings who are creative actors in their efforts to manage larger forces and constraints. Whether it be Isaiah building a home with friends in a city park, Lou circumventing the criminal-justice system by purchasing drugs "legally," street people innovating or participating in a range of income-generating activities, or addicts creating the rules of the street, these efforts represent individual or collective inventions under difficult circumstances. Moreover, some activities may be understood as forms of resistance, although they are often highly individualistic, privatized, and self-destructive. While the feelings and thoughts that trigger acts of resistance have the potential to be channeled into organized political action, this has not occurred among street addicts, who are held in check by social myth and the institutionalized web within which they are caught.

The very act of taking illicit drugs may be considered a form of resistance, a defiant gesture. In addition, addicts come together for various purposes (e.g., to socialize, to acquire drugs, to shoot up), which allows them to develop and use creative cultural tools like street lingo, ritualized patterns of behavior, and so on. Such gatherings of the defiant may indicate the presence of a "culture of resistance" or suggest the potential for alternative modes of collective organization and activity. In their present form, however, collections of street addicts (usually informal, loosely joined, and reactive) are highly accommodating to larger cultural norms and to the requisites of social reproduction, as discussed above. Street addicts may even embrace the social label of "deviant outcast" for what it means in terms of defying standard norms of "straight" society. Their defiance is limited, however, to symbolic suggestion and remains on the level of appearances.

The life-style of street addicts is *not* a viable alternative to mainstream ways. As has been shown throughout this book, street addicts are, in complex ways, active participants in the political, economic, social, and cultural life of the city. Their activities as workers, "dope fiends," clients, patients, criminals, and so on are congruent with and help to sustain the goals of global capitalism and national government. Following the logic of this discussion, street addicts are not a "threat to society." They have, de facto, joined hands with the larger public in *believing* in the ideology of deviance and the myth of the defiant dope fiend. As such, their roles in social reproduction are obscured, actual resistance is subverted, and other alternatives are suppressed.

The seeds of alternative forms of collective organization and activity are present in the current situation. Contradictions in the system provide gaps that allow for the possibility of these alternatives. For example, social-control practices are felt as oppressive, demeaning, and dehumanizing by those who are their object. The outrage and social criticisms thus provoked are necessary ingredients for effective struggle and active political mobilization. The "burdens and blessings" resulting from processes of social differentiation and "homogenization" also illustrate the possibilities that lie dormant in the contradictions. The "burden" of attaining more than one social identity lies in its role in displacing class conflict. Nevertheless, such a multiplicity of identity permits street addicts, for one, to view social conditions from more than one perspective—not merely as deviant dope fiends. Since consciousness requires emotional identification and empathy, the "blessing" of attaining more than one social identity lies in the awareness thus provoked. Similarly, although pressures toward "homogenizing" street addicts have helped create the "accommodating, deviant subculture" discussed above, the "blessing" of such an outcome lies with the possibility of collective solidarity and allegiance inspired by common experience.

POLICY AND POLITICS

This book suggests several potential areas for change in our understanding of the drug situation, and it therefore points in certain political and policy directions. In my view, broad social change is essential if the goal is to address significantly the problems posed by drug consumption among the poor and working class in the United States. Rather than maintain a narrow focus on "drugs," I suggest that we direct our efforts toward social action to address deeply entrenched class, racial, and gender inequalities and to make an honest assessment of the root causes of such chronic social problems as drug abuse, homelessness, teenage runaways, poverty, and feelings of hopelessness. As one step in this direction, I think it is important that existing labor organizations and social-action committees find ways of incorporating addicts and the drug issue generally into their activist efforts. Considering the ways drugs and addicts are used as a gloss for deeper social ills, it is imperative that they not be excluded from the activist agenda. Despite the fact that addicts are often highly individualistic, self-occupied, and impetuous, it may nevertheless be useful to consider that the problems they face (and the broad social context of addict life) are connected to those issues that affect the poor and the working class generally.

Political organizing among street addicts has not occurred, although this may change with the advent of the deadly disease AIDS (Gillman 1989; Friedman and Casriel 1988; Friedman, de Jong, and Des Jarlais 1988; Friedman et al. 1987). I believe collective efforts by street addicts would be useful in breaking down the dope-fiend stereotype and in demystifying the evils such people supposedly bring on society. Moreover, collective action of this kind may also help effect some change in the policies and practices of those institutions with which addicts have the most contact. In documenting "obstacles to self-organization among IVDUs" (intravenous drug users), Samuel Friedman and his colleagues note that participation in illegal activities is a crucial inhibiting factor (1987:

214). As long as street drugs are illegal, it would be difficult to imagine the emergence of a viable political organization of street addicts. A model for such a group has emerged in the Netherlands with the Federatie Nederlandse Junkie Bonden (Federation of Dutch Junkie Leagues), which was founded in 1980 (Bollag 1989; van Vliet 1988; Woudstra and Schade 1987; van de Wijngaart 1984). Although "hard" drugs like heroin and cocaine are not legal in the Netherlands, attitudes and policies toward addicts are also not as harsh as in the United States. Nevertheless, Junkie League political efforts have met with significant difficulties, not the least of which has been, according to Ingrid Woudstra and George Schade of the Junkie Bonden, "to communicate with a society that is hardly able to believe that a junkie is a real human being, with human feelings, with human needs, and human rights" (1987:2).

I also suggest improving existing treatment and prevention programs. As presented here, the street-addict population is rather diverse, although certain commonalities of experience cut across those differences. Nevertheless, diversity—particularly along lines of gender, race, culture, sexuality, and age—must be considered in the design and implementation of relevant treatment. While programs sensitive to these issues exist, they often do not receive adequate institutional and financial support (What Works Conference:1989).

Street addicts have a rich store of information and experience on "the life." Addicts like those who speak here have learned that involvement with illegal drugs brings the police on your back, the drug bosses breathing down your neck, and doctors and treatment counselors looking over your shoulder, as well as a myriad of other difficulties. This is valuable knowledge and experience that can be put to good use in prevention efforts. I recommend that in the course of political organizing (and connecting with other, existing groups), a grass-roots effort be made to tap this important resource for educating the most vulnerable in the urban community. I am reminded of a passage in Maya Angelou's autobiography (1974:181) in which she describes how a friend swayed her from "the life" in just such a way. Taking her down to the piers (a 1950s version of a shooting gallery), Troubadour forces her to watch him "jab and pick in his own flesh":

> I thought about the kindness of the man. I had wanted him before for the security I thought he'd give me. I loved him as he slouched, nodding, his mouth open and the saliva sliding down his chin as slowly as the blood had flowed down his arm. No one had ever cared for me so much. He had exposed himself to me to teach me a lesson and I learned it as I sat in the dark car inhaling the odors of the wharf. The life of the underworld was truly a rat race, and most of its inhabitants scurried like rodents in the sewers and gutters of the world. I had walked the precipice and seen it all; and at the critical moment, one man's generosity pushed me safely away from the edge.

Data Sources and Methodology

Dr. Goldstein's two studies, "Drug-Related Involvement in Violent Episodes" (DRIVE) and "Female Drug-Related Involvement in Violent Episodes" (FEMDRIVE), were funded by the National Institute on Drug Abuse (NIDA) through grants DA-03182, DA-04017, and DA-04017–02 (see Goldstein et al. 1987 and 1988 for interim final reports). The studies were carried out in a rented field site on Manhattan's Lower East Side from the summer of 1984 to the spring of 1987. According to Dr. Goldstein, most participants in the study were recruited from field contacts, snowball sampling, and active recruitment in local treatment programs (1987:35). Besides Dr. Goldstein, the principal investigator and project director, the members of the research team included Dr. Douglas S. Lipton, co-principal investigator; Dr. Barry J. Spunt and Patricia A. Bellucci, research associates; Thomas Miller, senior interviewer; and Nilda Cortez, Mustapha Khan, and Richard Durrance, interviewers.

In gathering the data, the team of researchers combined ethnographic and survey techniques, which resulted in a rich body of material on life histories, daily experiences in various situations, and special narratives on different aspects of life in New York City. Dr. Goldstein and his team developed three interview formats for gathering information. The life-history interview contained a series of bounded and open-ended questions dealing with an array of past and present demographic topics and with drug- and nondrug-related events and circumstances. (The interviews ranged from three to six hours each.) A second interview schedule was designed to elicit information on a range of daily activities. Participants were interviewed once a week over eight weeks on questions related to daily nondrug- and drug-related activities and events. (The average interview took one hour). Several participants were also given "special" open-ended interviews on topics that were of particular interest to the researchers. The "specials," as well as many of the life-history interviews, were tape-recorded and transcribed as hard copy. This material has provided the basis of my examination of street-addict life, and it forms the core of the ethnographic portraits presented throughout this book.

As a predoctoral fellow in the program of Behavioral Sciences Training in Drug Abuse Research at Narcotic and Drug Research, Inc., I was offered the opportunity to base my project on this rich data base. As an anthropologist, I was particularly interested in a study "thick" with ethnographic description. I consider it a testament to the quality of the work of Dr. Goldstein and his team that the data they collected could be so readily subject to alternative theoretical treatment by an "outside" scholar like me. I also developed and followed a specific set of procedures in the coding, writing, and analysis of the material. As a first step, I conceptualized the transcripts as archival data containing records of people's lives. Although these narratives are certainly of our times, I approached them as historical documents subject to interpretation. Once I became familiar with the material, I began to tease out certain key themes as articulated by street addicts, the narrators of the documents. These themes became the major topics of the book: housing and shelter, work, the criminal-justice system, drug treatment and medical care, interpersonal relations, and issues of drugs, culture, and society. I hand-coded each page according to these broad categories, which were further refined to consider issues of race/ethnicity, gender, age, class, and the nature of interaction between addicts and other people of various categories. In the coding process, I also separated addicts' articulations of thoughts, ideas, and feelings from their descriptions of activities and actions. In some cases, respondents may have discussed aspects of their work lives in detail, with less mention of their housing situation or interpersonal relations; in other cases, they may have provided detailed descriptions of shelter life or experiences with the criminal-justice system. For this reason, each chapter cites individuals who may or may not be heard in other chapters. In addition, more people than those quoted provided information on each of these themes. In all, an average of twenty-five individuals addressed each of the main topics.

The ethnographic sections of each chapter are based on quotations from street addicts, as culled from the transcripts and organized according to the categories I developed. (The real names of participants and all DRIVE/FEMDRIVE codenames have been changed.) Because the participants' words are so expressive and their stories so vivid, I chose to present them as narratives unto themselves, leaving my analysis until the discussion at the close of each chapter.

Notes

PREFACE

1. The Appendix contains a more detailed discussion of Dr. Goldstein's two studies.

2. This book may come to be seen as an early example of an anthropological effort at secondary analysis of qualitative data. Faced with the practical concerns and costs of anthropological fieldwork, and given the increased availability of computerized data sets, more and more anthropologists may undertake secondary analyses. At this time, the National Institute of Justice is the only federal agency to require that qualitative and quantitative data sets it supports be made available to researchers for secondary analysis. Other agencies will probably follow suit. Another signal of a move in this direction is the 1991 volume *Sharing Social Science Data: Advantages and Challenges*, edited by Joan E. Sieber (Newbury Park, Calif.: Sage Publications), in which some of the methodological issues related to secondary analysis are addressed.

CHAPTER II

1. The highly negative portrayals presented here may reflect street addicts' recollections of the more dramatic aspects of shelter existence rather than the ordinary course of their daily lives. The negative portrayals may also reflect biases in the research effort in which the difficulties of street-addict life were emphasized.

CHAPTER III

1. In reality, street addicts flow in and out of drug work, prostitution, and "legal" day work, as well as other criminal activities. While

some people report moving in stages from one "hustle" to the next, others are involved in various jobs simultaneously. Regardless of the pattern, street addicts make distinctions between different jobs they perform (e.g., drug selling, handyman work, etc.). These are differentiations not only of work activity, duties, and responsibility but also of meanings attached to them. While each descriptive category illustrates aspects of street-addict involvement in the working-class economy of the city, these classifications should not obscure the important assertion of this study that street addicts are a laboring segment within a differentiated market, a status concealed by processes operating within and outside the labor market.

2. The organization of drug work on the street may be more flexible than is suggested by the presentation here. In fact, several studies point to a diversity of structures in the organization of street drug work (Johnson et al. 1985; Williams 1989; Sullivan 1989).

CHAPTER IV

1. For an overall description of the criminal-justice process on the local and national levels, see Steven Belenko (1980) and Bureau of Justice Statistics (1983).

References

AGAR, MICHAEL H. 1973. *Ripping and Running: A Formal Ethnography of Urban Heroin Addicts*. New York: Seminar Press.

AKINS, CARL, and GEORGE BESCHNER. 1979. *Ethnography: A Research Tool for Policymakers in the Drug Field*. Rockville, Md.: National Institute on Drug Abuse.

ALBERT, JUDITH C., and STEWART A. ALBERT, eds. 1984. *The Sixties Papers: Documents of a Rebellious Decade*. New York: Praeger.

ALCALY, ROGER E., and DAVID MERMELSTEIN, eds. 1977. *The Fiscal Crisis of American Cities: Essays on the Political Economy of Urban America, with a Special Reference to New York*. New York: Vintage Books.

ALETTI, VINCE. 1988. "There's a Riot Goin' On." *Village Voice*. August 16.

ALKSNE, HAROLD. 1981. "The Social Bases of Substance Abuse." In *Substance Abuse: Clinical Problems and Perspectives*. Joyce H. Lowintin and Pedro Ruiz, eds. Baltimore, Md.: Williams and Wilkins.

ALLISON, MARGARET, ROBERT L. HUBBARD, and J. VALLEY RACHAL. 1985. *Treatment Process in Methadone, Residential, and Outpatient Drug-Free Programs*. Rockville, Md.: National Institute on Drug Abuse.

ANGELOU, MAYA. 1974. *Gather Together in My Name*. New York: Bantam Books.

ANSLINGER, HARRY J. 1951. "Relationship between Addiction to Narcotic Drugs and Crime." *Bulletin on Narcotics* 3:1–3.

ARELLA, LORINDA R., SHERRY DEREN, and JOAN RANDELL. 1987. *Issues Affecting the Utilization of Vocational/Educational Services in Drug Treatment*. New York: Narcotic and Drug Research, Inc., and New York State Division of Substance Abuse Services.

258 ■ References

ARENDT, HANNAH. 1978. *The Jew as Pariah*. New York: Grove Press.

BARBANEL, JOSH. 1988. "Number of Homeless Far Below Shelter Forecasts." *New York Times*. January 26.

BAXTER, ELLEN, and KIM HOPPER. 1981. *Private Lives/Public Spaces: Homeless Adults on the Streets of New York City*. New York: Community Service Society.

BECKER, HOWARD S. 1963. *Outsiders: Studies in the Sociology of Deviance*. New York: Free Press.

————. 1964. *The Other Side: Perspectives on Deviance*. New York: Free Press.

BELENKO, STEVEN. 1980. *Pretrial Service in Criminal Court: An Evaluation of the New York City Criminal Justice Agency*. New York: Criminal Justice Coordinating Council.

BELL, ROBERT R. 1971. *Social Deviance: A Substantive Analysis*. Homewood, Ill.: The Dorsey Press.

BLACKBURN, ROBIN, ed. 1973. *Ideology in the Social Sciences*. New York: Monthly Review Press.

BLOCK, FRED, RICHARD A. CLOWARD, BARBARA EHRENREICH, and FRANCES FOX PIVEN. 1987. *The Mean Season: The Attack on the Welfare State*. New York: Pantheon Books.

BLUMBERG, ABRAHAM S. 1973. "The Politics of Deviance: The Case of Drugs." *Journal of Drug Issues* 3(2):105–14.

BOLLAG, BURTON. 1989. "To the Swiss and Dutch, Tolerance Is Anti-Drug." *New York Times*. December 1.

BORIS, EILEEN, and PETER BARDAGLIO. 1983. "The Transformation of Patriarchy: The Historic Role of the State." In *Families, Politics, and Public Policy: A Feminist Dialogue on Women and the State*. Irene Diamond, ed. New York: Longman.

BOURDIEU, PIERRE. 1977. *Outline of a Theory of Practice*. Cambridge: Cambridge University Press.

BOURDIEU, PIERRE, and JEAN-CLAUDE PASSERON 1977. *Reproduction in Education, Society, and Culture*. London: Sage.

BOURGOIS, PHILLIPPE. 1989. "Just Another Night on Crack Street." *New York Times*. November 12.

BRAVERMAN, HARRY. 1974. *Labor and Monopoly Capitalism: The Degradation of Work in the Twentieth Century.* New York: Monthly Review Press.

BREWINGTON, VINCENT, SHERRY DEREN, LORINDA ARELLA, and JOAN RANDELL. 1987. *Obstacles to Vocational Rehabilitation: The Clients' Perspectives.* New York: Narcotic and Drug Research, Inc., and New York State Division of Substance Abuse Services.

BROOK, R. C., and I. C. WHITEHEAD. 1980. *Drug-Free Therapeutic Community.* New York: Human Sciences Press.

BROWN, ROGER M., THEODORE M. PINKERT, and JACQUELINE P. LUDFORD. 1983. *Contemporary Research in Pain and Analgesia, 1983.* Rockville, Md.: National Institute on Drug Abuse Research Monograph 45.

Bureau of Chemotherapy Services. 1988. *New York State Division of Substance Abuse Services, Waiting List Summary Sheet.* New York.

Bureau of Justice Statistics. 1983. *Report to the Nation on Crime and Justice.* Washington, D.C.: U.S. Department of Justice.

BURGESS, ERNEST W., and DONALD J. BOGUE. 1964. "Research in Urban Society: A Long View." In *Contributions to Urban Sociology.* Ernest W. Burgess and Donald J. Bogue, eds. Chicago: University of Chicago Press.

———. 1964. *Contributions to Urban Sociology.* Chicago: University of Chicago Press.

BURROW, JAMES G. 1963. *Voice of American Medicine.* Baltimore, Md.: Johns Hopkins University Press.

CARR., C. 1988. "Night Clubbing. Reports from the Tompkins Square Police Riot." *Village Voice.* August 16.

CASTELLS, MANUEL. 1975. "Immigrant Workers and Class Struggles in Advanced Capitalism: The Western European Experience." *Politics and Society* 5:33–66.

———. 1977. *The Urban Question.* London: Edward Arnold.

CHAVEZ, LYDIA. 1988. "Despite Bitter Cold, Many of Homeless Shun Shelters." *New York Times.* January 7.

CHEIN, ISIDOR, DONALD L. GERARD, ROBERT S. LEE, and EVA ROSEN-FELD. 1964. *The Road to H: Narcotics, Juvenile Delinquency, and Social Policy*. New York: Basic Books.

CLARKE, JOHN, STUART HALL, TONY JEFFERSON, and BRIAN ROBERTS. 1975. "Subcultures, Cultures, and Class: A Theoretical Overview." In *Resistance through Rituals: Youth Subcultures in Postwar Britain*. Stuart Hall and Tony Jefferson, eds. London: Hutchinson.

CLAYTON, RICHARD R., and HARWIN L. VOSS. 1981. *Young Men and Drugs in Manhattan: A Causal Analysis*. Rockville, Md.: National Institute on Drug Abuse.

CLECKNER, P. J. 1977. "Cognitive and Ritual Aspects of Drug Use among Young, Black Urban Males." In *Drugs, Rituals, and Altered States of Consciousness*. B. M. DuToit, ed. Rotterdam: A. A. Balkema.

CLINARD, MARSHALL B., ed. 1964. *Anomie and Deviant Behavior*. New York: Free Press.

CLOWARD, RICHARD A., and LLOYD E. OHLIN 1960. *Delinquency and Opportunity*. New York: Free Press.

CONRAD, P., and J. W. SCHNEIDER. 1980. *Deviance and Medicalization: From Badness to Sickness*. St. Louis, Mo.: Mosby.

COOMBS, ROBERT H., LINCOLN J. FRY, and PATRICIA G. LEWIS, eds. 1976. *Socialization in Drug Abuse*. Cambridge, Mass.: Schenkman.

COOPER, J. R., ed. 1983. *Research in the Treatment of Narcotic Addiction: State of the Art*. Rockville, Md.: National Institute on Drug Abuse.

DAI, BINGHAM. (1937) 1964. "Opium Addiction: A Socio-Psychiatric Approach." In *Contributions to Urban Sociology*. Ernest W. Burgess and Donald J. Bogue, eds. Chicago: University of Chicago Press.

DE BEAUVOIR, SIMONE. 1952. *The Second Sex*. New York: Vintage Books.

DeGiovanni, Frank F. 1987. *Displacement Pressures on the Lower East Side.* New York: Community Service Society.

DeLeon, George, and J. T. Ziegenfuss, eds. 1986. *Therapeutic Communities for Addictions.* Springfield, Ill.: Charles C. Thomas.

Diamond, Stanley, Bob Scholte, and Eric Wolf. 1975. "Anti-Kaplan: Defining the Marxist Tradition." *American Anthropologist* 77:870–76.

Dickstein, Morris. 1989. *Gates of Eden: American Culture in the Sixties.* New York: Penguin Books.

Ehrenreich, Barbara, and Deidre English. 1978. *For Her Own Good: 150 Years of the Experts' Advice to Women.* Garden City, N.Y.: Anchor Books.

Erikson, Kai T. 1966. *Wayward Puritans: A Study in the Sociology of Deviance.* New York: Wiley Press.

Feldman, Harvey W. 1968. "Ideological Supports to Becoming and Remaining a Heroin Addict." *Journal of Health and Social Behavior* 9 (June):131–39.

Fiddle, Seymour. 1967. *Portraits from a Shooting Gallery.* New York: Harper & Row.

Finder, Alan. 1988. "Lower East Side Housing: Plans and Conflict." *New York Times.* May 14.

Finestone, Harold. 1957. "Cats, Kicks, and Color." *Social Problems* 5 (July):3–13. Reprinted in *Readings in General Sociology,* 4th ed. 1964. R. W. O'Brien, ed. Boston: Houghton Mifflin.

Friedman, Samuel R., and Cathy Casriel. 1988. "Drug Users' Organizations and AIDS Policy." *AIDS and Public Policy Journal* 3(2):30–36.

Friedman, Samuel R., Wouter M. de Jong, and Don C. Des Jarlais. 1988 "Problems and Dynamics of Organizing Intravenous Drug Users for AIDS Prevention." *Health Education Research* 3(1):49–57.

Friedman, Samuel R., Don C. Des Jarlais, Jo L. Sotheran, Jonathan Garber, Henry Cohen, and Donald Smith. 1987. "AIDS and Self-Organization among Intravenous Drug Users." *International Journal of the Addictions* 22(3):201–19.

GILLMAN, CHERNI. 1989. "Genesis of New York City's Experimental Needle Exchange Program." *International Journal on Drug Policy* 1(2):28–32.

GIROUX, HENRY A. 1983. *Theory and Resistance in Education.* London: Heinemann Educational Books.

GITLIN, TODD. 1987. *The Sixties: Years of Hope, Days of Rage.* New York: Bantam Books.

GLADWIN, THOMAS. 1967. *Poverty U.S.A.* Boston: Little, Brown.

GOLDSMITH, DOUGLAS S., DANA E. HUNT, DOUGLAS S. LIPTON, and DAVID STRUG. 1984. "Methadone Folklore: Beliefs about Side Effects and Their Impact on Treatment." *Human Organization* 43(4):330–40.

GOLDSTEIN, PAUL J., PATRICIA A. BELLUCCI, BARRY J. SPUNT, THOMAS MILLER, NILDA CORTEZ, MUSTAPHA KHAN, RICHARD DURRANCE, and ALICE VEGA. 1988. *Female Drug-Related Involvement in Violent Episodes (FEMDRIVE): Interim Final Report.* New York: Narcotic and Drug Research, Inc.

GOLDSTEIN, PAUL J., DOUGLAS S. LIPTON, BARRY J. SPUNT, PATRICIA A. BELLUCCI, THOMAS MILLER, NILDA CORTEZ, MUSTAPHA KHAN, and ANDREA KALE. 1987. *Drug-Related Involvement in Violent Episodes (DRIVE): Interim Final Report.* New York: Narcotic and Drug Research, Inc.

GOVE, WALTER R., ed. 1975. *The Labelling of Deviance: Evaluating a Perspective.* Beverly Hills, Calif.: Sage.

GRIFFITH, H. WINTER. 1988. *Drugs: Side Effects, Warnings, and Vital Data for Safe Use.* Los Angeles: Body Press.

HALL, STUART, and TONY JEFFERSON, eds. 1975. *Resistance through Rituals: Youth Subcultures in Post-War Britain.* London: Hutchinson.

HAMID, ANSLEY, ed. 1988. *Drugs and Drug Abuse: A Reader.* Littleton, Mass.: Copley.

HANNERZ, ULF. 1980. *Exploring the City: Inquiries Toward an Urban Anthropology.* New York: Columbia University Press.

HARDING, SANDRA. 1986. "The Instability of the Analytical Categories of Feminist Theory." *Signs: Journal of Women in Culture and Society* 2(4):645–64.

HARRIS, OLIVIA, and KATE YOUNG. 1981. "Engendered Structures: Some Problems in the Analysis of Reproduction." In *The Anthropology of Pre-Capitalist Societies.* Joel S. Kahn and Josep R. Llobera, eds. Atlantic Highlands, N.J.: Humanities Press International.

HART, KEITH. 1973. "Informal Income Opportunities and Urban Employment in Ghana." *Journal of Modern African Studies* 11:61–89.

———. 1985. "The Informal Economy." *Cambridge Anthropology* 10(2):54–78.

HASKELL, MOLLY. 1988. "Paying Homage to the Spinster." *New York Times.* May 8.

HELMER, JOHN. 1975. *Drugs and Minority Oppression.* New York: Seabury.

HERBSTEIN, JUDITH. 1983. "The Politicization of Puerto Rican Ethnicity in New York: 1955–1975 *Ethnic Groups* 5:31–54.

HILL, RICHARD CHILD. 1978. "Fiscal Collapse and Political Struggle in Decaying Central Cities in the United States." In *Marxism and the Metropolis: New Perspectives in Urban Political Economy.* William K. Tabb and Larry Sawers, eds. New York: Oxford University Press.

HOPPER, KIM. 1988. "More than Passing Strange: Homelessness and Mental Illness in New York City." *American Ethnologist* 15(1):155–67.

HOPPER, KIM, ELLEN BAXTER, STUART COX, and LAURENCE KLEIN. 1982. *One Year Later: The Homeless Poor in New York City.* New York: Community Service Society.

HOPPER, KIM, and JILL HAMBURG. 1984. *The Making of America's*

Homeless: From Skid Row to New Poor, 1945–1984. New York: Community Service Society.

HOPPER, KIM, EZRA SUSSER, and SARAH CONOVER. 1986. "Economies of Makeshift: Deindustrialization and Homelessness in New York City." *Urban Anthropology* 14:183–236.

HUBBARD, R. L., M. ALLISON, R. M. BRAY, S. G. CRADDOCK, J. V. RACHAL, and H. M. GINZBURG. 1983. "An Overview of Client Characteristics, Treatment Services, and During-Treatment Outcomes for Outpatient Methadone Clinics in the Treatment Outcome Prospective Study (TOPS)." In J. R. Cooper, ed. *Research on the Treatment of Narcotic Addiction: State of the Art.* Rockville, Md.: National Institute on Drug Abuse.

HUGHES, PATRICK H., and JEROME H. JAFFE. 1971. "The Heroin Copping Area: A Location for Epidemiological Study and Intervention Activity." *Archives of General Psychiatry* 24(5) (May):394–400.

INCIARDI, JAMES A. 1986. *The War on Drugs: Heroin, Cocaine, Crime, and Public Policy.* Mountain View, Calif.: Mayfield.

JOHNSON, BRUCE D. 1980. "Towards a Theory of Drug Subcultures." In *Theories on Drug Abuse: Selected Contemporary Perspectives.* Dan J. Lettieri, Mollie Sayers, and Helen W. Pearson, eds. Rockville, Md.: National Institute on Drug Abuse.

JOHNSON, BRUCE D., PAUL J. GOLDSTEIN, EDWARD PREBLE, JAMES SCHMEIDLER, DOUGLAS S. LIPTON, BARRY SPUNT, and THOMAS MILLER. 1985. *Taking Care of Business: The Economics of Crime by Heroin Abusers.* Lexington, Mass.: Lexington Books.

JOHNSON, BRUCE D., and EDWARD PREBLE. 1978. *ETHNOS: Final Report.* New York: Narcotic and Drug Research, Inc., and New York State Division of Substance Abuse Services.

JONES, DELMOS J. 1972. "Incipient Organizations and Organizational Failure in an Urban Ghetto." *Urban Anthropology* 1(1):51–67.

———. 1989. "The Almost Homeless." *Practicing Anthropology* 11(2):11–12.

JOSEPH, HERMAN, P. APPEL, R. MARX, J. PEREZ, F. TARDELO, and L. WATTS. 1988. *Evaluation of Pre-KEEP (Key Extended Entry Pro-*

gram) in Three Facilities of the New York City Department of Corrections on Riker's Island. New York: New York State Division of Substance Abuse Services, Bureau of Research and Evaluation.

JOSEPH, HERMAN, and HILDA ROMAN-NAY. 1988. "The Homeless Intravenous Substance Abuser and the AIDS Epidemic." Paper prepared for the Technical Review Meeting on AIDS and Intravenous Drug Use: Future Directions for Community-Based Prevention and Research. Rockville, Md.: National Institute on Drug Abuse.

Journal of Drug Issues. 1983. *The Political Economy of Drugs and Alcohol.* Special Issue, vol. 13 (Winter).

KARABEL, JEROME, and A. H. HALSEY. 1977. *Power and Ideology in Education.* New York: Oxford University Press.

KAVALER, FLORENCE, DONALD C. KRUG, ZILI AMSEL, and ROSEMARY ROBBINS. 1968. "A Commentary and Annotated Bibliography on the Relationship between Narcotics Addiction and Criminality." *Municipal Reference Library Notes* 42:45–63.

KELLY, JOAN. 1979. "The Doubled Vision of Feminist Theory." *Feminist Studies* 5(1):216–27.

KITSUSE, JOHN I. 1980. "The 'New Conception of Deviance' and Its Critics." In *The Labelling of Deviance: Evaluating a Perspective.* Walter R. Gove, ed. Beverly Hills, Calif.: Sage.

KLEIN, DORIE. 1983. "Ill and against the Law: The Social and Medical Control of Heroin Users." *Journal of Drug Issues* 13(1) (Winter): 31–55.

KOSKIKALLIO, ILPO. 1983. "On the Special Characteristics of Drugs and Drug Markets." *Journal of Drug Issues* 13(1) (Winter): 167–77.

KRAMER, JOHN C. 1976. "From Demon to Ally—How Mythology Has, and May Yet, Alter National Drug Policy." *Journal of Drug Issues* (Fall):390–406.

LASCH, CHRISTOPHER. 1977. *Haven in a Heartless World: The Family Besieged.* New York: Basic Books.

LAURIE, PETER. 1967. *Drugs: Medical, Psychological, and Social Facts.* Baltimore, Md.: Penguin Books.

LEACOCK, ELEANOR BURKE, ed. 1971. *The Culture of Poverty: A Critique.* New York: Simon and Schuster.

LEEDS, ANTHONY. 1971. "The Concept of the 'Culture of Poverty': Conceptual, Logical, and Empirical Problems, with Perspectives from Brazil and Peru." In *The Culture of Poverty: A Critique.* Eleanor Burke Leacock, ed. New York: Simon and Schuster.

———. 1973. "Locality Power in Relation to Supra-Local Power Institutions." In *Urban Anthropology: Cross-Cultural Studies of Urbanization.* Aidan Southall, ed. New York: Oxford University Press.

LIPTON, D. I., and M. J. MIRANDA. 1983. "Detoxification from Heroin Dependency: An Overview of Method and Effectiveness." In B. Stimmel, ed. *Evaluation of Drug Treatment Programs.* New York: Haworth Press.

LOMNITZ, LARISSA. 1977. *Networks and Marginality: Life in a Mexican Shantytown.* New York: Academic Press.

Lower East Side Service Center (personal communication). March 1990.

LOWINTIN, JOYCE H., and PEDRO RUIZ, eds. 1981. *Substance Abuse: Clinical Problems and Perspectives.* Baltimore, Md.: Williams and Wilkins.

McBRIDE, ROBERT B. 1983. "Business as Usual: Heroin Distribution in the United States." *Journal of Drug Issues* 13(1) (Winter):147–66.

MacLEOD, JAY. 1987. *Ain't No Makin' It: Leveled Aspirations in a Low-Income Neighborhood.* Boulder, Colo.: Westview Press.

MAGURA, STEPHEN, DOUGLAS S. GOLDSMITH, CATHY CASRIEL, DOUGLAS S. LIPTON, PAUL J. GOLDSTEIN, BARRY J. SPUNT, and DAVID L. STRUG. 1988. "Patient-Staff Governance in Methadone Maintenance Treatment: A Study in Participative Decision Making." *International Journal of the Addictions* 23(3):253–78.

MARCUS, GEORGE E., and MICHAEL M. J. FISCHER. 1986. *Anthropology as Cultural Critique: An Experimental Moment in the Human Sciences.* Chicago: University of Chicago Press.

MARCUSE, PETER. 1985. "Gentrification, Abandonment, and Displacement: Connections, Causes, and Policy Responses in New York City." *Washington University Journal of Urban and Contemporary Law* 28:195–240.

MARGLIN, STEPHEN. 1974. "What Do Bosses Do? The Origins and Functions of Hierarchy in Capitalist Production." *Review of Radical Political Economics* (Summer).

MARTINEZ, ELIZABETH. 1989. "Histories of 'The Sixties': A Certain Absence of Color." *Social Justice: A Journal of Crime, Conflict, and World Order* 16(4):175–85.

MARX, KARL. 1967. *Capital*, vol. 1. New York: International Publishers.

MARX, KARL, and FREDERICK ENGELS. 1951. *Selected Writings*, vol. 1. Moscow.

MATZA, DAVID. 1964. *Delinquency and Drift*. New York: Wiley Press.

———. 1966. "The Disreputable Poor." In *Social Structure and Mobility in Economic Development*. Neil J. Smelser and Seymour M. Lipset, eds. Chicago: Aldine.

———. 1969. *Becoming Deviant*. Englewood Cliffs, N.J.: Prentice-Hall.

MEILLASSOUX, CLAUDE. 1975. *Maidens, Meal, and Money: Capitalism and the Domestic Economy*. Cambridge: Cambridge University Press.

MILLS, JAMES. 1965. *The Panic in Needle Park*. New York: Farrar, Straus and Giroux.

MORGAN, H. WAYNE. 1974. *Yesterday's Addicts*. Norman: University of Oklahoma Press.

MORGAN, JAMES P. 1966. "Drug Addiction: Criminal or Medical Problem?" *Police* (July–August):6–9.

MORGAN, PATRICIA A. 1983. "The Political Economy of Drugs and Alcohol: An Introduction." *Journal of Drug Issues* 13(1) (Winter):1–7.

MULLINGS, LEITH, ed. 1987. *Cities of the United States: Studies in Urban Anthropology*. New York: Columbia University Press.

MUSTO, DAVID F. (1973) 1987. *The American Disease: Origins of Narcotic Control.* New York: Oxford University Press.

———. 1981. "Review of Narcotic Control Efforts in the United States." In *Substance Abuse: Clinical Problems and Perspectives.* Joyce H. Lowinson and Pedro Ruiz, eds. Baltimore, Md.: Williams and Wilkins.

NASH, JUNE. 1979. *We Eat the Mines and the Mines Eat Us.* New York: Columbia University Press.

———. 1983. "The Impact of the Changing International Division of Labor on Different Sectors of the Labor Force." In *Women, Men, and the International Division of Labor.* June Nash and Maria Patricia Fernandez-Kelly, eds. Albany: State University of New York Press.

New York Academy of Sciences. 1989. *Population Profile of AIDS Shifts in New York City* (Spring):7.

New York City Department of Corrections, Office of Substance Abuse Intervention (personal communication), March 1990.

New York City Office of Special Services for Adults (personal communication), March 1990.

New York State Division of Substance Abuse Services. 1988. *Management Information System, Summary Management Report of Clients in Treatment Programs.* New York.

———. Department of Health, Office for the Aging, and the New York Medical Society, Drug Abuse Committee. 1984. *Desk Reference on Drug Misuse and Abuse.* Albany: State of New York.

NICOLAUS, MARTIN. 1973. "The Professional Organization of Society." In *Ideology in the Social Sciences.* Robin Blackburn, ed. New York: Monthly Review Press.

OLLMAN, BERTELL. 1971. *Alienation: Marx's Conception of Man in Capitalist Society.* Cambridge: Cambridge University Press.

———. 1979. *Social and Sexual Revolution: Essays on Marx and Reich.* Boston: South End Press.

OLLMAN, BERTELL, and EDWARD VERNOFF, eds. 1982. *The Left Academy.* New York: McGraw-Hill.

ORTNER, SHERRY B., and HARRIET WHITEHEAD, eds. 1981. *Sexual Meanings: The Cultural Construction of Gender and Sexuality.* Cambridge: Cambridge University Press.

PERLMAN, JANICE E. 1976. *The Myth of Marginality: Urban Poverty and Politics in Rio de Janeiro.* Berkeley: University of California Press.

PORTES, ALEJANDRO. 1983. "The Informal Sector: Definition, Controversy, and Relation to National Development." *Review* 7(1) (Summer):151–74.

PREBLE, EDWARD. 1981. *Who's Nodding Now?* Verbatim transcript from recording of presentation at Beth Israel Medical Center: New York.

PREBLE, EDWARD, and JOHN J. CASEY, JR. 1969. "Taking Care of Business." *International Journal of the Addictions* 4(1):1–24.

PREBLE, EDWARD, and THOMAS MILLER. 1977. "Methadone, Wine, and Welfare." In *Street Ethnography.* Robert S. Weppner, ed. Beverly Hills, Calif.: Sage Publications.

QUINN, NAOMI. 1977. "Anthropological Studies on Women's Status." *Annual Review of Anthropology* 6:181–225.

QUINNEY, RICHARD. 1977. *Class, State, and Crime: On the Theory and Practice of Criminal Justice.* New York: David McKay.

RAPP, RAYNA. 1978. "Family and Class in Contemporary America: Notes Toward an Understanding of Ideology." *Science and Society* 42(3):278–300.

———. 1987. "Urban Kinship in Contemporary America: Families, Classes, and Ideology." In *Cities of the United States. Studies in Urban Anthropology.* Leith Mullings, ed. New York: Columbia University Press.

RAPP, RAYNA, ELLEN ROSS, and RENATE BRIDENTHAL. 1979. "Examining Family History." *Feminist Studies* 5(1):174–200.

REINARMAN, CRAIG. 1983. "Constraint, Autonomy, and State Policy: Notes Toward a Theory of Controls on Consciousness Alteration." *Journal of Drug Issues* 13(1) (Winter):9–30.

ROSALDO, RENATE. 1989. *Culture and Truth: The Remaking of Social Analysis.* Boston: Beacon Press.

ROSEBERRY, WILLIAM. 1988. "Political Economy." *Annual Review of Anthropology* 17:161–85.

ROSENBERG, TERRY J. 1987. *Poverty in New York City: 1980–1985.* New York: Community Service Society.

RUBIN, LILIAN BRESLOW. 1976. *Worlds of Pain: Life in the Working Class Family.* New York: Basic Books.

RUBINGTON, EARL. 1967. "Drug Addiction as a Deviant Career." *International Journal of the Addictions* 2(1):3–20.

SALAMON, JEFF. 1988. "Leaflets from Nowhere." *Village Voice.* August 16.

SASSEN KOOB, SASKIA. 1980. "Immigrant and Minority Workers in the Organization of the Labor Process." *Journal of Ethnic Studies* 8(1):1–34.

———. 1981. "Towards a Conceptualization of Immigrant Labor." *Social Problems* 29(1):65–83.

———. 1984. "The New Labor Demand in Global Cities." In *Cities in Transformation.* Michael P. Smith, ed. Beverly Hills, Calif.: Sage.

SCHILLER, NINA GLICK. 1977. "Ethnic Groups Are Made, Not Born: The Haitian Immigrant and American Politics." In *Ethnic Encounters: Identities and Contexts.* G. Hicks and P. Leis, eds. Boston, Mass.: PWS-Kent Publishing–Duxbury Press.

SCHLOSSMAN, S. L. 1974. "The 'Culture of Poverty' in Ante-Bellum Social Thought." *Science and Society* 38:150–66.

SCHUR, EDWIN M. 1965. *Crimes without Victims: Deviant Behavior and Public Policy.* Englewood Cliffs, N.J.: Prentice Hall.

SHARFF, JAGNA WOJCICKA. 1980. *Life on Dolittle Street: How Poor People Purchase Immortality.* Final Report: Hispanic Study Project. Department of Anthropology, Columbia University. New York.

———. 1986. "Para el Futuro." Paper presented at the 108th annual meeting, American Ethnological Society. Wrightsville Beach, N.C.

———. 1987. "The Underground Economy of a Poor Neighborhood." In *Cities of the United States: Studies in Urban Anthropology.* Leith Mullings, ed. New York: Columbia University Press.

SHAW, MARTIN. 1973. "The Coming Crisis of Radical Sociology." In *Ideology in the Social Sciences.* Robin Blackburn, ed. New York: Monthly Review Press.

SIEBER, JOAN E., ed. 1991. *Sharing Social Science Data: Advantages and Challenges.* Newbury Park, Calif.: Sage Publications.

SIMMONS, J. L. 1969. *Deviants.* Berkeley, Calif.: Glendessary Press.

SMITH, MICHAEL PETER, ed. 1984. *Cities in Transformation: Class, Capital, and the State.* Beverly Hills, Calif.: Sage.

STAFFORD, WALTER W. 1985. *Closed Labor Markets: Under-representation of Blacks, Hispanics, and Women in New York City's Core Industries and Jobs.* New York: Community Service Society.

STEGMAN, MICHAEL. 1985. *Housing in New York: Study of a City, 1984.* New York: Department of Housing Preservation and Development.

STEPHENS, RICHARD C. 1987. *Mind-Altering Drugs: Use, Abuse, and Treatment.* In Law and Criminal Justice Series, vol. 9. Beverly Hills, Calif.: Sage.

STEPHENS, RICHARD, and STEPHEN LEVINE. 1971. "The 'Street Addict Role': Implications for Treatment." *Psychiatry* 34(4):351–57.

STERNLIEB, GEORGE, and JAMES W. HUGHES. 1983. "The Uncertain Future of the Central City." *Urban Affairs Quarterly* 18(4):455–72.

STORMES, JIM. 1988. "The Poor in the United States: A Class-Analytic Approach." *Rethinking Marxism* 1(2) (Summer):76–102.

STUART, JACKIE. Lower East Side Service Center, Methadone Maintenance Treatment Progam (personal correspondence), March 1990.

SULLIVAN, MERCER L. 1989. *"Getting Paid": Youth Crime and Work in the Inner City.* Ithaca, N.Y.: Cornell University Press.

SUSSER, IDA. 1982. *Norman Street: Poverty and Politics in an Urban Neighborhood.* New York: Oxford University Press.

——. 1986. "Political Activity among Working-Class Women in a U.S. City." *American Ethnologist* 13(1):108–17.

TABB, WILLIAM K. 1982. *The Long Default: New York City and the Urban Crisis.* New York: Monthly Review Press.

TABB, WILLIAM K., and LARRY SAWERS, eds. 1978. *Marxism and the Metropolis: New Perspectives in Urban Political Economy.* New York: Oxford University Press.

THORNE, BARRIE, and MARILYN YALOM. 1982. *Rethinking the Family: Some Feminist Questions.* New York: Longman.

TIMMER, DOUG. 1982. "The Productivity of Crime in the U.S.: Drugs and Capital Accumulation." *Journal of Drug Issues* 7(4) (Fall): 383–96.

TOBIER, EMANUEL. 1984. *The Changing Face of Poverty: Trends in New York City's Population in Poverty, 1960–1990.* New York: Community Service Society.

TREADWAY, W. L. 1930. "Some Epidemiological Features of Drug Addiction." *British Journal of Inebriety* (October).

TURNER, JOAN. 1984. "Building Boundaries: The Politics of Urban Renewal in Manhattan's Lower East Side." Ph.D. dissertation. City University of New York.

VALENTINE, CHARLES A. 1968. *Culture and Poverty: Critique and Counter-Proposals.* Chicago: University of Chicago Press.

VAN DE WIJNGAART, G. F. 1984. "The 'Junkie League:' Promoting the Interests of the Dutch Hard-Drug User." Paper presented at the 14th International Institute on the Prevention and Treatment of Drug Dependence. Athens.

VAN VLIET, HENK JAN. 1988. "Syringe-Exchange: AIDS Prevention and Drug Policy in the Netherlands." Paper presented at the Annual Meeting of the Society for the Study of Social Problems. Atlanta, Ga.

WALDORF, DAN. 1973. *Careers in Dope.* Englewood Cliffs, N.J.: Prentice-Hall.

WALKER, ALICE. 1984. *In Search of Our Mothers' Gardens.* New York: Harcourt, Brace, Jovanovich.

WEINBAUM, BATYA. 1983. *Pictures of Patriarchy*. Boston: South End Press.

What Works: An International Perspective on Drug Abuse Treatment and Prevention Research: A Conference to Set the Agenda for the 1990s. 1989. Session on the Impact of AIDS on the Partners and Children of Intravenous Drug Users, with speakers Judith B. Cohen (Project A.W.A.R.E.), Janet L. Mitchell (Harlem Hospital), and Dooly Worth (anthropologist).

WIERSEMA, BRIAN, W. S. WILSON HUANG, and COLIN LOFTIN. 1990. *Data Resources of the National Institute of Justice*, 4th ed. (February). College Park, Md.: Institute of Criminal Justice and Criminology.

WILLIAMS, TERRY. 1989. *The Cocaine Kids*. Reading, Mass.: Addison-Wesley.

WILLIS, PAUL. 1977. *Learning to Labor: How Working Class Kids Get Working Class Jobs*. New York: Columbia University Press.

WOLF, ERIC R. 1969. "American Anthropologists and American Society." In *Reinventing Anthropology*. Dell Hymes, ed. New York: Vintage Books.

———. 1982. *Europe and the People without History*. Berkeley: University of California Press.

WOUDSTRA, INGRID, and GEORGE SCHADE. 1987. Personal Correspondence to Samuel Friedman from the Federatie Nederlandse Junkie Bonden, May 22.

ZIMBALIST, ANDREW. 1979. *Case Studies in the Labor Process*. New York: Monthly Review Press.

Index